THE DISTRIBUTION
OF AUTOMOBILES,
AN ECONOMIC ANALYSIS
OF THE FRANCHISE SYSTEM

1960 Award Winner

THE FORD FOUNDATION DOCTORAL DISSERTATION SERIES

*A dissertation submitted in partial
fulfillment of the requirements
for the degree of Doctor of Philos-
ophy at the Massachusetts Institute
of Technology*

1959 Award Winners

Kalman J. Cohen
Computer Models of the Shoe, Leather, Hide Sequence
Dissertation submitted to Graduate School of Industrial Administration,
Carnegie Institute of Technology
Present Position: Associate Professor of Economics and Industrial Ad-
ministration, Graduate School of Industrial Administration, Carnegie In-
stitute of Technology

Bob R. Holdren
*The Structure of a Retail Market and the Market
Behavior of Retail Units*
Dissertation submitted to Department of Economics, Yale University
Present Position: Assistant Professor of Economics, Iowa State College,
Ames, Iowa

Frank Proschan
*Polya Type Distributions in Renewal Theory, with an
Application to an Inventory Problem*
Dissertation submitted to Department of Statistics, Stanford University
Present Position: Staff Member, Mathematics Laboratory, Boeing Sci-
entific Research Laboratories

Andrew C. Stedry
Budget Control and Cost Behavior
Dissertation submitted to Graduate School of Industrial Administration,
Carnegie Institute of Technology
Present Position: Second Lieutenant, United States Army, Operational
Mathematics Branch, Research & Engineering Div.

Victor H. Vroom
Some Personality Determinants of the Effects of Participation
Dissertation submitted to Department of Psychology, University of
Michigan
Present Position: Assistant Professor of Psychology, University of
Pennsylvania

THE DISTRIBUTION
OF AUTOMOBILES,
AN ECONOMIC ANALYSIS
OF THE
FRANCHISE SYSTEM

BEDROS PETER PASHIGIAN

1961

P R E N T I C E - H A L L ,   I N C .

Englewood Cliffs, N. J.

To my mother and father

L. C. Catalog Card Number: 61–16540

Foreword

This volume is one of five doctoral dissertations selected for publication in the second annual Doctoral Dissertation Competition sponsored by the Program in Economic Development and Administration of The Ford Foundation. The winning dissertations were completed during the academic year 1959–60 by doctoral candidates in business administration, in the social sciences and other fields relevant to the study of problems of business.

The dissertation competition is intended to generalize standards of excellence in research on business by graduate students. It should give widespread professional recognition to persons recently awarded doctorates in business whose dissertation research is especially distinguished by its analytical content and strong roots in underlying disciplines. It is also intended to give recognition to a selected number of persons outside business schools who in their doctoral dissertations pursued with distinction interests relevant to the field of business.

The dissertations selected include, in addition to Dr. Pashigian's monograph:

Decentralization of Authority in a Bureaucracy
     Bernard H. Baum
     Department of Sociology
     University of Chicago

The Choice of Wage Comparisons
     Martin Patchen
     Department of Social Psychology
     University of Michigan

Marketing in an Underdeveloped Economy:
The North Indian Sugar Industry
     Leon V. Hirsch
     Graduate School of Business Administration
     Harvard University

v

A Heuristic Program for Assembly Line Balancing
Fred M. Tonge
Graduate School of Industrial Administration
Carnegie Institute of Technology

In the first year of the competition four of the five dissertations selected made extensive use of mathematical and statistical tools. This may have led some to the mistaken impression that mathematically-oriented dissertations are unduly favored in the selection process. The results of the second year's competition should serve to correct any such misapprehension. Four of the five dissertations published this year are largely non-mathematical, thus underscoring our conviction that many disciplines, including mathematics, can make important contributions to rigorous business research.

On behalf of The Ford Foundation, I wish to express my gratitude to the Editorial Committee for the care and thought its members devoted to the selection process. The same scholars who served on the Committee for the first year's competition gave us the benefit of their experience by serving a second year. They are: Professors Robert Ferber of the University of Illinois, Sherman J. Maisel of the University of California (Berkeley), and William Foote Whyte of Cornell University.

As in the first year, the Editorial Committee's task was considerably lightened by the assistance of ten readers, experts in the wide range of disciplines covered in the Competition, who carefully screened each of the dissertations submitted. The Foundation joins the Committee in acknowledging their debt to Professors Austin C. Hoggatt, Julius Margolis and Lyman W. Porter of the University of California (Berkeley), Richard M. Cyert of the Carnegie Institute of Technology, Harry V. Roberts of the University of Chicago, Frank Miller and Henry Landsberger of Cornell University, Myron J. Gordon of the Massachusetts Institute of Technology, Samuel Goldberg of Oberlin College, and Robert B. Fetter of Yale University, for serving as readers in the second year of the competition.

Finally, my colleagues and I wish to acknowledge the substantial contribution of Prentice-Hall, Inc., to the publication and distribution of the selected dissertations.

THOMAS H. CARROLL
VICE PRESIDENT
THE FORD FOUNDATION

New York, New York
December, 1960

Preface

This study was accepted in 1960 in partial fulfillment of the requirements for the Ph.D. Degree at the Massachusetts Institute of Technology. A few minor revisions have been made, for the most part consisting of qualifications of previous conclusions. However, Chapter 2 has been expanded and revised.

Many people have contributed to the completion of the study. Unfortunately, I will not be able to acknowledge everyone. I am indebted to Professor Morris Adelman, my thesis supervisor, for his comments and his criticisms of the first draft. Special thanks are extended to Professor Robert Bishop for directing my attention to the franchise system, and to Professor Sidney Alexander for reading a section of the thesis and clarifying several obscure points.

I would be guilty of a serious omission if I did not express my thanks to Mr. Paul Herzog, Director of Research of the National Automobile Dealers Association for rekindling my interest at a time when I was about to drop "automobile distribution" from the list of serious thesis topics. His work in preparing and administering the dealer questionnaire deserves special thanks.

I would like to express my gratitude to the many individuals, both inside and outside of the auto industry, who, at one point or another, discussed distribution problems with me, or supplied me with data or answered my many letters. Often, they did not agree with me, but they were as helpful as they could be. At times I wondered whether my thesis or my thesis correspondence would be longer—a testimony to the sympathetic response my letters received. I am also indebted to the many dealers who completed and returned the dealer questionnaire.

B. Peter Pashigian

Contents

ix

CHAPTER 4

THE DEVELOPMENT OF MARKET REPRESENTATION
POLICIES IN AUTOMOBILE DISTRIBUTION   72

CHAPTER 5

DETERMINANTS OF DEALER PLACEMENT
IN SMALL AND LARGE MARKET AREAS   124

CHAPTER 6

AN ANALYSIS OF THE RETAIL AUTOMOBILE MARKET
IN GREATER CLEVELAND (CUYAHOGA COUNTY)   162

CHAPTER 7

THE RELATIONSHIP BETWEEN DEALERSHIP SIZE AND PROFITABILITY *196*

CHAPTER 8

DISTRIBUTION AS A BARRIER TO ENTRY IN THE AUTOMOBILE INDUSTRY *217*

CHAPTER 9

THE MARKET PERFORMANCE OF FRANCHISE DEALERS IN THE REPLACEMENT PARTS AND SERVICE MARKET *242*

APPENDIX A

DEALER REPLIES TO THE DEALER QUESTIONNAIRE   267

APPENDIX B

PRODUCTS AND SERVICES INCLUDED IN THE
DEFINITION OF THE REPLACEMENT PARTS
AND SERVICE MARKET   283

APPENDIX C

A COMPARISON OF ACTUAL FORD FRANCHISES
WITH CHILTON ESTIMATES   287

THE DISTRIBUTION
OF AUTOMOBILES,
AN ECONOMIC ANALYSIS
OF THE FRANCHISE SYSTEM

CHAPTER 1

Introduction

This is a study of the distribution sector of the automobile industry. Because it is an empirical study, the reader should be prepared for the coming onslaught of charts and tables. Sorting through pages of tables and charts can be dull, confusing and, at times, appear to be without purpose. Perhaps the confusion can be minimized by specifying at the outset the aims of the study and also by giving a summary of some background information. In several instances, references will be made to existing structural conditions in automobile manufacturing. Rather than interrupt the main argument each time, it seems preferable to summarize these structural conditions at the very beginning as well.

1.1. Problems to be Discussed

The Franchise System. Chances are the theorist will be most interested in the explanation of why the automobile companies have adopted a franchise system. Why do the automobile companies restrict the number of dealers below the number which would exist with entry? One might expect a manufacturer would allow entry into the retail sector and thereby benefit from the increase in retail price competition through higher sales. More generally, one might expect the manufacturer would prefer more price competition among wholesalers, and the wholesaler would prefer more price competition among retailers, and so on. Yet, the automobile companies restrict the number of dealers who can sell their autos. This is likely to decrease rather than increase the extent of price competition among their dealers. So why do the automobile companies use the franchise system?

Economies of Scale in Automobile Distribution. There are usually thousands of retailers in the distribution sector of any industry. Some individuals infer from this that retail markets approach perfectly competitive markets. This is usually far from the truth, although each industry must be analyzed separately. What are the market characteristics of local automobile markets? Are there few or many sellers in retail automobile markets? The extent of economies of scale in retailing often preclude the existence of many sellers in any local market. How important are these economies in automobile distribution? A major portion of the study will be devoted to the measurement of the economies of scale in automobile distribution, which is not an easy task. Generally, an intensive cost study is called for. The author had neither the data nor the funds to engage in such a study. Rather, the author has used several alternative techniques to estimate the shape of the long-run dealer cost function. The reader will be familiar with some of these techniques since they have been used before. Other techniques, as far as the author knows, have not been relied on in past studies.

Distribution as a Barrier to Entry. Knowledge of the extent of economies of scale in automobile distribution is important for two reasons. First, this will determine, within limits, the number of sellers which can profitably exist in a local market. Certain structural characteristics of local markets can then be specified. From this, inferences can be made of whether competition will take price or non-price forms. Second, and more important, the extent of the economies of scale in automobile distribution will partly determine the ease with which a new manufacturer can enter the auto industry. Some students of the auto industry have claimed that the establishment of a dealer organization is a major entry barrier, which a new entrant will find difficult to overcome. However, little has been said as to how its importance could be measured and under what conditions distribution can be an entry barrier. The matter need not be left to conjecture. Certain tests can be proposed and carried out to determine the quantitative importance of this barrier to entry. After several false starts, the author did stumble upon one method of measuring the importance of distribution as a barrier to entry. Essentially, the method measures the relationship between the per unit cost of selling autos and the manufacturer's volume, that is the extent of economies in distribution cost. An estimate of the extent of economies in distribution cost will be presented. Hence, the schedule distribution cost can be superimposed on the production cost schedule to determine the economic advantage of size in the auto industry.

These are the major questions or problems which will be discussed. Several other problems arise, but these are for a reader particularly interested in automobile distribution. The general reader will probably wish to concentrate on the problems and questions discussed above. At times the reader may find this difficult to do. There will be many tables and figures to study. The author has attempted to follow a simple rule on the question of whether a table or chart should be included. If a conclusion is derived from a table, the table has been included. In most cases, the reader should be able to agree or disagree with my conclusion without the aid of additional data.

1.2. Limitations of the Data

Before proceeding to issues of substance, several comments concerning the limitations of the data are appropriate. Any study of distribution is difficult because it involves a study of and the collection of data from so many local markets. Very seldom are these data readily available, which appears to be particularly true for automobile distribution. Various data sources have been used. In several instances, data were supplied by the automobile companies, but, unfortunately, this was not always the case. Furthermore, it has often been difficult to make an independent check of each set of data. Where possible, the author has developed additional data to cross-check the results and has not tried to go beyond the data. However, this is easier to say than to show. The reader should keep the following warning in mind. The older the data, the greater the probability of error or systematic bias in the data and hence in the conclusions derived. The relative accuracy of the different data sources is difficult to assess. The data collected by the trade magazines are probably less accurate though there appear to be exceptions. The data obtained from the companies were thought to be accurate. However, it should be noted that the automobile companies have a great deal of difficulty obtaining accurate data from their own dealers. Therefore, to some extent, one is treading on thin ice when the available data are used. The author has tried to be cautious in deriving conclusions. Nevertheless, it is well to admit from the very beginning that some of the conclusions rest on a less secure foundation.

1.3. Market Structure in the Automobile Industry

A concise summary of the structural characteristics in the automobile industry is presented in this section.

Relative Size of Firm. In 1958 there were six domestic manufacturers in the automobile industry. The market share of total new car registrations from 1955 to 1958 has varied from a low of 45 to a high of 51 per cent for the General Motors Corporation, from 26 to 30 per cent for the Ford Motor Company, and from 14 to 18 per cent for the Chrysler Corporation. The share of the Big Three has varied from a low of 87 per cent to a high of 95 per cent. Thus, the industry is and has been highly concentrated.

Barriers to Entry. Barriers to entry are generally thought to be high. Professor Bain estimates that between 5 to 10 per cent of total new car registrations in a six million unit car year is necessary for most efficient production. These estimates increase to between 10 to 20 per cent of the national low price market and between 30 to 60 per cent of the upper middle price market.[1] Little is known of the possible economies in distribution and sales promotion expenditure. Perhaps a more important barrier to entry is the extent of product differentiation. Attributing the differentiation to brand allegiances based on advertising, product reputation, dealer service organization, and differential trade-in values, Bain believes a new entrant would be at a 5 to 15 per cent disadvantage in price or extra sales promotion expenditure for ten years. He estimates a new entrant to the automobile industry would expect to lose $200 million or more during a decade to obtain 3 to 4 per cent of the market at the end of the decade.[2] Bain's findings suggest the industry should be viewed as a differentiated oligopoly in which the larger firms recognize their inter-dependence when determining their price, sales promotion, and product policies. Competitive strategy dictates the use of styling, product innovation, and product service as competitive techniques in preference to price competition.[3]

Product Differentiation. It is generally believed that automobiles are differentiated products. Most studies of consumer

---

[1] These estimates are outdated because of the recent relative decline in the size of the upper middle class.

[2] J. S. Bain, *Barriers to New Competition* (Cambridge: Harvard University Press, 1956), pp. 296–308.

[3] Some observers believe the automobile industry is highly competitive because of the extensive and frequent styling changes. It is not clear that this is the relevant criteria. It is likely product styling and product improvement would persist even if there were many producers in the industry.

purchases of automobiles indicate that repeat sales are a large component of total sales. However, caution is urged since the data upon which these studies are based are decidely limited. Data showing repeat sales are presented in Table 1. They indicate approximately one-half of new cars purchased of a given make during a year are purchased by individuals or families who own an automobile of the same make.[4]

General Motors makes tend to have somewhat higher repeat sales than other makes in the years for which we have data. However, little is known about the stability of these percentages over time. Given the limited amount of data, the only valid conclusions seem to be that repeat sales account for slightly more than 50 per cent of total sales in the low price class and possibly, for a somewhat lower percentage in the middle price class.

---

[4] The data in Table 1 should be carefully evaluated. In a major face lift year, more buyers will switch makes than in a minor face lift year. For example, suppose an unusually large number of Chevrolet buyers switch to Ford in a given year. Of the total buyers of new Fords in that year, only a small percentage will appear as repeaters, that is, trade in a Ford and buy a Ford even though, most Ford owners repurchase Fords. Hence, the data for any one year may underestimate or overestimate the extent of repeat sales. There was a relatively large change in market shares in 1957. Therefore, the percentages in Table 1 are probably understated. An alternative method of measuring the importance of repeat sales would be to classify all new car buyers by the make of trade in. Then, the percentage of these buyers who purchased the same make could be determined. In effect, this measure shows the percentage of owners of a given make who remain loyal to the make. Although these data are available, they are considered as confidential data by the companies. At the request of the author, a special tabulation was made of the *U.S. News and World Report* data. Buyers were classified by the make traded in. Then, the percentage of these buyers who purchased the same make was determined. The results are presented below.

Make	Per cent Purchasing the Same Make (1957 Survey)	Response Rate
Ford	71.7	67.6
Chevrolet	65.1	66.6
Buick	57.6	63.6
Chrysler	40.3	69.2

TABLE 1. REPEAT BUYERS BY MAKE—PER CENT OF NEW CAR BUYERS
WHO OWNED SAME MAKE AS PURCHASED

1957 Survey

Low price class	
Chevrolet	61.7
Ford	55.0
Plymouth	43.6
Middle price class	
Buick	67.8
Pontiac	60.7
Oldsmobile	61.9
Chrysler	44.3
Mercury	55.1
Desoto	38.9
Dodge	36.6
High price class	
Cadillac	77.6
Lincoln	39.0

[a] n.a. denotes not available.
[b] Estimated from a small base.
Sources : U.S. News and World Report and Benson & Benson, Inc., *A Market Study of the People Buying New Automobiles* (New Jersey : U.S. News and World Report, 1957).

Moreover, if buyers considered each make in each price class as a perfect substitute and hence selected their autos at random, one would expect a smaller percentage of repeat sales.[5]

Another indicator of product differentiation is the behavior of the resale prices of used automobiles. Differences in the resale price, as a per cent of the original wholesale price, show the differential evaluation by consumers of the different makes. If these differentials in used prices persist, they would indicate each make is not considered a perfect substitute for other makes. It is pos-

---

[5] Suppose each buyer considered Fords, Chevrolets and Plymouths as perfect substitutes. Then, one would expect that 33 per cent of all Chevrolet owners to repurchase a Chevrolet, and so on. This assumes the repurchase is confined to the low price class. Until the advent of the compact car, this was a reasonable assumption.

sible to trace these price differentials to differences in quality.[6] Then, it is difficult to explain why producers whose automobiles persistently depreciate at a faster rate do not copy those automobiles with superior features. Patents are freely exchanged among the producers. There appears to be no technological or economic reason why this could not be done. It follows that persistant price differentials among the different makes of used cars of similar age, style, and so on are an indication that each make is not a perfect substitute for other makes in the same price class.

During the 1946–1950 period, Bain found that General Motors' brands occupied preferred positions in trade-in values over the brands of the Ford Motor Company and the Chrysler Corporation.[7] The advantage of General Motors in this regard was smallest in the middle price class. In turn, he found that the independents are at a general disadvantage compared to Ford and Chrysler. Bain studied 1950 and earlier models. To determine if these price differentials persisted, a similar test was applied to 1955 and 1956 models. These data are reproduced in Table 2. They basically substantiate Bain's findings. General Motors' autos invariably have lower depreciation rates, although General Motors' advantage does not seem to be any greater in the low price class than in the middle price class.

The available data, which show repeat sales and used prices of different makes, support the contention that automobiles are differentiated products. It would appear that the autos of the Big Three are differentiated from the autos of the independents and that the autos of the Big Three are differentiated among themselves.

Price and Income Elasticities. The demand for automobiles is thought to be highly sensitive to changes in disposable income.

---

[6] For example, used Fords may have been driven more than used Chevrolets of the same age. Hence, Fords may depreciate at a faster rate. While possible, there is no reason why this should be true, but this is no proof that it is not.

[7] Bain, *op. cit.,* p. 304.

TABLE 2. RESALE PRICE OF USED AUTOMOBILES BY MAKE

	1955 Models Wholesale Value as a Per cent of Factory Invoice (as of May 1, 1956)	1956 Models Wholesale Value as a Per cent of Factory Invoice (as of May 1, 1957)
Low price class		
Chevrolet	76	79
Ford	72	74
Plymouth	70	65
Rambler	—	69
Middle price class		
Oldsmobile	75	76
Buick	74	74
Pontiac	73	71
Mercury	72	68
Dodge	70	69
Desoto	68	69
Hudson	67	60
Nash	55	60
Studebaker	63	63
Upper middle and high price class		
Cadillac	91	90
Chrysler	69	71
Chrysler (N.Y.)	66	70
Lincoln	63	70
Packard	60	55

Source: *Depreciation Analysis of American Automobiles July 1957* (Teaneck, New Jersey: Yegen Associates, no publication date).

A reason for this is that the stock of automobiles held con-sumers is related to the level of income. Therefore, changes in the stock of automobiles, that is, new car sales, will be related to changes in the level of income. Because of this, the sales of automobiles can be expected to show greater variability than the sales of most other products for any given change in in-come.

The Commerce Department conducted a study of the in-come sensitivity of consumption expenditures for a large number of goods and services. Dollar expenditure on each good or service was correlated with disposable income and a trend variable.[8] Expenditure for new cars and net purchases of used cars was shown to be highly sensitive to changes in disposable income. A 10 per cent change in disposable income produces a 20 per cent change in consumer expenditure. Of the many goods and services included in the study, the expenditure of only three other goods was more sensitive to changes in disposable income than the expenditure on automobiles. Thus, total expenditure on new automobiles appears to change by a greater percentage for any given percentage change in disposable income than the total expenditure on most other goods and services.

There have been several conventional studies of the demand for automobiles. The price and income elasticities estimates are summarized in Table 3. Generally, the estimates of the price elasticity of demand are near minus one and in several instances somewhat larger.

TABLE 3. THE DEMAND FOR AUTOMOBILES, PRICE AND INCOME ELASTICITIES

Study	Income Elasticity	Elasticity with Respect to Price-per Month	Elasticity with Respect to Retail Price
1. Suits			
Equation 2.1t	4.16	−.59	
Equation 2.2t	4.59		+.40
Equation 2.3t	3.80	−.55	
2. Roos and von Szeliski	2.5–3.8 [a]		−.65 [a]
3. Atkinson	2.455		−1.31
4. Cohen	2.283		
5. Nerlove	2.8		−.9
6. Chow	1.7		−1.1

[a] Adjusted by Suits for comparability.

Sources: Estimates 1 through 4 are reproduced from Daniel B. Suits, "The Demand for New Automobiles in the United States 1929–1956," *The Review of Economics and Statistics* (August, 1958), pp. 273–280. Estimates 5 and 6 are reproduced from *Administered Prices*. Hearings before the Subcommittee on Antitrust and Monopoly of the Committee on the Judiciary, U.S. Senate, 85th Congress, 2nd Sess., pursuant to S. Res. 57 and S. Res. 231, Part 7, Appendix, p. 4176.

[8] Clement Winston and Mabel N. Smith, "Income Sensitivity of Consumption Expenditure," *Survey of Current Business* (January, 1950), pp. 17–20.

CHAPTER 2

The Restrictive Franchise System in Automobile Distribution

2.1. Introduction

Before a businessman can become a new car dealer, he must apply for and obtain a franchise from an automobile manufacturer. The number of franchises is usually restricted. Throughout most of the postwar period there has been a waiting line of qualified applicants for the franchises of the Ford Motor Company and the General Motors Corporation. Why do these automobile companies find it more profitable to adopt a restrictive franchise system? Why do they not allow entry into automobile retailing and sell automobiles to any qualified businessman who expects to make an economic profit? In this chapter a theoretical analysis of the restrictive franchise system is presented. Tests are made of the alternative explanations of why a restrictive franchise system is used in automobile distribution.

2.2. Definition of the Restrictive Franchise System

Throughout this study, a distinction will be made between a restrictive franchise system and a franchise system. There is a reason for this distinction. It is easy to think of the franchise, and many individuals do, as a contract, a piece of paper, authorizing the retailer to be a representative of the manufacturer in a particular market. The economist considers the issuance of franchises as a formality. In general, he is interested in the number of franchises issued and, in particular, whether the number of franchises issued is equal to or less than the number which would be issued if the manufacturer allowed every qualified businessman who desired to sell the product. Many manufacturers issue franchises and claim they distribute their products under a franchise system. In most instances, closer inspection will show that they have already issued enough franchises so that there is no longer a demand for their franchises. It is evident that the issuance of franchises does not indicate whether the franchise system is or is not restrictive. It is desirable to distinguish between situations where the number of franchises is restricted from situations where the number of franchises is not restricted. The phrase—restrictive franchise system—refers to those situations where the number of franchises is restricted. To some extent, the use of the word restrictive is unfortunate. The unsuspecting reader may believe an ethical judgment is implied. This is the last thing the author has in mind. The use of the word restrictive does not imply any ethical judgment. Rather, it is simply used to distinguish those market situations where the number of franchises is restricted from those market situations where the number of franchises is not restricted.[1]

A central characteristic of a restrictive franchise system is that entry is blocked A franchise system is restrictive whenever ex-

---

[1] Often however, the author will delete the term restrictive for brevity.

cess demand for entry exists at expected profit rates. If the profit rates of a company's retailers have been relatively high and if there is evidence that the company has restricted the number of retailers, then it is likely that the franchise system is restrictive.

2.3. The Restrictive Franchise System In Automobile Distribution

A persistent waiting line of qualified applicants at the manufacturer's door is one sign that a restrictive franchises system has been adopted. The following statement by Mr. Gossett, Vice President and General Counsel of the Ford Motor Company, suggests the automobile companies have adopted a restrictive franchise system:

> The right to be an authorized dealer is valuable because the dealership is the only place in most communities where the consumer can buy the manufacturer's product and obtain authorized service. Although there often are a number of authorized dealerships of a given make of vehicle in the larger metropolitan areas, these dealerships, nevertheless, are limited in number compared to the number there would be if the manufacturer chose to sell to all who elected to handle its products.[2]

Mr. Gossett's statement suggests there was an excess demand for Ford franchises at the time of his statement. Whether there is a persistent excess demand for Ford and General Motors franchises is not known and can only be conjectured. The smaller auto manufacturers have probably not observed a persistent excess demand for their franchises. On the whole, this is an area where data are practically nonexistent. For this reason, an alternative set of performance tests must be specified to determine whether the franchise system in automobile distribution has been restrictive.

---

[2] Statement by Mr. Gossett, Vice President and General Counsel, Ford Motor Company, *Automobile Dealer Franchises,* Hearings before the Antitrust Subcommittee (Subcommittee No. 5) of the Committee on the Judiciary, House of Rep., 84th Cong., 2nd Session on H. R. 11360 and S. 3879, p. 286.

Profitability. Since the franchise system blocks entry into the distribution sector, it limits the number of final sellers below the number that would be observed with entry. With entry restricted, it is likely the retail price will persistently exceed the long-run average cost of the retailer.[3] In general, the profit rates of retailers operating under a franchise system should be higher than the competitive rate of return.

One objective test has been proposed. Are the profit rates in automobile distribution higher than the competitive rate? There are three sources of dealer profit data: from the company sources, *Statistics of Income,* and the *National Income Supplement.*[4] It is difficult to estimate just what is a competitive rate of return. A proxy variable will be substituted. The profit rate of the corporate retail trade sector will be substituted for the competitive rate return. It is not a perfect substitute for several reasons. First, there is reason to suspect that retail markets are imperfect because of scale and location variables. Profit rates of the retail trade sector are likely to be above the competitive rate. Second, the profit rate of the corporate retail trade sector will be used as the proxy variable. The reason for this is the inadequacies of the data. Profit rates in the corporate retail sector appear to be higher on average than the estimates of profit rates in the unincorporated retail trade sector. This is an important point because the ratio of the sales of corporate auto dealers to the total sales of all auto dealers is higher than the ratio of the sales of all corporate retailers to total retail sales. Thus, a comparison of the profit rates of corporate auto dealers with the profit rates of all corporate retailers will tend to minimize the differences between the average profit rate in automobile distribution and the average profit rate in retail trade. Any comparison of the corporate rates of return to determine whether the profit rate

---

[3] Later this statement will be modified.

[4] A more detailed description of the limitations of these data are presented in Chapter **7**.

of auto dealers are higher than the profit rate of the retail trade sector is biased against that finding.[5]

One final point should be made. Profit rates of unincorporated retailers have not been published. However, estimates can and have been made. Although these estimates may not be very accurate for any one year, they probably are reasonably accurate estimates of the average returns obtained by unincorporated retailers over the period of observation.[6]

The profit rates of automobile dealers, of incorporated retailers and of unincorporated retailers are presented in Table 4. Profit rates are computed before and after deductions of officers'

---

[5] For example, in 1954 the sales of corporate automobile dealers accounted for 66 per cent of total retail sales of automobile dealers. The sales of incorporated retailers accounted for only 48 per cent of total retail sales. In 1954 the profit rate before payment of officers' salaries was 14.6 for corporate automobile dealers and 18.6 for incorporated retailers. (See Table 4, p. 17.) One might infer from these figures that in 1954 the average profit rate in retailing was some 4 percentage points higher than the average profit rate in automobile distribution. Yet, this estimate of the difference in profit rates would be too large. The profit rate of unincorporated retailers was 11.1 per cent in 1954. Assume the profit rate of unincorporated auto dealers was equal to the profit rate of unincorporated retailers. (It was probably higher.) Then, the profit rates of the incorporated and unincorporated sectors can be weighted by the proportion of total sales each sector accounts for. This can be done for automobile retailing and the retail trade sector. A difference of 4 percentage points was found in the corporate profit rates. The weighted profit rate of the retail trade sector would be 14.7 per cent, and the weighted profit rate of automobile retailing would be 13.4 per cent, a difference of just 1.3 per cent. The reader will wish to keep this in mind when he studies Table 4.

[6] The estimates can be obtained by making judicious use of data found in *Statistics of Income, Census of Business,* and the *National Income Supplement.* The profit rates of the unincorporated sector of retail trade can be estimated in the following manner. Income per unincorporated enterprise in retail trade was computed from data published in the *National Income Supplement.* This is equivalent to corporate profits before deductions of officers' compensation and income taxes. Net worth per unincorporated enterprise can be estimated in the following manner. Assume the ratio of net worth per unincorporated retail firm to the net worth per retail corporation is equal to the ratio of sales per unincorporated retail firm to the sales per retail corporation. This procedure yields an estimate of net worth per unincorporated retail firm. Probably it is a high estimate because the sales-net worth ratio is lower for incorporated firms than unincorporated firms.

salaries. The reason for this is that it is difficult to separate the compensation of officers from profits.[7] Officers tend to overstate their salaries in order to minimize their total tax liability. The author prefers to use profit rates before deductions for officers' compensation when making the desired comparisons. In this way, the effect of artificial allocations between profits and officers' compensation can be minimized.

Inspection of Table 4 shows that the total return rates (before-tax profits plus officers' compensation) in automobile distribution have tended to exceed the total return rates in the retail trade sector. In the prewar period, the total return rates were substantially above the total return rates of the retail trade sector. As is well known, the profit rates of automobile dealers in the immediate post-war period were exceptionally high. From 1953 to 1955, the two series of corporate total return rates have tended towards equality. As was noted above, an equality of the corporate returns rates implies the average profit rates in automobile retailing has exceeded the average profit rate in retail trade. Nonetheless, these data do suggest a narrowing in the difference, and one might have reason to question whether the franchise system was restrictive during this period.

For this reason, a more intensive analysis was made of the *Statistics of Income* data. There is reason to suspect the reported profits in the *Statistics of Income* have a downward bias. One additional comparison will shed light on the defects of the corporate tax data and permit more accurate estimates of the returns in automobile distribution. The General Motors Corporation and the Ford Motor Company have released after-tax profit rate data. These profit rates are computed after officers' compensation has been deducted. These rates are probably better indicators of the actual returns in automobile distribution since they are more likely to be free from any serious distortion which

---

[7] The interested reader may wish to skip ahead and read Chapter 7. A more detailed description of the difficulty of measuring profits in the retail sector is given in that chapter.

TABLE 4. COMPARISON OF PROFIT RATES OF AUTOMOBILE DEALERS AND OF THE CORPORATE AND UNINCORPORATED RETAIL TRADE SECTOR, 1938-1955[a]

| Year[b] | Profit Rates before Payment of Officers' Salaries | | | Profit Rates after Payment of Officers' Salaries | | |
| | Corporate Automobile Dealers | Retail Trade | | Corporate Automobile Dealers | Retail Trade | |
		Corporate	Unin-corporate		Corporate	Unin-corporate[c]
1938	12.6	10.6	5.1	—5.9	4.0	—.9
1939	26.4	13.6	5.3	5.0	7.1	0.0
1940	32.5	15.5	5.9	10.9	8.8	.7
1941	49.5	22.6	7.2	25.0	15.3	2.2
1946	67.3	36.3	14.2	51.4	28.6	8.0
1947	65.6	34.6	12.0	55.4	26.3	5.1
1948	62.1	30.3	11.5	45.3	22.1	4.4
1949	38.0	23.4	...[d]	23.4	15.3	...[d]
1950	45.9	28.4	11.7	30.9	20.1	4.4
1951	33.3	23.3	10.7	19.3	15.3	3.3
1952	n.a.	21.5	10.5	n.a.	13.7	2.7
1953	19.9	19.8	10.8	7.5	11.9	2.6
1954	14.6	18.6	11.1	3.0	10.8	2.4
1955	21.7	21.4	11.6	9.2	13.1	2.3

[a] Profits are given as a per cent of net worth.
[b] From 1938 to 1950 the profit rates are for the retail trade sector. From 1951 to 1955 the profit rates are for the combined retail and whole-sale trade sector. This change was caused by a change in the method of data presentation.
[c] Salary of the proprietor of each unincorporate firm was assumed to equal the full time earnings of an employee in retail trade.
[d] These data are available, however, the author was not able to obtain them at the time the computations were made.

Sources: U.S. Internal Revenue Service, Statistics of Income, Part II, annual issues; U.S. Bureau of the Census, Census of Business (1939, 1948, 1954); U.S. Office of Business Economics, National Income and Product of the United States (1929, 1950, 1951 Edition); U.S. Office of Business Economics, U.S. Income and Output (1958).

17

may be found in the tax data. They cannot be compared directly with the *Statistics of Income* after-tax profit rates. Quite likely, the after-tax profit rates of incorporated retailers are understated. Retailers will overstate the compensation of officers and other expenses to lower their tax liabilities. The real question is how much are they able to do this. No simple answer can be given. However, an extreme assumption can be made. Suppose the total of reported officers' compensation in the retail trade sector really represents profits. Suppose the total of reported officers' compensation of all retail corporations is added to reported after-tax profits of all retail corporations (the sum will be referred to as adjusted after-tax profits). Why is this an extreme assumption? In recent years, reported officers' compensation of retail corporations tends to be about equal to (actually somewhat larger) reported after-tax profits. Adjusted after-tax profits are about twice as large as reported after-tax profits. After-tax profits are adjusted upward to compensate against the apparent overstatement in expenses and officers' compensation. The real question is whether retailers are able to add expenses in sufficient amount to cut their after-tax profits in half. Roughly speaking, this is the amount that has been added to reported after-tax profits to arrive at the adjusted figure. Of course, there is no direct test of this. Possibly, they can. Yet, it is hard to believe the Internal Revenue Service is so lax that retailers are consistently able to understate their actual profits by as much as 50 per cent.

However, suppose incorporated retailers are able to overstate their expenses and thereby lower their actual after-tax profits by 50 per cent. By adding reported officers compensation to reported after-tax profits, an estimate of actual after-tax profits can be obtained. Then, a comparison can be made between the General Motors and Ford dealer profit data, which are after taxes and after deductions for officers' compensation, and the Internal Revenue Service profit data of corporations in retail trade, which are after tax but *before* deduction of officers' compensation. If the profit rates of General Motors and Ford dealers still exceed the adjusted Internal Revenue Service profit rates, it is likely the profit rates of General Motors and Ford dealers have exceeded the profit rates of incorporated retailers. The profit rates of all General Motors and all Ford dealers (after tax and before deductions of officers' compensation) are presented in Table 5. The profit rates of incorporated retailers

TABLE 5. PROFIT RATES OF GENERAL MOTORS AND FORD MOTOR CO. DEALERS COMPARED TO PROFIT RATES OF CORPORATIONS IN RETAIL TRADE [a]

	All Corporations in Retail Trade [b]		General Motors Dealers [c]	Ford Motor Co. Dealers [d]
Year	After Tax but *before* Deduction for Officers' Compensation	After Tax and *after* Deduction for Officers' Compensation	After Tax and *after* Deduction for Officers' Compensation	After Tax and *after* Deduction for Officers' Compensation
1938	9.5	3.0	n.a.	
1939	12.1	5.6	n.a.	
1940	13.2	6.4	27.2	
1941	16.5	9.1	n.a.	
1946	26.0	18.3	87.2	
1947	25.1	16.8	98.5	
1948	22.2	14.0	64.8	
1949	17.6	9.4	38.0	
1950	20.1	11.8	42.4	
1951	15.5	7.5	24.6	
1952	14.5	6.6	15.3	
1953	13.3	5.5	14.4	
1954	12.8	5.0	9.04	11.27
1955	14.9	6.6	13.81	16.28

[a] Profits are given as a per cent of net worth.
[b] *Statistics of Income,* Part II, annual issues 1938–1955.
[c] *General Motors,* Hearings before the Subcommittee on Antitrust and Monopoly of the Committee on the Judiciary, U.S. Senate, 84th Cong., 1st Sess., pursuant to S. Res. 61, Part 8, p. 4055; 4470.
[d] *Automobile Dealer Franchises,* Hearings before the Antitrust Subcommittee (Subcommittee No. 5) of the Committee on the Judiciary, House of Representatives, 84th Cong., 2nd Sess. on H.R. 11360 and S. 3879, pp. 386–387.

(after tax but before deductions of officers' compensation and after tax and after deductions of officers' compensation) are also presented. There is only one prewar observation. In 1940, the profit rate of General Motors dealers far exceeded the adjusted profit rate of the retail trade sector.

Whether this was a persistent characteristic of the prewar

period is not known. There is evidence that it was. Fortune Magazine reported the after-tax profit rates of General Motors dealers averaged 12 per cent of net worth from 1932 to 1936.[8] Profit rates in the retail trade sector for the same period are not known. The only comparison that can be made (and it is a crude comparison) is with the average of the profit rates of leading manufacturing corporations compiled and computed by the National City Bank. From 1932 to 1936 the average after-tax profit rate of these leading manufacturers averaged 4.7 per cent on net worth. Admittedly, this is a crude comparison, but it does suggest that General Motors dealers were able to earn a higher rate of return on their investment throughout most of the depression decade than most corporations. If correct, this is an interesting finding. Later, there will be reason to return to this point.

In the postwar period, the profit rates of all General Motors dealers (incorporated and unincorporated) have exceeded the *adjusted* profit rates of incorporated retailers in every year except 1954–1955. As was noted above, the profit rates of unincorporated retailers are usually lower than the profit rates of incorporated retailers. The General Motors and Ford data include the returns of their incorporated and unincorporated dealers, whereas the Internal Revenue Service data only include the returns of incorporated retailers. If an adjustment were made, the adjusted profit rates of incorporated retailers would exceed the profit rates of General Motors dealers only in 1954. These data suggest that the profit rates of General Motors and (quite likely) Ford dealers have generally exceeded the profit rates of incorporated retail firms, even under the assumption that all deductions for officers' compensation of retailers should be considered as retailer profits. If this assumption is relaxed, that is, if a larger and larger proportion of the compensation of officers is allocated to the salary account as bona fide payments, there

---

[8] "General Motors III: How to Sell Automobiles," *Fortune* (February, 1939), p. 106.

is even more reason to believe the profit rates of General Motors and (quite likely) Ford dealers have persistently exceeded the profit rates of incorporated and unincorporated retailers.[9]

Turnover Rates. Another test of the profitability hypothesis is whether turnover rates are lower in automobile distribution than the turnover rates in other industries. Again, basic data problems exist, but several comparisons can be made. The turnover rates of General Motors dealers are available and are presented in Chapter 3, Table 9. The turnover rates of General Motors dealers ranged from 5.4 per cent in 1951 to 9.9 per cent in 1954. The average annual turnover rates from 1951 to 1955 for other major industry groups are presented in Table 6A. The turnover rates are defined as the number of discontinued plus transferred businesses as a percentage of the number of firms in existence in each industry. Data showing turnover rates for more detailed industries than those shown in Table 6A are also available, though they are not presented. Out of 45 sub-industries (classified in manufacturing, retail trade, and wholesale trade), only two had lower turnover rates from 1951 to 1955 than the average annual turnover rates of General Motors dealers from 1951 to 1954. These unadjusted turnover rates do suggest that lower turnover rates are experienced by General Motors dealers. However, turnover rates are a function of many variables, for example, the average size of the firm in the industry, and the growth rate of the industry. The available data do not allow an adjustment for each of these factors. One crude method of correcting for differences between industries in the average size of the firms is to compare turnover rates of General Motors dealers with turnover rates of incorporated firms. Generally, incorporated firms are larger than unincorporated firms, and, more often than not, they are manufacturing firms. The author does not know of any data which show turnover rates of incorpo-

---

[9] However, it should be noted that the differential has narrowed in the 1953–1955 period. It is likely this differential has narrowed even further since 1955.

TABLE 6A. AVERAGE ANNUAL TURNOVER RATES IN SELECT INDUSTRIES (1951-1955)[a]

Industry	(Per cent) Turnover Rate
ALL industries	16.0
Manufacturing	13.2
Retail	20.2
Wholesale	9.9
Finance, insurance and real estate	8.4
Service	13.5
Mining and quarrying	14.1
Contract construction	14.6

TABLE 6B. COMPARISON OF TURNOVER RATES OF GENERAL MOTORS DEALERS WITH TURNOVER RATES OF ALL INCORPORATED FIRMS

Year	ALL Incorporated Firms (Per cent)	General Motors Dealers (Per cent)
1951	9.3	5.4
1952	9.5	6.7
1953	10.0	8.0
1954	10.3	9.9

[a] Defined as the number of discontinued plus transferred businesses as a percentage of businesses in operation.

Sources: Betty C. Churchill, "Business Population by Legal Form of Organization, *Survey of Current Business* (April, 1955), pp. 14–20; Betty C. Churchill "Rise in the Business Population," *Survey of Current Business* (May, 1959), pp. 15–19. *General Motors,* Hearings Before the Subcommittee on Antitrust and Monopoly of the Committee on the Judiciary, U.S. Senate, 84th Cong., 1st Sess., pursuant to S. Res. 61, Part 8, pp. 4381–4382.

rated firms by industry. However, the turnover rates of all incorporated firms are available. These data are presented in Table 6B. The turnover rates of incorporated firms are generally lower than the turnover rates of unincorporated firms. Only crude comparisons can be made with these data. It would appear that the turnover rates of incorporated firms have tended to exceed the turnover rates of General Motors dealers (both corporate and unincorporated). These data are consistent with the hypothesis that turnover rates have been lower among General Motors dealers than the turnover rates in most other industries, at least for the period under observation.

Age Distribution of Dealers. Just as one would expect turn-over rates to be lower in automobile distribution, one would also expect the life expectancy of automobile dealerships to be greater than the life expectancy of the business population as a whole. Life expectancy data are not available. However, data showing the age distribution of dealers are available. All other things being equal, one would expect a larger percentage of auto dealers to be in business for x years or more than for the business population as a whole. The reason for this follows directly from the use of the franchise system. Since turnover rates are likely to be lower under a franchise system, this means that, once dealers are appointed, they are more likely to remain in business for a longer period. But, all things do not remain constant. The age distribution of firms in any given industry will also depend, among other variables, on the rate of growth of the industry. Hence, if an industry has recently experienced rapid growth, many new firms will enter the industry. A larger percentage of the firms in a growing industry should be relatively young. The automobile industry was one of the faster growing industries in the postwar period (at least from 1946 to 1955). Therefore, if a larger percentage of auto dealers have been in business, say ten years or more than all firms classified in retail trade, it cannot be argued that this is because sales of autos grew at a slower rate than total retail sales, and, hence, there has been no need for entry into the industry.

The age distributions of firms in various industries are compared to the age distributions of automobile dealers in Table 7. It is evident that the average or median age of auto dealers exceeds that of firms in other industries. It appears that the life expectancy of automobile dealers is higher than the life expectancy of firms in other industries.

To summarize, several independent tests have been made to determine if the franchise system adopted by the larger auto companies has been restrictive. The data are imperfect. Only a tentative conclusion can be advanced at this time. Nevertheless,

TABLE 7. THE AGE DISTRIBUTION OF FIRMS, A COMPARISON OF AUTOMOBILE DEALERS
WITH FIRMS IN OTHER INDUSTRIES (PER CENT)

Percentage of Firms in Business	All Industries	Manu-facturing	Whole-sale Trade	Retail Trade	Service Industries	Finance etc.
Under 5 years	43	39	40	47	37	31
5–9 yrs.	26	25	30	26	24	20
10–19 20 or more	{31	{36	{30	{27	{39	{49

Median Age (Dec. 31, 1954)

	All Industries	Manu-facturing	Whole-sale Trade	Retail Trade	Service Industries	Finance etc.
	6.75	7.50	7.25	6.00	7.75	10.25

Percentage of Dealers Holding Franchises	General Motors Dealers	Chevrolet Dealers	Ford Motor Co. Dealers	Chrysler Corp. Dealers
Under 5 years	24.6	24	n.a.	28.4
5–9	22.5	19	n.a.	18.1
10–19	22.9	20	{50	31.2
20 or more	30.0	38		22.3

Median Age

	General Motors Dealers	Chevrolet Dealers	Ford Motor Co. Dealers	Chrysler Corp. Dealers
	10+	10+	10	10+

Sources : *Industry sectors:* Betty C. Churchill, "Age and Life Expectancy of Business Firms," *Survey of Current Business* (December, 1955), pp. 15–19.
General Motors Dealers: The Development and Growth of General Motors, statement by Harlow H. Curtice, President, General Motors, before Subcommittee on Antitrust and Monopoly of the U.S. Senate Committee on the Judiciary, December 2, 1955, p. 20.
Chevrolet Dealers: personal letter from Mr. John L. Cutter, Public Relations Director, Chevrolet Central Office, dated March 24, 1958.
Ford Motor Company Dealers: Automobile Marketing Practices, Hearings before a Subcommittee of the Committee on Interstate and Foreign Commerce, U.S. Senate, 84th Cong., 2nd Sess. pursuant to S.Res. 13 Continued by S.Res. 163, Part 1, p. 978.
Chrysler Corporation Dealers: Automobile Marketing Practices, Hearings before a Subcommittee of the Committee on Interstate and Foreign Commerce, U.S. Senate, 84th Cong., 2nd Sess. pursuant to S.Res. 13 Continued by S.Res. 163, Part 1, p. 444.

the results of these tests suggest that the franchise system in automobile distribution has been restrictive at least over the period under examination. Mr. Gossett's statement appears to be an accurate description of distribution policy of the larger auto companies.

2.4. Reasons for the Use of a Restrictive Franchise System

The larger automobile companies have apparently adopted some form of restrictive franchise system. As yet, nothing has been said about why a restrictive franchise system might be used. In this section a theoretical analysis of the restrictive franchise system is presented. Under what conditions and in what types of market might a manufacturer want to adopt a restrictive franchise system?

Throughout the analysis, the number of retailers will be considered a variable controlled by the manufacturer. In the first part of the analysis, the manufacturer (for simplicity, a monopolist) quotes a wholesale price (uniform to all retailers) and allows each retailer to determine the number of units to be purchased. In the second part of the analysis, the manufacturer not only quotes a wholesale price but also specifies a sales quota for each retailer which the retailer must fulfill; that is, the manufacturer specifies an "all or nothing" bargain. For conciseness, this practice will be referred to as forcing.[10]

The Restrictive Franchise System in Perfect Retail Markets. Perfect retail markets seldom exist. Yet, it is instructive to see if a restrictive franchise system would be adopted if perfect retail markets did exist. Given the retail demand for the manufacturer's product, the manufacturer would be interested in selecting that number of retailers which would minimize the distribution cost of any given volume of sales. Distribution costs would be minimized by selecting enough retailers so that each retailer operated at the minimum point of his long-run average cost schedule. Hence, the manufacturer will merely subtract from the retail demand curve a distribution cost margin to derive a

---

[10] Because the question of dealer-manufacturer relations is such a sensitive issue, the author would like to stress that the use of the word forcing does not imply an ethical judgment.

net demand curve and then maximize his profits with respect to this net demand function. In equilibrium

(1) $$P_R = AC_L{}^* + w = MC_L{}^* + w$$

where P_R is the retail price, $AC_L{}^* = MC_L{}^*$ is the minimum per unit distribution cost (excluding the cost of the product to the retailer), and w is the wholesale price charged by the manufacturer to the retailer. Equation (1) will be satisfied if, and only if, each retailer operated at the minimum point of the long-run average cost schedule. The manufacturer will select the profit maximizing wholesale price and sell to all retailers at that price. The number of retailers will increase until the retailers' profits are competed away. At this point, there will be no further demand for entry by potential retailers. There is no incentive for the manufacturer to restrict the number of retailers. Under these conditions, the adoption of a restrictive franchise system implies some non-maximizing behavior. To find a rational justification for the use of a restrictive franchise system, some market imperfection must exist.

The Restrictive Franchise System in Relatively Small Local Markets. Most retail markets are not perfect. One imperfection arises from the extent of economies of scale in the distribution sector which often precludes the existence of many efficient retailers in each local market. Although more than one retailer may be able to operate profitably in the market, the maximum number that could is sufficiently small. Each retailer will recognize the interdependence between his and his competitor's price policy. For simplicity, a collusive market-sharing solution will be assumed to be reached by the oligopolists. In the author's opinion, this is a convenient and often realistic solution to the oligopoly problem, especially when the number of sellers is small. Will the manufacturer adopt a restrictive franchise system under these conditions? Assume the demand curve facing any given retailer is given by

(2)
$$P_R = f(nq)$$

where P_R is the retail price, q is the sales of each retailer, and n is the number of retailers in the market (to be determined by the manufacturer). The profits of the retailer are

(3)
$$\pi_R = f(nq)q - C(q) - wq \qquad \pi_R \gtreqless 0$$

where $C(q)$ is the retailer's long-run distribution cost schedule. The first order equilibrium condition is

(4)
$$\frac{d\pi_R}{dq} = qnf' + f - C' - w = 0$$

where

$$f' = \frac{df}{d(nq)}$$

and

$$C' = \frac{dC}{dq}$$

The profits of the manufacturer are

(5)
$$\pi_M = wqn - M(nq) = q^2 n^2 f' + qnf(qn) - qnC'(q) \\ - M(nq)$$

where $M(nq)$ is the manufacturer's long-run cost schedule. The manufacturer selects n and q so as to maximize Equation (5). Differentiating Equation (5) with respect to n and q and making several substitutions, one obtains the condition

(6)
$$C''(q) = 0$$

What is the economic interpretation of Equation (6)? The manufacturer may continue to add retailers to the market as long as it does not force any one retailer to operate at an output where the retailer's marginal cost is falling or rising. If the manufacturer allowed more retailers into the market, the total derived demand of the n retailers for the manufacturer's product would be less. Hence, the manufacturer would find it profitable to restrict the number of retailers even though this allowed the operating retailers to earn profits. These profits are a signal for potential retailers to enter the retail sector. However, the manufacturer forestalls this by refusing to sell the product to them. In general, the manufacturer will prefer to have a few large retailers than several smaller retailers which would exist if free entry were allowed.

Two additional points are worth mentioning. First, this argument does not depend on the natural monopoly argument. More than one retailer could and would operate profitably in the market if the manufacturer permitted entry. Second, suppose the manufacturer finds it profitable to have only one retailer in a market. The manufacturer would prefer the single retailer to charge a lower price than the monopoly price. The manufacturer may threaten to add another retailer to the market. The retailer may well choose to ignore the manufacturer's bluff. For, if it is not profitable for the manufacturer to add another retailer, the retailer need not fear that the monopoly price will attract entry.

The Restrictive Franchise System in Large Local Markets where the Retailers are Differentiated Sellers. In the larger retail markets many retailers can exist in each market. The manufacturer would not adopt a restrictive franchise system if each retailer were a perfect substitute for every other retailer. However, what if the consumer considered each retailer as a differentiated seller? Suppose the demand schedule facing each retailer is downward sloping even though the retailer accounts for a small percentage of total market sales. Would the manufacturer ever find it profitable to adopt a restrictive franchise system under these conditions?

Suppose the manufacturer has n retailers in a given market. By hypothesis, each retailer is an imperfect substitute for every other retailer. The demand curve for the kth retailer can be written as

$$(7) \qquad P_k = A_k - a_{kk}q_k - \sum_{\substack{i=1 \\ i \neq k}}^{n} b_{ki}q_i \qquad k = (1 \ldots n)$$

where q_k are the sales of the kth seller and q_i are the sales of the ith seller.[11] Though some realism is lost, for simplicity, all retailers will be assumed to have identical demand and cost functions; that is, $b_{ki} = b$ for all k and i except $k = i$, $a_{kk} = a$, $A_k = A$ and $C_k(q_k) = C(q_k)$ for all k.

For any wholesale price w charged by the manufacturer, the retailer will determine q_k so that the retailer's marginal revenue equals the retailer's marginal cost; that is,

$$(8) \qquad A - 2aq_k - b \sum_{\substack{i=1 \\ i \neq k}}^{n} q_i = C'(q_k) + w$$

The second order condition requires

$$(9) \qquad -2a < C''(q_k)$$

Because of the symmetry assumption, each retailer will reach the same solution, hence $q_k = q_i$. The equilibrium condition, Equation (8), becomes

$$(10) \qquad A - [2a + b(n-1)]q_k = C'(q_k) + w \qquad {}^{12}$$

Suppose the manufacturer allows free entry into the retail sector. The manufacturer will quote a wholesale price. Given that wholesale price, retailers will enter the retail sector until retailers' profits are competed away. Put somewhat differently, the manufacturer quotes a wholesale price and then allows the number of retailers to adjust until retailers' profits are zero.

The retailer's profits will be zero when the retailer's demand curve is tangent to his average cost curve which, in turn, is the

---

[11] This formulation is taken from James M. Henderson and Richard E. Quandt, *Microeconomic Theory* (New York: McGraw-Hill Book Co., Inc., 1958), pp. 192–195. The a's and the b's are assumed to be constant. They are likely to change as n varies. In this inquiry the effects of these changes are ignored. However, it would be interesting to consider a more general model where the coefficients are a function of n.

[12] This condition, together with the zero profit condition,

$$(10a) \qquad \pi_R = 0 = Aq_k - [a + (n-1)b]q_k^2 - C(q_k) - wq_k$$

will determine q_k and n to satisfy the familiar Chamberlin tangency solution.

sum of the per unit processing cost and the wholesale price; that
is,

(11) $\dfrac{C(q_k)}{q_k} + w$

Note that the *slope* of the average cost curve is independent of
the wholesale price w. Hence, no matter what wholesale price
the manufacturer quotes, each retailer, who remains in business,
will sell the same output.[13] However, the number of retailers
will fall if the manufacturer should select a higher wholesale
price.

Each retailer sells a given number of units, and this number
is independent of the wholesale price. Hence, the per unit processing cost (or selling cost) is determined, and this is independent
of the wholesale price. If the per unit processing cost is sub-
tracted from the industry demand curve at each output, the
derived demand curve facing the manufacturer is obtained.
Given this demand curve, the profits of the manufacturer will be
"maximized" at that output where the marginal revenue of this
derived demand schedule is equal to marginal manufacturing
cost. This will determine a wholesale price (say) w^*. The retail price R^* will be equal to $w^* + AC = R^*$, where AC is
the per unit processing cost of the retailer at the tangency output. The number of retailers in the industry will be determined
by the equation $Q = nq$, where q is that output at which AC
$= AC^*$.

Suppose the manufacturer determines w by this process.
The number of retailers n^* is determined by the retailer zero
profit condition.

Under what conditions would the manufacturer's profits *increase* if he refused to sell to one of the n^* retailers? Suppose

---

[13] This can also be seen by solving the two equilibrium equations
$$A - [2a + b(n-1)]q_k = C'(q_k) + w$$
$$0 = Aq_k - [a + b(n-1)]q_k^2 - C(q_k) - wq_k$$
for q_k, the second equation is the zero profit condition. The solution for q_k is
independent of w.

the manufacturer does not change the wholesale price, w^* but decides to sell to one less retailer. Suppose it can be shown that total retail sales by the remaining $(n^* - 1)$ retailers would be higher than the sales of the n^* retailers. Then, the manufacturer's profits must increase. Since the wholesale price is assumed to be constant at w^* and since the $(n^* - 1)$ retailers will wish to sell more total units than the n^* retailers, it follows that

$$(12) \qquad w^* = MR > M'(nq)$$

where MR is the marginal revenue received by the manufacturer, and $M'(nq)$ is the marginal cost incurred by the manufacturer. Hence, the manufacturer's profits must increase for small changes in total sales.

Total sales will increase if the sum of the increase in each remaining retailer's sales is greater than the sales of the retailer who is excluded from the market; that is,

$$(13) \qquad n\frac{dq}{dn} < -q \qquad \text{or} \qquad -n\frac{dq}{dn} > q$$

From Equation (10), derive

$$(14) \qquad \frac{dq}{dn} = -\frac{bq}{2a + (n-1)b + c''(q)}$$

Substituting into Equation (13) and simplifying, one obtains

$$(15) \qquad \frac{nb}{2a + (n-1)b + c''(q)} > 1$$

or

$$\frac{nb}{2a - b + nb + c''(q)} > 1$$

Under what conditions will this ratio be greater than 1? The second order condition for a profit maximum requires that $-2a < C''(q)$. Therefore, the inequality, $-[2a + (n-1)b] < C''(q)$, will be satisfied. This implies

$$(16) \qquad -[2a + (n-1)b + C''(q)] < 0$$

Therefore,

$$2a + (n-1)b + C''(q) > 0$$

Hence, the denominator of Equation (15) will be positive. The stability condition, plus the condition that the ratio be greater than one, implies that the slope of the marginal cost curve must satisfy the following condition

(17) $- 2a < C''(q) < - (2a - b)$

The manufacturer's profits will increase if at the zero profit output of the retailer $C''(q) < - (2a - b)$ [14]

Condition (17) will not always be satisfied at the zero profit output of the retailer. If the inequality holds at the zero profit output of the retailer, it would be profitable for the manufacturer to exclude a retailer from the market even though this permits the remaining retailers to earn economic profits. More generally, whether the manufacturer's profits will increase by restricting a retailer from the market will depend upon (a) the slope of the retailer's marginal cost curve, (b) the effect on the retailer's price as he increases his sales, and (c) the effect on the retailer's price when another retailer increases his sales.

Hence, a manufacturer may adopt a restrictive franchise system if there are economies of scale in retailing, and if consumers consider the retailers as differentiated sellers. These conditions must exist before a manufacturer will consider using a restrictive franchise system.

As noted above, the manufacturer may have an "efficiency" bias. The manufacturer may prefer to have fewer retailers in the retail sector than would exist with free entry. This is true in small local markets and also in large local markets where consumers are attached to retailers. Thus, the manufacturer may act as an "efficiency regulator" by decreasing the number of retailers and thereby increasing the size and efficiency of the remaining retailers. This may be what company officials are think-

---

[14] This result can be reached more directly but with less intuitive appeal in the following manner. Form the manufacturer's profit function
$$\pi_m = wnq - M(nq) = Anq_k - [2a + b(n-1)]nq_k^2 - C'(q_k)nq_k - M(nq)$$
Differentiation with respect to n and q and a substitution will yield the condition
$$-2a + b = C''(q)$$

ing about when they say they prefer to establish fewer and bigger retailers.

In summary, the use of a franchise system by a manufacturer can be shown to be a rational policy under certain retail demand and retail cost conditions. From the usual static assumptions of given demand and cost functions, it is possible to show that the profits of a manufacturer could increase rather than fall by restricting the number of retailers.

The Restrictive Franchise System and the Bargaining Position of the Manufacturer. These models suffer from two important defects. First, the usefulness of the analysis for empirical testing is limited. The adoption of a restrictive franchise system in any particular industry cannot be explained unless the values of certain slopes are known. Very seldom is it possible to make accurate estimates of these slopes. Second, the models ignore another marketing practice which is observed in automobile distribution. The automobile manufacturer appears to have a stronger bargaining position relative to the bargaining position of the dealer. The manufacturer not only can specify a transfer price but also can specify a sales quota which the dealer is required to fulfill. The dealer is encouraged to order more units than is consistent with his profit maximizing interests. This practice will be referred to as forcing and will be discussed in more detail in the next chapter. With a sufficiently strong bargaining position, a manufacturer could establish the dealer's sales quota so that the dealer's economic profits would be eliminated. In practice, this may be very difficult to achieve. Nevertheless, it is profitable for the manufacturer to adopt such a policy.

Forcing is a method of achieving the scale economies in the distribution sector.[15] These scale economies would not be real-

---

[15] This can be demonstrated in the following manner. Assume the manufacturer can specify not only a transfer price but also a retailer's sales quota. The retailer's sales quota will be determined so that $\pi_R = 0$. In the pure oligopoly case,

ized in the absence of forcing either because of the relatively small size of some local markets or because of the attachments of buyers to sellers.

The theoretical models presented and discussed in the last footnote assume the manufacturer is able to impose an "all or nothing" bargain on the retailer which eliminates the economic profits of the retailer. The tendency for the profit rates of automobile dealers to surpass the profit rates of the retail trade sector persistently indicates that automobile manufacturers have not been able to impose an "all or nothing" bargain on their dealers successfully. Thus, dealer economic profits have persisted.

However, one ought to ask the following question: Why

---

that is, with few sellers in the retail market, this implies

$$\pi_R = 0 = f(nq)q - C(q) - wq$$

The manufacturer's profit function can be determined from this equation. Differentiation of the manufacturer's profit function with respect to n and q will yield the following condition:

$$\frac{qC'(q) - C(q)}{q^2} = 0$$

The expression on the left side is the slope of retailer's average cost curve. Thus, the manufacturer will determine the number of retailers so that each one operates at the minimum point (or range) of the retailer's average cost curve. A somewhat similar result can be obtained if the monopolistic competition model is used. Suppose the manufacturer can specify not only a transfer price but also a retailer's sales quota. Again, the retailer's sales quota will be determined so that $\pi_R = 0$; that is,

$$\pi_R = 0 = Aq_k - [a + (n-1)b]q_k^2 - C(q_k) - wq_k$$

Once again, the manufacturer's profit function can be formed and the profit maximizing conditions can be specified. In this case, this condition reduces to

$$-a + b = \frac{q_k C'(q_k) - C(q_k)}{q_k^2}$$

The expression on the right side is the slope of the retailer's average cost curve. $-a$ is the slope of the demand curve. With entry, the Chamberlin tangency condition requires these slopes to be equal in equilibrium. However, this solution will not maximize the manufacturer's profits. In particular, suppose that the manufacturer can determine the retailer's sales quota, so that $\pi_R = 0$. The manufacturer will determine n so that at the retailer's equilibrium output the demand curve will cut the retailer's average cost curve. The retailer's equilibrium output will be greater than the retailer's output when free entry is allowed since the maximizing condition requires the slope of the average cost curve to equal $-a + b$, not just $-a$.

has not the manufacturer granted franchises to other business-men seeking to enter the automobile retailing? By permitting entry into automobile retailing, the manufacturer would be able to overcome or neutralize the bargaining position of the established dealers. The point can be put somewhat differently. The established dealers have sold fewer autos than the manufacturer might have liked them to sell and, hence, have sold them at higher retail prices than the manufacturer would like the autos to be sold. Why haven't the manufacturers placed new dealers and encouraged them to be low price dealers? In this way, the manufacturer could lower retail prices and generate added volume. The established dealers would have no option but to meet these lower retail prices. In this manner, the bargaining position of the established dealers could be overcome.

Little is known about the determinants of the bargaining position of the dealer, about the bargaining process that develops between the dealer and field representatives of the manufacturer, or about the costs involved in administering an effective forcing program. Until more information is available, few definite statements can be made. Nevertheless, several conjectures can be advanced to explain why the manufacturer may not find it profitable to issue additional franchises. Once a new dealer has been placed in a local market, he would have the same economic incentive as the established dealers to resist the manufacturer's pressure to sell added volume. The number of units the manufacturer will want the new dealer to sell will be larger than the number that will maximize the dealer's profits. The automobile companies have not been too successful in overcoming the bargaining position of their established dealers. There is no reason to believe they would be more successful with newly placed dealers. Once a dealer has been placed, he cannot easily be cancelled. The larger automobile companies are not going to antagonize the Justice Department or members of Congress by liberal use of the cancellation provision. Finally, a policy that encourages dealer turnover and lowers buyer-dealer attachments, and, hence, buyer-brand attachments, is likely to be frowned upon and costly to administer.[16]

If the manufacturer has no expectation of lowering retail prices by permitting entry into the retail sector, the manufacturer will have no incentive to allow entry into the retail sector. In particular, if there are economies of scale in retailing, the placement of additional retailers in the local markets would merely decrease the profits of the manufacturer. In effect, the placement of additional dealers in the market will result in smaller and less efficient dealers.

In summary, the reason for the relatively low dealer turnover rates and the relatively high dealer profit rates is not because the automobile companies have deliberately chosen to adopt a restrictive franchise system. Rather, the reason lies in the inability of the automobile companies to compete away dealer economic profit completely either by resorting to forcing or by issuing more franchises. However, the limitations of the analysis should be recognized. The institutional factors which have prevented the automobile companies from competing away the dealer's economic profits are difficult to evaluate. An intensive study of how dealer sales forecasts are made and then aggregated into a firm forecast and the way in which production is scheduled and distributed among dealers may reveal why the internal decision process of the firm makes it difficult to adopt a forcing

---

[16] The newly placed dealers may not be much of a threat to the established dealers if the newly placed dealers encounter substantial barriers to entry. If buyers are attached to established dealers or if scale economies are important, a new entrant (dealer) will find entry difficult. If entry is difficult, the manufacturer cannot expect retail prices to decrease with entry. Furthermore, if entry is difficult, there should be no excess demand for entry even though the economic profits of the established dealers persist. Though the available evidence is limited, it appears that an excess demand for franchises persisted from 1946 to 1955. Whether this excess demand has persisted since 1955 is not known. There has been a small decline in the number of Ford and Chevrolet franchises from 1956 to 1959. This decline suggests the waiting list for franchises has decreased or disappeared. However, the decline is small and perhaps not too much importance should be attached to it.

policy successfully. However, such a study could only be undertaken with the cooperation of the automobile companies. The author has spoken to several individuals and industry officials who have suggested that a real test of the bargaining strength of the dealer will be revealed by the trend and level of dealer profit rates since 1955. They argue that excess capacity first appeared and has persisted in the automobile industry since 1955. Prior to 1955, the automobile manufacturers did not have to exert much pressure on their dealers because of the favorable demand conditions. With the development of excess capacity, the manufacturers have placed more pressure on their dealers to accept more autos. Thus, they argue, the period since 1955 is an appropriate one to test the ability of the automobile dealers to resist the manufacturer's pressure for volume. If dealer profit rates still exceed the profit rates of the retail trade sector, the hypothesis of a strong dealer bargaining position will be sustained. Most of the evidence indicates that dealer profit rates have declined since 1955. However, it is not possible to determine with the evidence at hand just how low they have fallen. The author would prefer to reserve judgment. Excess capacity undoubtedly existed in the automobile industry throughout the 1930's. Yet, there is some evidence that General Motors dealers were able to earn superior returns on their net worth during this period. So, it may be somewhat hasty to assume dealer economic profits have been or will be competed away.

The Restrictive Franchise System as an Efficient Method of Developing Consumer-brand Attachments. The arguments which have been just presented were derived once the usual static assumptions of a given demand and cost function were made. There is another line of reasoning which attempts to explain why a manufacturer will adopt a restrictive franchise system. Briefly stated, the franchise system may develop consumer-retailer attachments and, hence, consumer-brand attachments more efficiently, that is, at lower cost to the manufacturer, than any other sales promotion policy. Industry officials generally agree with this position.

The consumer's selection of brand can be affected by the retailer from whom he purchases. Change the retailer and the consumer will change the brand purchased. For example, brand attachments may be more efficiently developed in the automobile industry by maintaining a stable group of dealers who remain in business year in and year out than by spending more on advertising. The automobile is a relatively complex instrument, and few consumers understand its mechanical operation. Because of his ignorance, the consumer must rely on the dealer to provide the necessary service to correct defects, to keep the auto in operating condition, and not to deceive him by selling him a "lemon." The automobile is a major capital expenditure. A poor selecton means a large loss. Under these conditions, the consumer may be a risk averter, preferring to purchase from a dealer who has been in business for a period of years and with whom he has had previous experience.

The maintenance of buyer-brand attachments may be more efficiently accomplished by the maintenance of buyer-retailer attachments than by more intensive reliance on other non-price promotional programs. This can be accomplished by maintaining a stable group of retailers. If so, the manufacturer would not be indifferent to the loss of an established retailer. The loss of a retailer, because he finds it unprofitable to continue in business, means that some buyers, who were previously indifferent between several brands and who previously purchased the manufacturer's brand because of the retailer, are more likely to switch to another brand. If these buyers account for a large percentage of the total market, the manufacturer will find it profitable to protect the established retailers from incurring losses, even though they may be temporary.[17]

---

[17] Automobile officials often argue that the franchise system is necessary to assure adequate service. They argue that if dealer profits were lower, as they would be with free entry, the dealer would not service the automobiles he sells.

What types of price and representation policies are likely to maintain a stable dealer organization over time in an industry as cyclical as the automobile industry? This could be accomplished by restricting entry into the retail sector. In this way, the dealer can be protected from losses resulting from unexpected shifts in demand.[18] This can be thought of as a risk premium which the manufacturer grants the retailer to minimize the probability of a loss.

A policy which restricts the number of retailers is more likely to be adopted in industries where (1) demand is cyclical and where (2) industry output is concentrated among a few manufacturers. If output is concentrated among several manufacturers, the wholesale price is more likely to be rigid. Bain concludes,

> As demand and cost curves shift back and forth with cyclical business fluctuations, an oligopoly is less likely to make short-run adjustments to the changing situation than is a single-firm monopoly and much less likely to do so than a purely competitive industry. This is in part because when price is controlled by agreement or price leadership, every change in price places some strain on the controlling mechanism and increases the probability of defections from the agreement. By maintaining a relatively rigid price, the oligopolists lessen the possibility that open price rivalry or price cutting will emerge.[19]

Thus, dealer profits are the incentive needed to bribe the dealer to provide service. The author is not particularly happy with this argument. There is no reason to believe the service market is an unprofitable one. There is reason to believe that a dealership which does not provide the necessary service can not persist in automobile retailing. Finally, the available evidence, meager as it is, does not indicate a positive relationship between dealer profit rates and dealer penetration of the service market.

[18] Since the dealer affects the consumer's brand choice, the dealer will be protected by the manufacturer. The franchise system is one way of protecting the dealer. In the automobile industry, other methods have been used at various times. A territorial security provision had been included in the dealer's contract until 1949. At the request of the Justice Department, this provision was removed. A territorial security provision tends to discourage out-of-market sales. The auto companies have also looked with disfavor on bootlegging. Hence, a variety of methods have been used to protect the dealer.

[19] Joe S. Bain, *Price Theory* (New York: Henry Holt & Company, Inc., 1952), p. 294.

As was noted in the last chapter, output is highly concentrated in the automobile industry. Hence, one would expect wholesale price rigidity. This has often been observed in the industry. Once the wholesale price has been established at the beginning of the model year, it has tended to be maintained. However, there have been controlled downward adjustments at the end of the model year in recent years.

Why should the wholesale price rigidity be related to the use of a franchise system? When wholesale prices are rigid, an error in estimating demand can lead to large losses or profits for retailers. For example, suppose demand is over-estimated and a relatively high wholesale industry price is established. If actual demand is less than predicted demand, dealers will suffer losses. Some dealers will be forced to go out of business. If, as has been postulated, the dealer is an important determinant of consumer brand selection, the manufacturer will have lost an asset and obtained less in return. To avoid this, the manufacturer will formulate his wholesale price and representation policy so that the existing retailers will be protected from large losses due to errors in demand prediction. This can be accomplished by not permitting entry into the retail sector. Thus, the manufacturer will quote a wholesale price which will allow the restricted number of retailers to earn profits if demand has been correctly forecast. If, however, predicted demand is greater than the actual demand, dealer profits will be eliminated and perhaps become negative if this discrepancy is large. However, the retailers' losses will be less than they would be if entry had been allowed into the retail sector. By restricting entry into the retail sector, the manufacturer lowers the probability that the retailer will suffer a large loss.[20]

In summary, when the dealer affects the consumer's brand choice, the dealer will be protected by the manufacturer. The

---

[20] The author is not particularly happy with this hypothesis. One might ask why the manufacturer who has a superior capital position does not lend funds to the dealer and enable him to survive these low profit years?

manufacturer will adopt price and representation policies which protect the dealer body from large losses. This is an even more likely policy when the wholesale price is rigid, that is, where industry output is concentrated among few sellers and demand prediction is difficult.

There is some reason to believe that demand prediction is more difficult in the automobile industry than in most other industries. The author is not aware of any studies of cross-industry demand predictions. Hence, it is difficult to prove this statement. In the last chapter, the demand for automobiles was shown to be sensitive to changes in disposable income, more so than for most products. Because of this, one can expect that a greater percentage error in demand prediction will occur in the auto industry than in other industries for every percentage point error in the prediction of disposable income. There is one bit of evidence available which shows how accurately the auto companies do predict. Predictions of annual sales of automobiles made by the Ford Division of the Ford Motor Company from 1950 to 1956 deviated from actual auto sales by an average of 9.5 per cent per year.[21] Whether this percentage error is large relative to the percentage errors in other industries is not known. There are several reasons to suspect so.

To review, both conditions which might lead to the use of a franchise system, rigidity in the wholesale price level and difficulty in demand prediction, apparently exist in the auto industry.

The Adjustment of Resources to Changes in Consumer Demand under a Restrictive Franchise System. What effect does the restrictive franchise system have on efficiency in automobile retailing? As noted above, the restrictive franchise system is designed to allow the existing retailers to operate at higher sales volumes than they would with entry. This efficiency bias is one

---

21 John A. Howard, *Marketing Management* (Homewood, Ill.: Richard D. Irwin, Inc., 1957), p. 129.

of the desirable aspects of the franchise system. There will be less excess capacity in the retail sector with a restrictive franchise system than with entry.

However, once a franchise system has been developed and used over a period of time, it is likely to delay and possibly exclude the introduction of more efficient resources into the retail sector. The franchise system not only restricts the number of retailers in the retail sector, but it also forestalls the introduction of more efficient retailers into the retail sector. There is no effective market mechanism which assures the replacement of a less efficient retailer by a more efficient retailer.

Is the franchise system more likely to provide the consumer with the desired mix between product and service? The product in retailing changes with the mood and fancy of the consumer. At times, the consumer is only interested in the commodity for sale with a minimum of services. At other times the consumer will pay for the commodity and additional services.[22]

The preference of consumers between product without service and product with service changes—often, quite rapidly. The price system is thought to act as an efficient regulator by eliminating those retailers who attempt to provide the consumer with too many or too few services. In this regard, the franchise system is likely to delay the adjustment of the retail sector to changes in the composition of demand. It is not clear that the consumer will be offered an effective choice between product and service. The entry of potential competitors cannot be relied on to provide low cost services or to institute a trend to more product and less service.[23] The pressure to do so will always exist. However, the franchise system can be expected to lag behind changes in the composition of consumer demand.

The number of retailers is restricted under a franchise system.

---

[22] M. A. Adelman, "The 'Product' and 'Price' in Distribution," *American Economic Review* (1957), pp. 266–273.

[23] This may be one of the reasons for the vehement charges by some dealers against the manufacturers for establishing low cost dealers in the market.

Because of this, it is more likely that retail competition will take non-price forms. This is a probable result because of three reasons. Under a restrictive franchise system, the retailers have a longer time horizon since retailer turnover rates are lower. Tacit price agreements are more likely under these conditions. Also, the existing retailers do not have to contend with the threat of entry. Finally, because there are fewer retailers in the market, tacit price agreements are more easily reached. Therefore, it is more likely that retail competition will be channeled into non-price forms under a franchise system.

The manufacturer may prefer competition to take non-price forms for several reasons. If greater reliance is placed on price competition, some high cost retailers will be forced to leave the industry. Consumer-dealer attachments and, hence, consumer-brand attachments, which have been established, will be broken. In the larger markets, where there are other retailers selling the same brand, there may be a simple transfer of consumers to another retailer selling the same brand. However, this is not an automatic result. These consumers must begin anew collecting market information about the retailer, the retail price, and the extent of non-price services. Some of these consumers, who had never shopped before, can become shoppers and collect market information about other brands. Hence, an increase in the turnover rate of retailers can be expected to increase the consumers' market information. In small markets there is usually only one retailer of each make. Therefore, the loss of a retailer by one manufacturer is likely to lead to a larger proportional loss of consumers to other brands.

In addition, the very process of price competition tends to break down consumer-dealer attachments. As price competition increases and price information increases, more consumers become price conscious and less influenced by brand or retailer. Sales promotion techniques will be relegated to the background. The importance of the dealer is likely to diminish in a market which emphasizes price.

To summarize, the franchise system uses existing resources more efficiently than a system which would allow entry into the retail sector. However, the franchise system is not likely to adjust as quickly to changes in the composition of consumer demand or to introduce more efficient resources into the retail sector at as fast a rate as a system which allows entry.

Structural Conditions in Automobile Distribution and the Use of the Restrictive Franchise System. The purpose of this section is to determine if those conditions which are most likely to favor the adoption of a restrictive franchise system exist in automobile distribution.

This is a difficult task. The data seldom exist to permit proper and complete testing of the hypotheses advanced in the first part of this chapter. Unfortunately, the inquiry will be decidedly limited.

At least one and possibly two conditions must exist before a manufacturer would consider adopting a restrictive franchise system. First, there should be economies of scale in distribution so that it is impossible for many sellers to operate efficiently in local markets. Second, the retailer may be considered a differentiated seller by the consumer.

Economies of Scale. The extent of economies of scale in automobile distribution is, in part, the subject matter of Chapters 4 through 8. Two dealer cost functions are estimated. The low estimate assumes that cost economies persist until the dealership sells 600 new units per year. The second estimate assumes that cost economies persist until the dealership sells 800 new units per year.

How large are most local markets? This is very difficult to determine because it is difficult to determine just what a market area is. As a first approximation, the estimated number of new units retailed per franchise by size of place has been estimated for a hypothetical manufacturer accounting for 2, 5, 10, 20, or 30 per cent of a 6,000,000 annual market. These data are presented in Table 72 (page 234). Inspection of this table will show that even a manufacturer who accounted for 20 per cent of the total market would find that approximately 60 per cent of these sales were made in markets where the manufacturer's dealers had not fully exhausted the economies of scale.[24] Granting that the Census definition of place is a poor definition of a market, it is nevertheless true that in very few markets are there more than one franchise of a given make per place. Tables 20, 23, and 26 show the number of franchises per place by make and according to the size of the place. In a few instances, there is more than one franchise per place. The data are imperfect, and this should be recognized. Nevertheless, there is some evidence to believe that in many local markets many sellers of one make cannot exist. Local markets, because of their small size, must be concentrated. Hence, it is conceivable that a manufacturer would restrict the number of dealers in these local markets so that the remaining dealers would be more likely to exhaust the economies of scale.

Dealership Differentiation. With available data it is very difficult to show dealership differentiation. To obtain any results at all, some very strong assumptions must be made.

There are two sets of data from which hypotheses about the extent of dealership differentiation can be tested. First, there are shopping data: how many buyers shop how many dealers. Second, there are dealer repeat sales data: how many buyers, who repurchase the same make they trade in, repurchase from the same dealer.

What can be inferred about dealership differentiation from shopping data? When a consumer buys a new car, he can shop dealers of a given make once the make has been selected, or he

---

[24] This must be considered a high estimate because the definition of market is limited.

can shop makes while only going to one dealer of each make, or he can shop both make and dealer, shopping many makes and many dealers of each make.

Auto buyers can be divided into four shopping groups (the percentages, in brackets, represent the percentage of all buyers in that group):

1. *Attachments to dealer and possibly to make:* buyers who shop only one dealer and hence shop only one brand. These buyers do not shop many dealers of the make purchased. Hence, they may be attached to the dealer (47 per cent).
2. *Attached to make but not to dealer:* buyers who shop only one make but two or more dealers of the make. Because these buyers shop only one make, they are likely to be attached to the make. Since they shop several dealers of that make, they are likely to be sensitive to price differentials (20 per cent).
3. *Possible attachments to dealer but not to make:* buyers who shop two or more makes but only one dealer of the make purchased. These buyers do not appear to be attached to a given make. However, these buyers do not shop more than one dealer of the make purchased. Hence, it does not appear that they would be sensitive to price differentials between dealers selling the same make the buyer purchased. Possibly, buyers in this group make their selection because of the dealer. Otherwise, it is difficult to explain why the buyer does not shop more dealers of the make purchased (19 per cent).
4. *No attachments to makes or dealers:* these buyers shop two or more makes and two or more dealers of the make purchased. These buyers have no apparent attachments to makes and are probably sensitive to price differentials (14 per cent).[25]

These shopping data are difficult to evaluate. Shopping represents one method of collecting market information. By visiting a dealership, the consumer is likely to obtain accurate and relevant market data. Telephone calls or information from friends

---

[25] These data were obtained from the Ford shopping study. This study is discussed in greater detail in Chapter 5.

represent other sources. However, these sources are likely to be less accurate.[26] Those buyers who are effective bargainers are most likely to make use of their talents by visiting dealerships and not by telephoning. Perhaps, their shopping behavior is correctly measured by these data. Those buyers, who are not effective bargainers and who accept the first quotation as the final quotation, may have secured price information by calling, and then visiting, and finally buying either from the same dealer from whom they bought their last auto or from the one who offered the lowest quotation over the phone. Hence, 47 per cent that shopped only one dealer, and, hence, one brand, is likely to be a high estimate of the actual size of this apparently inert nonshopping group.

The buyers in Group 1 and possibly Group 3 are likely to be attached to a dealer. Together, these groups add up to 66 per cent of total buyers. If Group 3 is excluded, at most 47 per cent of total buyers are attached to dealers.

Suppose the Census definition of place is considered as a market area definition. Then, approximately 60 to 70 per cent of total market sales are made in markets where there is only one dealer of a given make. This is a high estimate because the Census definition of place underestimates the market area. These percentage figures are consistent with the observed shopping behavior of buyers. By this test, one would have to conclude that there is little dealer differentiation since actual shopping behavior is about equal to expected shopping behavior.

In contrast, suppose the metropolitan area is considered as a market area. Well over 50 per cent of total sales of any given make are made in markets where there are two or more dealers of that make. This is particularly true of the low price class. Inspection of Table 35, shows the distribution of total sales by size of metropolitan area and several estimates of the

---

26 However, Allen Jung has found that telephoning is an efficient way of securing automobile prices. See the series of articles by Allen Jung on automobile pricing beginning with the October, 1959 issue of *The Journal of Business.*

number of dealers (of a given make) the buyer could apparently purchase from without incurring a large (imputed) transport cost. Approximately 20 per cent of total sales would be recorded in markets where there is one dealer per make, and even in these markets there will be dealers of other makes. Hence, in very few markets will there be just one dealer. One cannot infer from the expected shopping behavior and the actual shopping behavior that buyers do consider all dealers selling the same make as perfect substitutes. Otherwise, one would expect greater shopping by buyers among dealers selling the same make. Retail automobile markets are far from perfect. Effective shopping is likely to bring lower net prices. Also, an automobile is purchased infrequently. Hence, up-to-date market information must be collected each time an auto is purchased. Market information collected three to four years earlier is irrelevant. Because retail markets are not perfect and because market information is limited, one would expect more shopping by customers. Thus, the inferences one makes about dealer differentiation from shopping data depends on which definition of market is used.

What can be inferred about dealership differentiation from dealership repeat sales? Two questions are of interest. First, what per cent of total sales of each make are made to buyers who trade in the same make and who purchase both cars from the same dealer? In other words, what percentage of total sales are made to buyers who repurchase the same make from the same dealer. These buyers are most likely to be attached to the dealer. If these buyers account for a large share of the market, then it is more likely that the manufacturer would be interested in adopting a franchise system. Second, of those buyers who repurchase the same make as the make traded in, what percentage repurchased from the same dealer? If dealerships were differentiated, consumers would tend to repurchase from the same dealership. Hence, one can infer from dealer repeat sales data, the existence of dealership differentiation.

What percentage of total sales are made to buyers who repurchase the same make as the make traded in from the same dealer? This percentage will depend on the extent to which buyers switch brands during the year. For example, in any one year, buyers who previously purchased Fords may switch to Chevrolets. Hence, the percentage of total Chevrolet sales which are made to buyers trading in Chevrolets will be low because in that year many previous Ford buyers have switched to Chevrolets. In the same year the percentage of total Ford sales which are made to Ford buyers trading in Fords will either stay constant or decline depending on whether owners of Chevrolets switch to Fords. The greater the switching of buyers among makes, the lower the percentage of dealership repeat sales.

The data available on switching are for 1957. The market share of General Motors dropped by about 6 percentage points from 1956. The market share of Ford and Chrysler increased to account for most of the change. There was considerable switching of makes by consumers in 1957. Hence, the percentage of total sales which are made to buyers who repurchase the same make as the make traded in from same dealer is probably understated in 1957 over the percentage one would observe in a normal year.

The percentage of buyers of 1957 new cars who repurchased the same make as the make traded in and who purchased both from the same dealer are given in Table 8. As would be expected, the percentages for the Chrysler Corporation makes are relatively low. Moreover, as was just noted, the figures are generally understated in 1957. These data would suggest that between 30 to 40 per cent of all buyers return to the same dealer to repurchase the same make as the make traded in; that is, both autos are purchased from the same dealer. Unfortunately, it is difficult to evaluate the significance of these numbers. Three-tenths to four-tenths of the market is made up of dealer repeat sales, not an insignificant share. However, it is not possible to say whether this share is large enough to encourage the manufacturer to adopt a franchise system. It is clear that a sizeable portion of the total

TABLE 8. PERCENTAGE OF ALL NEW BUYERS WHO RETURN TO SAME DEALER TO
REPURCHASE THE SAME MAKE AS MAKE OF TRADE-IN

Make	Percentage	Response Rate
Low price makes		
Chevrolet	35.7	66.6
Ford	27.6	67.6
Plymouth	26.0	68.5
Middle price makes		
Pontiac	37.6	63.3
Dodge	28.0	62.4
Mercury	35.4	66.3
Desoto	31.2	70.0
Oldsmobile	37.8	69.3
Chrysler	33.7	69.2
Buick	41.1	63.6
High price makes		
Cadillac	62.9	60.5
Lincoln	30.8	64.6
Imperial	37.8	66.9

Source : *A Market Study of the People Buying New Automobiles,* conducted jointly
by Market Research Division, Advertising Department, U.S. News & World Report and
Benson & Benson, Inc., Princeton, New Jersey (place or publisher not listed, 1957).
A separate report is presented for each make.

market is made up of dealer repeat sales. Unfortunately, little
is known about the stability of these percentages over time.

It remains to be seen if those buyers who repurchase from the
same dealer select their dealer by chance or systematically repurchase from the same dealer. Those buyers who repurchase the
same make as the make traded in have been segregated from other
buyers. The percentage of these buyers who repurchase from the
same dealer is presented in Table 35. These data indicate that
approximately 50 per cent of these buyers repurchase from the
same dealership.

To infer something about dealership differentiation from
these data, it is necessary to assume something about how these
buyers choose the dealership from which they purchase. Suppose
they select the dealership at random once the make is selected.
Once this assumption is made, it is possible to estimate the expected percentage of dealer repeat sales. Then, if the actual

dealer repeat sales are greater than the expected dealer repeat sales, it is possible to infer that buyers do not select dealerships at random but show some evidence of repeating their purchases from the same dealership. This hypothesis is tested in Chapter 5.[27] The results suggest that actual dealer repeat sales are somewhat higher than the predicted dealer repeat sales. Hence, there is some reason to believe dealerships are differentiated. However, there does not seem to be any pronounced dealer differentiation.[28] The basic data are subject to several limitations. Therefore, this must be considered a tentative conclusion.

In summary, there is some reason to believe that dealerships are differentiated. Both the consumer shopping data and dealer repeat sales data lend some support to this conclusion. However, the strength of consumer attachments to dealerships does not appear to be particularly strong.

---

[27] The interested reader will wish to skip ahead.

[28] This is one reason why the author doubts the importance of the dealer in determining the consumer's selection of brand. These data tend to reject the hypothesis that consumers are strongly attached to dealerships. However, there appears to be some dealership differentiation.

CHAPTER 3

Aspects of Retail and Wholesale Price Behavior

3.1. Introduction

The purpose of this chapter is to study some aspects of price determination in the automobile industry. The chapter is divided into two sections. In the first part, the determination of the wholesale price of new autos, that is, the transfer price from the manufacturer to the dealer, will be discussed.[1] The second part of the chapter will be devoted to a comparative study of new car retail price behavior in large and small local markets.

3.2. Wholesale Price Determination

The theory of vertical pricing has received extensive treatment in the literature and can be used for present purposes.[2]

---

[1] The discussion will be limited to the vertical price policy of a single manufacturer who sells to a group of retailers and to some extent duplicates the discussion in Chapter 2. A related problem is the effect of the cost structure of the distribution system on the stability of wholesale price-output solution reached by an oligopoly. For example, all or most of the dealers of one oligopolist may have higher costs than the dealers of another oligopolist. Wholesale price agreements would be less easy to reach under such conditions.

[2] For example, see William H. Nicholls, *Imperfect Competition Within Agricultural Industries* (Ames, Iowa: The Iowa State College Press, 1941) Chapter 10; William Fellner, "Prices and Wages Under Bilateral Monopoly," *Quarterly Journal of Economics,* 61 (August, 1947), pp. 503–532.

A complete review of the theory is not necessary. Rather, two limiting cases will be summarized.

For simplicity, the number of dealers of each make is assumed to be given. Hence, the demand curve facing the manufacturer is made up of the lateral summation of the individual dealer demand schedules. In turn, each dealer's demand schedule is derived from the local market demand schedule in the dealer's market and the dealer's cost schedule.

Each dealer is assumed to be a monopolist in his local market. Obviously, this assumption distorts reality. Yet, it simplifies the analysis by avoiding the oligopoly problem and does not negate the basic findings of the analysis. The fundamental point to be demonstrated is that there is a conflict of interest between the dealer and the manufacturer. The volume of sales which maximizes dealer's profits does not simultaneously maximize the manufacturer's profits. As long as the dealer has some monopoly control in the product market, the dealer will always wish to sell fewer units than the manufacturer would like to have sold in the dealer's market.

This point arose during an exchange between Chairman Celler and Mr. William T. Gossett, Vice President and General Counsel of the Ford Motor Company over a proposed bill designed to diminish the manufacturer's dominant position.

> The Chairman: You say you will lose volume. Why will you lose volume?
>
> Mr. Gossett: We will lose volume, Mr. Chairman, because without the influence of the manufacturer, the normal persuasive sales influence of a manufacturer on the dealers will not sell the same volume of cars that they now sell.[3]

The point was stated somewhat more emphatically by one dealer. He replied, in response to a Senate Committee questionnaire,

---

[3] *Automobile Dealer Franchises,* Hearings before the Antitrust Subcommittee of the Committee on the Judiciary, House of Representatives, 84th Cong., 2nd Sess. on H.R. 11360 and S. 3879, p. 288.

Michigan

DeSoto-Plymouth. Enforce manufacturers to curtail production only to the extent that each dealer has only as many cars as he personally can handle profitably. Stop this forcing, by different ways, of dealers to handle cars they do not ·really want. Give them all they want and no more.[4]

The theory of vertical pricing explains why the discrepancy exists between the interest of the manufacturer and the interest of the dealer.

Derivation of the Dealer's Demand Schedule for New Autos. Each dealer faces a given market demand schedule which shows the number of new cars the dealer can sell at various retail prices. In addition, each dealer has a long-run cost schedule. This schedule is defined to include all operating costs. It excludes the cost of new cars purchased by the dealer from the manufacturer. By subtracting total costs from total revenue, a dealer gross profit schedule can be derived. This schedule shows the dealer's gross profit at each volume of sales. (The gross profit is shown because the cost of the new cars purchased by the dealer from the manufacturer has not been deducted.) The gross profit schedule is shown in the left panel of figure 1. M.G.P. denotes

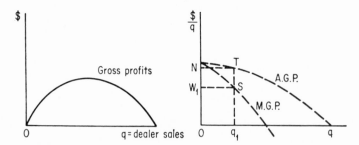

Fig. 1. Gross and average profits schedules of dealer

[4] *Automobile Marketing Practices,* Hearings before a Subcommittee of the Committee on Interstate and Foreign Commerce. U.S. Senate, 84th Cong., 2nd Sess. pursuant to S. Res. 13. Continued by S. Res. 163, Part 1, p. 1147. The reader may wish to correct the grammar but little fault can be found with the analysis.

the marginal gross profits schedule. A.G.P. denotes the gross profit per new car retailed. These schedules are shown in the right panel of Figure 1. The dealer's demand schedule for new cars is given by the M.G.P. schedule. This schedule shows the increase in the dealer's gross profits for each unit increase in volume. The dealer's total profits will increase as long as the marginal gross profit is greater than the wholesale price of the car. For a given wholesale price, the dealer will continue to order cars from the manufacturer until the marginal gross profit equals the wholesale price of the car. The M.G.P. schedule traces out the dealer's demand for autos at alternative wholesale prices.

The Demand Curve Facing the Manufacturer. By summing the individual dealer demand schedules laterally, the manufacturer's demand schedule is derived. This schedule shows the total number of new cars that the manufacturer's dealers will demand at each wholesale price the manufacturer quotes. The demand schedule is labelled $D'D'$ and is shown in Figure 2. $D''D''$ denotes

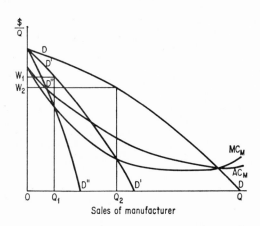

Fig. 2. Wholesale price determination by manufacturer

the corresponding marginal revenue schedule. AC_M and MC_M denote the long-run average and marginal manufacturing cost schedules, respectively.

The Determination of the Wholesale Price. Two limiting cases will be presented.

1. The manufacturer determines the wholesale price, and each dealer adjusts his sales volume. Suppose each dealer is allowed to determine the number of autos he will order, and the manufacturer ships only the number ordered. The manufacturer will maximize profits by establishing the wholesale price at OW_1 and will sell OQ_1 units. At this quoted wholesale price, each dealer will order only the necessary number of new cars to maximize his profits, that is, OQ_1 units. The profits of the dealer will be equal to the area $NWTS$ (see Figure 1).

2. The manufacturer determines the wholesale price and the dealer's quota. The manufacturer's profits can be increased if he has a superior bargaining position over the dealer. Suppose the manufacturer can not only determine the wholesale price but can also ship the dealer the number of new cars which the manufacturer "thinks" the dealer should sell. This is an all-or-nothing bargain. The manufacturer quotes the wholesale price and also imposes a sales quota which the dealer must fulfill. In essence, the manufacturer forces the dealer to equate price (in this case A.G.P.) to the wholesale price. If the manufacturer has this bargaining power, the manufacturer will quote OW_2 as the wholesale price and OQ_2 will equal the sales of the manufacturer.[5] The profits of the manufacturer will increase, and the profits of the dealer will decrease.

These two price-output results represent extreme solutions. The actual price-output result is actually reached somewhat between these two positions. Nevertheless, the model does show that the sales volume which maximizes the dealer's profits does not simultaneously maximize the manufacturer's profits.

The Superior Bargaining Position of the Manufacturer. As was noted above, the actual price-output result will depend on the relative bargaining strength of the manufacturer and the

---

[5] The $D'D'$ schedule is the marginal schedule of the DD schedule. Similarly, the $D''D''$ is the marginal schedule of the $D'D'$ schedule.

dealer. Most students of the automobile industry have commented on the superior bargaining position of the manufacturer. Each dealer accounts for an insignificant share of the company's total sales. Yet, the dealer depends on the franchise for the total earnings of the dealership. Under these conditions, the bargaining position of the manufacturer appears to be potentially superior to that of the dealer.

Two points have been made. First, the manufacturer has an incentive to "force" cars on dealers since the profits of the manufacturer are thereby increased. Second, the manufacturer appears to be in a superior bargaining position and, therefore, should be able to force cars on the dealer. Yet, this is only a possible result. Whether dealers are in fact forced to take autos and to what extent, has yet to be demonstrated.

Clearly, there are limits on the actions of the manufacturer. The manufacturer can only "force" cars on the dealer if the dealer has a profitable franchise. If the dealer is just earning a normal return and the manufacturer increases his quota, the dealer will find that his return has become subnormal. Consequently, the dealer would go out of business.

The existence of an economic profit is a necessary condition for the practice of "forcing." Until recently, Studebaker-Packard and American Motors franchises have not been profitable. In general, these companies have not been able to "force" cars on their dealers. Ford Motor Company and General Motors Corporation franchises have been profitable. Hence, these companies are in a better position to secure compliance with sales quotas, space requirements, and so on. Usually, there is a waiting list for the franchises of Ford Motor Company and General Motors Corporation. Under these conditions, the dealer has little alternative, other than giving up a profitable franchise, but to accept the factory suggestions. A dealer who disagrees with factory policies appears to be in a weak bargaining position.[6]

---

[6] It would appear that the factory could delay deliveries, lower shipments, or send the wrong mix of autos to a non-complying dealer. However, the point is difficult to document. It should not be inferred that the dealer has no bar-

To what extent have the manufacturers used their potentially dominant position to "force" autos on dealers? Suppose the manufacturers do in fact have a dominant bargaining position and exploit this position to the fullest. One would expect the dealers' profit rates to be no more than the competitive rate. However, dealer profit rates have not been that low. The difficulty of measuring and comparing profit rates in retailing industries has been discussed in Chapter 2. To insure comparability, the total return rate (profits plus officers' compensation) of automobile dealers was compared with the total return rate in retail trade. In general, the total return rate of automobile dealers has exceeded the total return rate in retail trade.[7] Also, it appears that the profit rates of General Motors and Ford dealers have exceeded the profit rates of retail firms. Granting the inadequacies of the data, the best estimate seems to be that dealer earnings have tended to be higher than the earnings of other businesses in retail trade.

The existence and persistence of the earnings differential is

gaining power. In some local markets, a dealer can account for a large percentage of the total sales. Many customers may be attached to the dealership. The replacements available to the manufacturer may be inferior to the existing dealer. In addition, the manufacturer must evaluate the cost of replacing an experienced dealer with another dealer. The replacement will have to be closely supervised by the field staff for a period in order to overcome startup difficulties. Hence, the existing dealer may be in a position to ignore some factory pressure. Furthermore, if the dealer has a reputation as an efficient dealer, he may be able to secure preferential treatment as to the filling of orders, mix and color of inventory. Finally, and most important, state and national dealer organizations are active political bodies and often seek redress in the halls of Congress. Some members of Congress are sympathetic to the dealer's cause. The automobile manufacturers are aware of this and try to avoid practices which will offend lawmakers and lead to congressional action. The adoption of the five-year franchise agreements after dealer and congressional criticisms of the "one-sided" one-year contracts is one such example. A careful reading of the recent hearings as well as earlier ones supports the contention that these practices have existed. However, these hearings have not demonstrated how prevalent these practices have been.

7 The author prefers to use the total return rate for this comparison. The reader may wish to use the profit rate for this comparison. In this case, the profit rate of auto dealers has exceeded the profit rate in retail trade except in the following years: 1938 and 1939, and from 1953 to 1955.

not consistent with the full use of "forcing" by the manufacturers. Hence, there is some support for the contention that the companies, if they have a dominant bargaining position, have not used it as effectively as they might. This does not mean there has been no "forcing." It just means that the manufacturer could have engaged in this practice to an even greater extent.

A second performance test may be used to support the contention that dealer earning rates have exceeded the earning rates in retail trade. Suppose earning rates are higher in automobile distribution than in retail trade. Then one would expect dealer turnover to be lower than turnover of all retail firms; that is, the higher the return, the greater the probability the firm will remain in business.

Adequate turnover data are available, and several comparisons can be made. From 1928–1937, total dealer changes in the number of General Motors dealers for *all* reasons averaged 12.8 per cent per year of total General Motors dealers. From 1933 to 1937 total changes in the number of General Motors dealers for *all* reasons averaged 11.0 per cent of total General Motors dealers.[8] Dealer terminations by the Ford Motor Company and the General Motors Corporation in the postwar period are presented in Table 9. These postwar data were discussed in some detail in Chapter 2. It appears that the turnover rates of General Motors dealers and, quite possibly, Ford dealers have been lower than the turnover rates in most other industries.[9]

In summary, these data are consistent with either of two conclusions. The manufacturers have not used their dominant bargaining position to the fullest extent possible. Hence, dealer turnover rates have been relatively low and dealer earning rates have been relatively high. Or, one can conclude that the bargain-

---

[8] *Hearings on House Resolution 389, Directing the Federal Trade Commission to Investigate Motor Vehicle Distribution Practices*, Hearings before a Subcommittee of the House Committee on Interstate and Foreign Commerce, U.S. House of Representatives, 75th Cong., 2nd and 3rd Sess., p. 167.

[9] The Ford data are not comparable with the General Motors data. The Ford data do not include voluntary terminations.

ing position of the manufacturer is not as dominant (relative to the bargaining position of the dealer) as is commonly supposed. The inability to "force" cars on to dealers and the restriction of entry

TABLE 9. DEALER TERMINATIONS, GENERAL MOTORS CORPORATION
AND FORD MOTOR COMPANY

General Motors Corporation

	Total General Motors Passenger Car and Truck Dealerships	Non Renewals	Involuntary Terminations	Voluntary Terminations	Total	Total Terminations as a Per cent of Total Dealerships
	(1)	(2)	(3)	(4)	(5)	(6)
Dec. 31, 1951	18,503	44	120	833	977	5.4
Dec. 31, 1952	18,509	72	135	1,042	1,249	6.7
Dec. 31, 1953	18,311	103	153	1,217	1,473	8.0
Dec. 31, 1954	18,137	113	152	1,534	1,799	9.9
Aug. 31, 1955	18,406	118[a]	165[a]	1,277[a]	1,560[a]	. . .

Ford Motor Company

	Average Number of Dealers per Year	Total Failures (Unprofitable Operations)	Inadequate Finances	Other	Terminations	Total
1946–1955	7,553	89	176	2	224	491

[a] Ten months, 1955.
Sources: *General Motors Corporation data: General Motors*, Hearings Before the Subcommittee on Antitrust and Monopoly of the Committee on the Judiciary, U.S. Senate, 84th Cong., 1st Sess., pursuant to S. Res. 61, Part 8, pp. 4381–82.
Ford Motor Company data: Automobile Dealer Franchises, Hearings Before the Antitrust Subcommittee (Subcommittee No. 5) of the Committee on the Judiciary, House of Representatives, 84th Cong., 2nd Sess., on H.R. 11360 and S. 3879, p. 386. The Ford data do not include voluntary terminations.

into the retail sector have permitted dealer earnings to be relatively high and dealer turnover rates to be relatively low.

3.3. New Car Price Behavior in Retail Markets

Local markets differ considerably in the number of new car registrations, number of dealers of each make, and the geographical size of market. In the large metropolitan area markets, there will be many dealers of each make. Frequently, a dealer in a large metropolitan market will account for a relatively small share of new car registrations within the market. In the smaller markets, there are fewer dealers of each make, and each dealer's share of the market correspondingly increases. Outside of the large metropolitan areas, the number of dealers per market area rapidly decreases.

Local automobile markets are further segmented because of the differentiation of the product. Within limits, price competition tends to be price competition among dealers selling the same make. This segmentation of the market by make is important because the number of sellers retailing the same "product" in each market area is thereby reduced drastically. This is a particularly relevant consideration in the smaller markets. In these smaller markets, there will be only one dealer representing each make. This fractionization of the market by make is of less importance in the larger markets. In these markets, the number of dealers of a given make is usually large enough so that each dealer's share of new car registrations of that make is relatively low.

Market Structure and Expected Price Behavior. As was just noted, market structures differ from market to market. What type of predictions concerning retail price behavior can be made from these differences in market structure? At this point, the reader may wish to turn to Tables 20, 23, and 26. These tables show the number of franchises per place by size of place. Clearly, most markets have few dealers. Indeed, in the low price class, cities with fewer than 50,000 inhabitants frequently have but one Ford or one Chevrolet dealer.

Clearly, this does not mean that each Ford or Chevrolet dealer is a monopolist. Often, there will be one or more competing dealers in surrounding communities. Nevertheless, the dealers in these smaller markets will account for a large percentage of the sales in the market. In such markets, sellers are likely to recognize the interdependence of their respective price policies. These markets will have many characteristics of oligopolistic market structures. In the large metropolitan area markets, there will be more sellers retailing each make. The dealer's share of the new car registrations of the dealer's make may be as high as 15 per cent. Most sellers will account for about 5 per cent of the market. Hence, the sales of any one dealer is less likely to affect the market price significantly. Under these conditions, the bonds of interdependence among sellers are likely to be weaker in metropolitan area markets. Hence, greater independence in the formulation of dealer price policy can be expected. If, in addition, there are differences in cost structure among dealerships, there will be further pressures for some dealers to establish an independent price policy. In summary, the probability of reconciling the different private interests of the numerous sellers in metropolitan area markets appears to be less likely than it would be in small cities and rural markets where there are fewer sellers.

This analysis leads to two predictions. First, new car prices can be expected to be lower in metropolitan area markets than in smaller city markets or rural markets. Second, new car prices can be expected to be more flexible in metropolitan area markets than in smaller city markets or rural markets.

New Car Price Behavior in Large and Small Markets. How accurate are these predictions? Data are available which permit partial testing of these two hypotheses.

New car price data in large and small cities are collected by the Bureau of Labor statistics for use in the construction of the Consumer Price Index. Because these data are confidential, they were not analyzed by the author. At the request of the author, a review of new car price data from mid-1954 to May, 1959, was made by the staff of the Division of Prices and Cost of Living of the Bureau of Labor Statistics.

Two general conclusions can be made from these data. First, the average of the dealers' new car prices has tended to be higher in isolated towns than in large cities. Second, there has been less price flexibility during the model year in small cities than in large cities.[10]

A test of the second hypothesis can be made. The Department of Agriculture has published times series data of prices paid by farmers for new autos. These data are collected from franchise dealers located in rural markets. The Consumer Price Index data are collected from dealers located in metropolitan areas. These two sets of data can be compared to determine if new car prices are more flexible in cities than in rural markets throughout the model year.

The Department of Agriculture collects new car price data in November, January, and July. They are collected by means of a mail survey and an enumerated survey conducted by the personnel of the Department.[11]

For each year an index was constructed. New car prices at the beginning of the model year (in November from 1956 to 1959 and in January in 1955) were set equal to 100. Then, the value of index in January and July of succeeding year was recorded. This procedure was applied to both price indexes. These data are presented in Table 10.

It appears that prices are more flexible in city markets than in rural markets. In each year, new car prices in metropolitan

---

10 Personal letter dated July 6, 1959 from Mr. Sidney A. Jaffe, Acting Chief, Division of Prices and Cost of Living, Bureau of Labor Statistics.

11 Personal letter dated June 25, 1959 from Mr. B. R. Stauber, Chief, Agricultural Price Statistics Branch, Agricultural Marketing Service.

TABLE 10. PRICE FLEXIBILITY IN NEW CAR PRICES, A COMPARISON OF CITY
AND RURAL MARKETS

		Prices Paid by Farmers	
Year and Month	Consumer Price Index	6 cylinder [a]	8 cylinder [b]
1955 January	100.0	100.0	100.0
July	93.8	98.0	98.1
1956 November (1955)	100.0	100.0	100.0
January	95.8	98.6	97.8
July	94.6	97.6	97.0
1957 November (1956)	100.0	100.0	100.0
January	99.2	100.0	95.6
July	95.6	98.6	97.2
1958 November (1957)	100.0	100.0	100.0
January	96.2	99.1	99.3
July	94.5	96.9	97.2
1959 November (1958)	100.0	100.0	100.0
January	97.3	100.8	98.4

[a] Model designations include Ford Custom 300, Chevrolet Biscayne, Plymouth Savoy, and comparable model designations prior to 1959.
[b] Model designations include Ford Fairlane, Chevrolet Belair, Plymouth Belevedere, Buick LeSabre and comparable model designations prior to 1959.
Sources : U.S. Bureau of Labor Statistics, *Indexes of Retail Prices of New Automobiles* (mimeographed tables) ; U.S. Agricultural Marketing Service, *Agricultural Prices* (June 15, 1959), p. 37.

area markets decline by a larger percentage than new car prices in rural markets. These results are similar to those reached by the staff of the Division of Prices and Cost of Living of the Bureau of Labor Statistics from the Consumer Price Index data.

In summary the available price data suggest that (1) new car prices are generally lower in metropolitan areas than in small city or rural markets, and (2) new car prices are more flexible during the model year in metropolitan area markets than in rural markets. These results correspond favorably with the predictions of price behavior which can be made from an examination of the market structure in local markets.

Department of Justice Views and Dealer Attempts to Stabilize Prices. The Department of Justice has taken a somewhat different view. Recently, the Justice Department has brought indictments against local dealer associations in large metropolitan areas. It is claimed that each group has conspired to raise, fix, and stabilize retail prices of new automobiles.

Local dealer organizations often attempt to stabilize prices. This is usually justified on some moral grounds of a "fair" price. It is hard to imagine a dealer meeting during which some mention of profits, margins, and prices is not made.[12] It is clear that city dealers, as a group, have more of an incentive to arrive at some form of price agreement. Prices in the city are generally lower and more flexible downward during the model year. It is also evident that dealers in the larger markets are less able to fix and maintain prices. Not that they do not try, they do.[13] In many instances, the large volume dealers do not become members of the local dealer associations. They wish to operate their dealerships on low margins in order to obtain volume. Hence, they have less interest in maintaining margins. Apparently, there are important differences in cost structure among dealerships. Hence, price agreements are that much more difficult to execute. On the demand side there are many dimensions to the price of an automobile, for example, finance terms, price of accessories, used car valuation, and so on. An effective price agreement among dealers must include an agreement on each of these dimensions. Finally, and most important, price is usually well above marginal

---

[12] The indictments of the Department of Justice indicate that attempts are made. For a description of other attempts by dealers to control price competition, see Federal Trade Commission, *Report on Motor Vehicle Industry*, H. R. Doc. 468, 76th Congress, First Session (Washington, D.C.: U.S. Government Printing Office, 1939), pp. 365–418.

[13] An amusing incident was related to the author by one member of a dealer organization. He said that at each dealer meeting an informal resolution would be introduced. This resolution would favor the establishment of minimum prices. Without fail, each dealer would solemnly raise his hand indicating his concurrence. For a week or two, prices would be maintained; then one dealer would begin to shade prices. Soon, all dealers were matching the price cuts. At the next meeting each dealer would solemnly raise his hand in favor of another resolution setting minimum prices. A week or two later prices were being cut again, and so on.

cost. Personal price discrimination can be and is practiced. A sale to one buyer need not affect the terms of sale to another buyer. The incentive to discriminate is ever present.[14]

Several automobile pricing studies have been published, and each shows that personal price discrimination is a persistent characteristic of retail automobile markets. A price study conducted in Denver in 1955 showed that 67 per cent of new Fords (of a given specification) were priced in a range varying from no discount to a discount of $300. A similar study conducted in Houston revealed that 86 per cent of the prices quoted by authorized Ford dealers were priced in a range varying from a discount of $150 to a discount of over $300.[15] Johnson found a $630 differential in prices paid for clean deals, that is, those with no trade in, by buyers in Michigan in 1954 for the same automobile.[16] Jung has found substantial personal price discrimination in the Chicago retail market.[17] Discounts from list price for a new Ford (of a given specification) ranged from $159 to $539 and a new Chevrolet (of a given specification) ranged from $239 to $569. It appears that personal price discrimination is a continuing characteristic of retail automobile markets. In the

---

[14] This is reflected by those dealer advertisements which urge the potential buyer to return to the dealership after the consumer has shopped. Presumably, the dealership is willing to match or undercut any other quotation.

[15] "Report on Pilot Study of Bootlegging" published in *Automobile Marketing Practices*, Hearings, *op. cit.*, Part 1, p. 1103.

[16] Ronald S. Johnson, "What Price Your Ego? When to Trade a Car," *Michigan Business Review* (May, 1955), p. 11.

[17] Allen F. Jung., "Price Variations among Automobile Dealers in Chicago, Illinois," *The Journal of Business*, Vol. XXXII, No. 4 (October, 1959), pp. 315–326. This article has been supplemented by a series of additional articles dealing with similar pricing studies. These articles appear in subsequent editions of the same journal. These articles have expanded our knowledge of automobile pricing considerably. However, Professor Jung has made some unwarranted conclusions from the results of his price studies about the degree of efficiency in automobile distribution. He has found that gross markups are lower in automobile distribution than in other retailing industries. He has concluded that automobile dealerships in Chicago are efficient agencies of distribution. No such inference can be made. Without knowing something about the turnover of capital, no inferences can be made about the degree of efficiency. Markups just do not supply information for this purpose.

author's opinion, this type of discrimination improves the performance of local markets.[18]

Bootlegging of New Automobiles. A tacit price agreement among dealers located in any given market may not be successful if an alternative supply of automobiles is available. Bootlegging represents a method of increasing the supply of autos into a market area. A sale of a new car by a franchise dealer to another buyer, other than another franchise dealer, for subsequent resale is known in the trade as bootlegging. Basically, little is known about the practice. This is regrettable because the important question of the definition of a market cannot be

---

[18] The extent to which personal price discrimination is a disrupting force, tending to drive prices lower, can be measured, in part by the efforts of dealer groups to minimize it. The recent "price labeling" law which was sponsored by dealer groups, gives a ring of authority to the suggested list price. This is one reason why the labeling law has so little merit. It tends to discourage price discrimination. If there is a desire to provide the consumer with accurate price information, this could be accomplished by listing the wholesale price of the automobile, accessories, and so on. See Department of Justice views on price labeling, *Automobile Labeling,* Hearings before a Subcommittee of the Committee on Interstate and Foreign Commerce, House of Rep., 85th Congress, 2nd Sess., on S. 3500, pp. 3–4. However, the posting of the suggested retail price may have eliminated "price packing." The author has often wondered whether the purpose of the labeling law was to eliminate price packing or to help maintain the price structure. If "price packing" is profitable, it is not clear why dealers would like to eliminate it. If "price packing" is unprofitable, it would not be engaged in, and there would be no need to abolish it through the price labeling law. Hence, there is at least a suspicion that the reason for the dealer endorsement is their expectation that the price labeling law will help maintain the price structure. Whether it has or has not, is an entirely different matter.

Bain has noted the importance of price discrimination in improving the market performance of oligopolists. "Personal price discrimination tends to emerge rather naturally as a by-product of imperfect collusion, when individual sellers, though nominally adhering to a common posted price, make secret price concessions on individual orders or to individual buyers in order to enhance their own sales volume."

"An anomalous aspect of such price discrimination is that although it at least superficially resembles true monopolistic discrimination and may have some of the same undesirable results, it is actually a vehicle for a type of price competition which tends to improve the performance of oligopolistic industries." Joe S. Bain, *Price Theory* (New York: Henry Holt & Company, Inc., 1952), pp. 348–349.

determined until more is known about the extent and motivation of bootlegging.

Why does a dealer bootleg autos? Bootlegging represents a way whereby the dealer is able to discriminate between markets. Hence, bootlegging occurs if the dealer is able to segregate markets (third-degree price discrimination), or is able to segregate buyers (first-degree price discrimination).[19] It will always pay a dealer to bootleg an auto if the market price is higher in a distant market (assuming the sale in the distant market does not affect the price in that market) than the marginal revenue from selling an additional unit in his own market.

Very little data are available which show how far bootlegged cars are shipped? Nevertheless, several estimates can be made. To obtain some idea of the arbitrage possibilities, assume that each dealer takes the market price as given. The cost of transporting a car under its own power is between $.03 to $.05 per mile. The cost of transporting an auto by rail or haulway is between $.13 and $.14 per mile.[20]

What is the marginal cost of selling an auto in B from A? If the car is transported under its own power, the transport cost is $.05x, where x is the number of miles. Suppose there is a $100 price discrepancy between markets, then it would pay a dealer to ship to market B if market B is less than 200 miles from market A. Hence, one would be tempted to infer that market areas are much larger than metropolitan areas.

For example, suppose there is perfect flow of autos between markets. A $200 retail price differential between Detroit (say), a low price market, and Bay City (say), a high price market, could not persist since Bay City is only 103 miles from Detroit. A difference of more than $50 to $75 should not persist.

Whether wholesale markets are efficiently organized, is a different matter. The extent of bootlegging is difficult to estimate.

---

[19] The firm maximizes profits when $MR_1 = MR_2 = \ldots = MC$, where MR_1 is the marginal revenue in submarket 1, and so on, and MC is the marginal cost of selling another unit.

[20] *Automobile Marketing Practices*, Hearings, *op. cit.*, Part 1, p. 1104.

Mr. Crusoe estimated that 2 per cent of the total sales of new Fords in 1954 and 1955 were bootlegged autos.[21] Of course, the extent of bootlegging will vary considerably both by make and by market. For example, 102,000 new Volkswagons were regis- tered in the United States in 1958. Yet the company shipped only 85,000 units to its United States dealers. In general, a gross profit of $350 to $400 per auto could be realized by purchasing a Volkswagon in Europe, reconverting it in Europe, shipping and selling it in the United States market. Thus, it would appear that over 15 per cent of the Volkswagons sold in the United States in 1958 were bootlegged autos.[22]

Although bootleg sales may account for a small percentage of total sales, they may account for a large percentage of total sales within individual markets. A survey conducted by the Di- vision of Prices and Cost of Living of the Department of Labor reveals that 18 per cent of the new cars purchased by buyers in Houston were from sellers other than franchise dealers.[23] Ford estimated that bootlegged sales accounted for 9 per cent of total new Ford sales in Houston and 6 per cent in Denver during the beginning of the 1955 model year.[24] Thus, in some individual markets, bootleg sales represent a significant share of total sales. However, the results of the price studies conducted by Jung suggest that bootlegging is limited. He found that differences in the average price of Falcons and Corvairs between various cities were greater than the transportation cost between the cit- ies. This evidence suggests that wholesale markets do not func- tion perfectly or, at least, with some lag. This is an important finding and, if sustained by other price studies, justifies the use of a more limited definition of local automobile markets.[25]

There is some evidence which suggests that bootlegging arises

---

21 *Automobile Marketing Practices,* Hearings, *op. cit.,* Part 1, p. 1029.

22 *The New York Times* (April 5, 1959), p. 4A.

23 U.S. Bureau of Labor Statistics, *Monthly Labor Review* (March, 1957), pp. 336–341.

24 *Automobile Marketing Practices,* Hearings, *op. cit.,* Part 1, p. 1096.

25 Allen F. Jung, "Compact-Car prices in Major Cities," *The Journal of Business,* Vol. XXXIII, No. 3 (July, 1960), pp. 252–257.

not from price differences between markets but from imperfections within a given market. The Ford Motor Company conducted a study of bootlegging.[26] Their findings suggest that bootlegging may arise from segmentation of buyers within a given market and not solely from differences in prices between markets. The Ford study indicated that bootlegged autos tended (but not always) to be priced *higher* than new cars sold in the same market by franchise dealers. Buyers of bootlegged autos had lower incomes and paid higher finance charges than those buyers who purchased from authorized dealers. When surveyed, most buyers of bootlegged cars thought they had received a better price than they would have received from an authorized dealer. These data suggest that bootlegging arises because price discrimination exists within a market (first-degree price discrimination) and not necessarily because there are price differences between markets. Buyers of bootlegged autos thought they were purchasing at a lower than market price. Actually, most were buying at a higher than market price. It would appear that buyers of bootlegged cars are less informed and are low income buyers. Thus, a used car dealer in low priced markets may still purchase autos from a franchise dealer in his own market or even in a high price market because he is able to sell to these less informed buyers at higher than market prices. A difference between the average price in one market and the average price in an adjoining market may not be an accurate predictor of the amount of bootlegging.

It is unfortunate that so little is known about bootlegging. It is important to know just how efficiently these secondary market channels operate since the question of the definition of a market can only be determined after the extent and motivation of bootlegging has been determined. The Ford study suggests that bootlegging may arise more from imperfections on the demand side of the market. Sellers are therefore able to practice first-degree price discrimination. If this is the primary reason

---

[26] *Ibid.*, pp. 1094–1115.

for bootlegging, it would suggest the definition of a market area can be restricted to a city or a metropolitan area and not extended (say) 200 miles from the central city. The preliminary results obtained by Jung confirm this impression. Hence, there seems to be some justification for the use of the city or the metropolitan area as a market area.[27]

---

[27] In general the companies have frowned on bootlegging. Hence, one of the strongest deterrents to bootlegging may be the factories themselves. For factory views, see *Toward A New Era of Dealer Progress* by Harlow H. Curtice, President, General Motors, speech before the 40th Annual Convention, National Automobile Dealers Association, Civic Auditorium, San Francisco, California, January 29, 1957 (mimeographed). *A Statement* by Lewis D. Crusoe, Executive Vice President, Car and Truck Divisions, Ford Motor Company, *Automobile Dealer Franchises*, Hearings before the Antitrust Subcommittee of the Committee on the Judiciary, House of Representatives, 84th Cong., 2nd Sess. on H.R. 11360 and S. 3879, pp. 409–435.

CHAPTER 4

The Development of Market Representation Policies in Automobile Distribution

4.1. Introduction

The market representation policies now practiced in automobile distribution have evolved over a period of some thirty years. In the nineteen-twenties distribution received comparatively little attention. Very little centralized market research was carried out. Most decisions were made at zone offices with little centralized supervision. For a time, manufacturers delegated market representation policy to regionally appointed distributors.[1]

General Motors had been moving in the direction of systematizing their market representation policy in the late twenties. The depression speeded things along. Throughout the thirties there was much experimentation in market representation poli-

---

[1] Channels used in the distribution of automobiles are discussed in Paul F. Banner, "Competition in the Automobile Industry" (unpublished doctoral dissertation, Harvard University, 1950); and Clare Elmer Griffin, "Wholesale Organization in the Automobile Industry," *Harvard Business Review,* Vol. II (July, 1925), pp. 424–435.

cies. To a great extent, the experimentation was forced on by the collapse of sales. General Motors, striving to save the hard hit dealers of the middle price class, began doubling up franchises (better known in the trade as the BOP policy). Probably this was a depression expediency because it was quickly abandoned. Industry sales had declined by 72 per cent from 1929 to 1932. In 1933, sales began to rise and the question arose: How soon and how many dealers should be added? With dealer organizations depleted, most manufacturers added replacements. By 1937 industry sales had increased by 218 per cent over their 1932 low. Unexpectedly, the industry found itself in the midst of the severe 1937–1938 recession. Down sales went again, 46 per cent in one year. Once again, dealers dropped by the wayside. Fortunately, it was a short recession. Soon sales increased. Again the question was asked: How soon and how many dealers should be added? By this time, market representation policies had changed. The dealer organizations were not enlarged. In fact, the size of some dealer organizations was decreased. From that time on, dealers were to be encouraged to expand. They would be carefully appointed and the total number restricted. Franchises would be carefully rationed.

These policies were adopted by most companies and, for the most part, adhered to in the postwar period. The purpose of this chapter is to review these changes and try to explain why these policies were adopted. Some attention will be directed at differences among the company policies.

What is meant by the term market representation policy? [2]

In this study, the term will refer to the number of dealers, the distribution of dealers by size of town, and the use, if any, of multi-line dealerships, better known in the trade as dual dealerships. How many dealers should be appointed? Where should they be appointed, both regionally and by size of town? Should

---

[2] In several instances, the term "franchise policy" may be used interchangeably with the term "market representation policy."

the Chevrolet dealer be given an Oldsmobile franchise or should a separate Oldsmobile dealer be established? These are the decisions which are constantly made at the many zone, regional, and central offices of the companies.

It is desirable to clarify certain other terms. In some cases, a dealer will retail several makes. Such a dealer will have several franchises. In the tabulation of franchise statistics, such a dealer will be enumerated for each franchise. A Chevrolet-Oldsmobile dealer would be counted twice, once for each franchise. Consequently, the number of franchises exceeds the number of dealers. The reader can also see why it would be difficult to determine the number of new car registrations (sales) per Chevrolet dealer. In this case, it would be necessary to allocate a fraction of the total new car registrations of Oldsmobiles to Chevrolet dealers to determine the number of new car registrations per Chevrolet dealer. This cannot be done with available data. New car registrations per franchise are used as a substitute measure. This procedure does understate new car registrations per dealer.

Several comments should be made about the limitations of the data. The analysis begins in the late twenties and extends to the recent past. Very little is known of the market representation policies adopted by the automobile companies from 1920–1941 because there have been few, if any serious studies of automobile distribution. The primary reason for this is that the companies have not released much data or permitted a serious study of the formation and evolution of distribution policies during this period. Consequently, reliance has been placed on the data collected by trade magazines. Deriving conclusions from these data can be and is risky. It is difficult to determine the accuracy of these data or even to specify any systematic bias. The reader should consider many of the conclusions of this chapter as tentative and subject to revision.

Several checks of the data have been made. As a general proposition, one can say the older data are less accurate. This statement was based on two comparisons that have been made.

Data showing the number of franchises by division as of February, 1955, has been released by the General Motors Corporation.[3] These data were compared with the R. L. Polk data reported in Almanac issues of *Automotive News*. The average understatement in the Polk data was about 5 per cent. There was no understatement in the number of Chevrolet franchises but a 3 per cent understatement in the number of Pontiac franchises. Perhaps, the franchise data for the lower priced makes is more accurate. In the second comparison data showing the number of dealers in 1937 for each division of the General Motors Corporation and each division of the Chrysler Corporation were published by the Federal Trade Commission.[4] These data were compared with similar data published by the Trade List Department of the Chilton Company. The average understatement in the Chilton data was about 15 per cent. These two comparisons suggest the older data are less accurate.[5] Quite possibly, the understatement is concentrated in the small markets where a complete enumeration of dealers is difficult to achieve.

The Chrysler Corporation has published data showing the number of Chrysler Corporation dealers from 1926–1954. These data were compared to the Trade List data for prewar years. There is substantial understatement in 1928, 1929, 1933, and 1934. In the other years, the understatement is 10 per cent or less and averaged about 5 per cent. The two series generally move together after 1933. The franchise data for the twenties are subject to a very large error. Since 1934, the direction of change of franchises and the percentage change in franchises probably re-

---

[3] A study of the Antitrust Laws, Hearings before the Subcommittee on Antitrust and Monopoly of the Committee on the Judiciary, United States Senate, 84th Cong., 1st Sess. pursuant to S. Res. 61, Part 8, p. 4381.

[4] United States Federal Trade Commission, *Report on the Motor Vehicle Industry* (Washington, D.C.: Government Printing Office, 1939) pp. 435, 556.

[5] *Fortune Magazine* has often published articles about the automobile companies or divisions of the companies. Often, the number of dealers of the company or division has been reported. It is believed these figures were obtained from the companies. Data published by the trade magazines understated the number of dealers reported by *Fortune* by about 10 per cent.

flects the actual direction of change of franchises (over a period of two or three years) and the actual percentage change of franchises. The Trade List Department data will correctly reflect the larger long-term changes in actual franchises, especially since 1934. It is clear that very little in the way of a detailed analysis can be expected. Because of these data limitations, less confidence can be placed in the figures of dealer franchises. In turn, this means much of the analysis will consist of a study of trends.[6]

4.2. Trends in the Number of Dealers and New Car Registrations per Franchise

Total new car dealers and new car registrations per dealer in various years are presented in Table 11. Inspection of this table shows a gradual reduction in the number of dealers. Even in the prosperous late forties, when margins were unusually high, the total number of dealers was some 8,000 less than the number of dealers in the late twenties. The increase in the average size of dealer has been persistent, apparently (but spuriously) interrupted at intervals by recessions; more than doubling in the last thirty years. These data also suggest that the majority of dealers are small. The large dealer, selling over 800 new units is a rare animal. Most dealers are located in small markets and sell one-eighth that number. This point will be discussed in more detail in a later chapter.

What has been the trend in the number of dealers of specific makes? These data are somewhat more difficult to obtain because of dualing policy. Consider Ford, Chevrolet, and all

---

6 At the time of this revision, Ford franchise data were kindly made available to me by the Ford Motor Co. Because of the time limitation, I could not incorporate these data into the body of the text. However, I have presented the actual Ford franchise data along with the Chilton estimates in Appendix C. This comparison should impress upon the reader the limitations of the data and the tentative nature of the conclusions derived in this chapter. The Chilton data frequently understate the actual number of Ford franchises. In particular, there appear to be substantial errors in the Chilton data both in the number and the direction of change of franchises from 1932 to 1934.

TABLE 11. TOTAL NEW CAR DEALERS AND NEW CAR REGISTRATIONS PER DEALER,
ALTERNATE YEARS, 1925–1957
(1943 AND 1945 EXCLUDED)

Year	New Car Dealers (000)	New Car Registrations Per New Car Dealer
1925	46.7	64
1927	51.4	51
1929	51.6	75
1931	42.9	44
1933	34.1	44
1935	39.8	69
1937	43.7	80
1939	39.3	68
1941	38.7	96
1947	38.5	82
1949	43.1	112
1951	43.3	117
1953	44.4	129
1955	40.8	176
1957	37.6	159

Source: *Total New Car Dealers;* Trade List Department, Chilton Company. Data published in annual issues of *Automotive Industries. New Car Registrations,* R. L. Polk and Company.

Chrysler Corporation dealers. These makes have been selected because the relevant data are available. Although Chevrolet or Ford may be dualed with another make, it is likely this is done only to secure representation of the other make. Thus, in these cases, total franchises have been assumed equal to total dealers. The total number of new car dealers, the number of Chevrolet dealers, the number of Ford dealers and the number of Chrysler Corporation dealers are presented in Table 12. Indexes of growth are also presented. These data also show a decline in the number of dealers. Since 1929, there has been a reduction of at least 1,500 Ford dealers and probably more. These reductions have continued even though the number of new Ford registrations has been rapidly expanding. Since 1952, when the postwar peak in the total number of dealers was reached, there has been a 21 per cent decline. However, the extent of the decline has varied by make, as Table 12 indicates. A large part of the decline can

TABLE 12. TOTAL NUMBER OF DEALERS OF SPECIFIC MAKES FOR SELECTED YEARS 1925–1958

Year	New Car Dealers (000)	Index 1952 = 100	Chev- rolet Dealers (000)	Index 1952 = 100	Ford Dealers	Index 1952 = 100	Chrysler Corpo- ration Dealers (000)	Index 1952 = 100
1929	51.6	114	9.6	128	8.6	130	11.3	106
1933	34.1	75	8.9	119	7.5	114	9.7	91
1937	43.7	97	8.8	117	8.2	124	11.4	107
1941	38.7	86	7.8	104	7.0	106	10.0	94
1947	38.5	85	7.2	96	6.7	101	10.5	99
1951	43.3	96	7.2	96	6.7	101	10.8	101
1952	45.2	100	7.5	100	6.6	100	10.6	100
1953	44.4	98	7.5	100	6.6	100	10.4	98
1954	42.3	94	7.5	100	6.6	100	10.0	94
1955	40.8	90	7.6	101	7.0	106	10.1	95
1956	39.1	86	7.6	101	7.0	106	9.0	85
1957	37.6	83	7.5	100	7.0	106	8.7	82
1958	35.5	79	7.2	96	6.9	104	8.0	76

Sources : *Total New Car Dealers* (see Table 11).
Chevrolet and Ford Dealer: 1929–1941, Trade List Department, Chilton Company.
Chevrolet Dealers: 1947–1958, Almanac Issues, *Automotive News.*
Ford Dealers: 1947 and 1958, Almanac Issues, *Automotive News;* 1951–1957, data sup-plied by Ford Motor Company.
Chrysler Corporation Dealers: 1929–1954, *Some Facts About Chrysler Corporation* "*The Forward Look*" (Office of the Comptroller, Chrysler Corporation, May, 1955), p. 21 ; 1955–1958, Almanac Issues, *Automotive News.*

be accounted for by a decline in the number of dealers retailing middle price makes. The total number of Chrysler Corporation dealers has declined by about 24 per cent since 1952. As far as the author knows, this has not happened to Chrysler before.[7]

Reasons for the Decline in the Number of Dealers. There are several reasons for the decline in the total number of dealers. The decline which took place from the late twenties to the late thirties was prompted by the depression but was due, funda-

---

[7] Actually, the decline has been less. From 1926–1954 Chrysler Corporation data have been used. Since 1954, data from *Automotive News* have been used. *Automotive News* probably underestimates the number of dealers. Hence, the decline may not be as large as the data suggest. Nevertheless, Chrysler has not experienced a decline of this magnitude prior to this.

mentally, to the adoption of a more conservative market representation policy by the leading firms in the industry. Documentation of this last point will soon be presented. The recent decline, since 1952, is due in part to the temporary eclipse of the independents and the evolution of low margin volume dealers. A series of developments have encouraged the growth of the large volume dealer. Available evidence indicates there are economies of scale in automobile distribution. This means that, as the market size grows, margins will tend to fall. Small volume dealers will be under price pressure. Second, there have been shifts in population from rural areas to urban places. In 1920, 48 per cent of the population was located in rural areas, that is, towns with less than 2,500 inhabitants. By 1950, this had been reduced to 41 per cent. The density of the population has increased. In 1920, there were 36 people per square mile. In 1950, there were 51 people per square mile, a 42 per cent increase. As the density of population increases, dealer cost of securing new customers decreases. The increase in the percentage of rural roads surfaced has increased and with it the cost of movement has decreased. Each of these factors lowers the cost of consumer movement and expands market areas. Each encourages consumer mobility and the development of the low margin dealer.[8]

The Evolution of Current Market Representation Policies. Market representation policies have changed over time. As was noted above, the current policies resulted from experimentation during the thirties. In what way did market representation policies change in the thirties and were these changes uniformly adopted by all manufacturers?

New car franchises by make are presented for selected years in Table 13. In the low price class, a general decline in franchises

---

[8] For one of the better public statements by an industry official on these topics, see *Remarks* by Ivan L. Wiles, executive Vice President, General Motors, before Detroit Sales Executive Club, Sheraton-Cadillac Hotel, Detroit, Michigan, November 19, 1957, pp. 3–8 (mimeographed).

TABLE 13. NEW CAR FRANCHISES BY MAKE, 1929–1955

	1929	1937	1941	1950	1955
Low price class					
Chevrolet	9,553	8,752	7,795	7,238	7,612
Ford	8,598	8,245	7,034	6,716	7,009
Middle and upper price class					
(Big Three)					
Dodge-Plymouth	2,994	4,380	3,883	3,628	4,118
Pontiac	4,545	4,006	3,370	3,813	4,123
Mercury	—	—	4,300	1,682	3,046
DeSoto-Plymouth	1,133	2,926	2,465	2,879	2,726
Oldsmobile	1,668	2,588	2,543	3,178	3,774
Buick	3,241	2,750	2,544	3,119	3,534
Chrysler-Plymouth	3,337	3,837	3,333	3,343	3,256
Cadillac-LaSalle	722	803	748	1,334	1,715
Lincoln	—	—	2,516	1,030	1,449
Independents					
Hudson and Essex	3,488	3,390	2,342	2,017	1,574
Nash	2,123	1,753	1,792	1,358	1,524
Studebaker and Rockne	2,242	2,335	2,792	2,510	2,317
Graham-Paige	1,751	877	—	—	—
Hupmobile	1,296	302	—	—	—
Kaiser-Frazer	—	—	—	2,565	1,608
Packard	776	1,283	1,117	1,390	1,282

Sources : 1929–1941, Chilton Trade List Department, data published in annual issues of *Automotive Industries,* 1950–1955, R. L. Polk and Co., data published in Almanac issues of *Automotive News,* 1950–1955, Ford Motor Company Franchises from Ford Motor Company.

is observed. In the middle price class, there have been increases and decreases depending on the make. New car registrations per franchise by make for selected years are presented in Table 14. Again, the general impression is one of a persistent increase in the number of new car registrations per franchise.

What determines the size of a dealer? At first, the author thought the size could be determined merely from the size of the market. For example, it was thought that the new car registrations per Ford dealer could be predicted from new Ford registrations. This would be consistent with the hypothesis that there are no significant diseconomies of scale at least for large increases in sales. Then, one would expect the average size of dealership

TABLE 14. NEW CAR REGISTRATIONS PER FRANCHISE BY MAKE, 1929–1955

	1929	1937	1941	1950	1955
Low price class					
Chevrolet	82	88	113	196	216
Ford	153 [b]	96 [b]	86	174	225
Middle and upper price class					
(Big Three)					
Dodge-Plymouth[a]	48	93	94	133	121
Pontiac	42	53	85	116	129
Mercury	—	—	23 [c]	210 [c]	134 [c]
DeSoto-Plymouth [a]	78	78	98	103	122
Oldsmobile	56 [e]	73	91	117	156
Buick	53 [d]	75	121	172	209
Chrysler-Plymouth [a]	34	64	88	100	114
Cadillac-LaSalle	49	50	81	76	82
Lincoln	[b]	[b]	[c]	[c]	[c]
Independents					
Hudson and Essex	73	27	31	67	27
Nash	50	39	43	129	61
Studebaker and Rockne	37	30	41	107	33
Graham-Paige	35	16	—	—	—
Hupmobile	34	2	—	—	—
Kaiser-Frazer	—	—	—	38	4
Packard	58	74	62	53	22

[a] Plymouth registrations were divided equally among Dodge, DeSoto and Chrysler dealers. In recent years this is a good approximation. In 1929 this procedure may produce biased results since it is not clear that all Chrysler Corporation dealers retailed Plymouths.
[b] Lincoln registrations were assumed to be made by Ford dealers from 1929 to 1937.
[c] Lincoln registrations were assumed to be made by Mercury dealers from 1937 to 1955. Continental registrations were also assumed to be made by Mercury dealers in 1955.
[d] Includes Marquette registrations.
[e] Includes Viking registrations.
[f] Includes Oakland registrations.
Sources : *Registrations*, R. L. Polk and Co. ; *Franchises*, see Table 13.

would increase with an increase in new car registrations. However, the analysis is complicated by the delayed reaction of management to the recognition of the existence of economies of scale. Throughout the twenties and early thirties, management placed many more dealers for any given level of new car registrations than it has since the late thirties.

Market Representation Policy in the Low Price Class. The changes in total number of new car dealers and the number of new car registrations per dealer can be seen by considering the relationship between new car registrations of Chevrolets and Chevrolet franchises. These data are plotted for selected years from 1927 to 1958 in Figure 3. Similar data for Ford are plotted in Figure 4. These figures show the different policies which have been practiced throughout the 1927–1958 period.

First, we shall concentrate attention on Chevrolet. Note three different responses by Chevrolet management in three separate growth periods during the 1927–1941 period. New car registrations increased from 1927 to 1929, from 1933 to 1936, and from 1938 to 1941. The increase in new car registrations of Chevrolets in each of these growth periods was approximately 450,000 units. Yet, the response, the change in franchises, apparently was different in each period. With each succeeding growth period fewer franchises were added. Apparently, in the 1939–1941 period, there was an actual reduction. In this twenty-five year period, three distinct market representation policies were practiced. Each successive policy was somewhat more cautious than the former policy. By the end of the thirties, market representation policy had changed. It was designed to encourage the growth of large dealers. The postwar policy represents a continuation of this policy. Franchises were again reduced.

Ford's market representation policies are, in large part, similar to those of Chevrolet. However, several important differences exist. Chevrolet has consistently issued more franchises than Ford. For the same level of new car registrations, the fewer Ford franchises means that new car registrations per Ford franchise are higher than new car registrations per Chevrolet franchise. The decline in Ford franchises during the 1927–1931 period was due to the lower new car registrations of Ford which were experienced in the late twenties compared to the higher new car registrations of Ford recorded in the early twenties.

Figures 3 and 4 show the delayed reaction of management in recognizing the existence and importance of economies of scale in automobile retailing. One comparison may be particu-

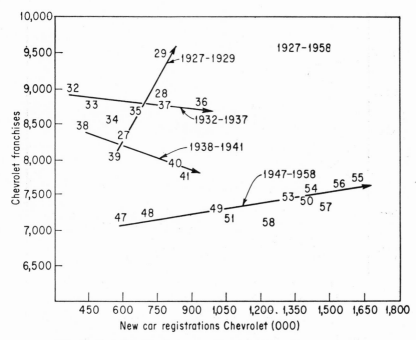

Fig. 3. Relationship between Chevrolet franchises and new car registrations of Chevrolet

larly instructive. In 1929 and 1956, new car registrations of Ford were about equal. Yet, there were approximately 1,500 more Ford franchises in 1929 than in 1956.

Why was franchise policy changed in the late thirties? Why not earlier? To a great extent, these questions must be left unanswered. There simply is not enough information available to answer these questions. It should be stressed that these policies were adopted only after much experimentation. It cannot be said that the particular franchise policies now practiced by the companies were selected by chance. Various methods and alternatives were considered, used, and subsequently discarded. Assuming each company is profit motivated, each has adopted the franchise system, as it is known today, because of its superiority over others. However, it does not follow that the franchise system is necessarily the optimum distribution system.

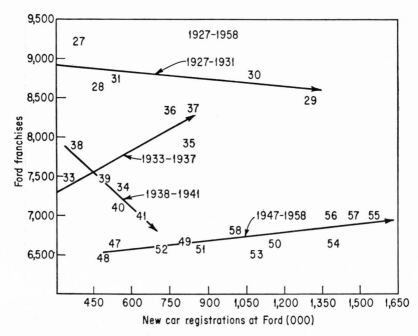

Fig. 4. Relationship between Ford franchises and new car registrations of Ford

Reasons for the adoption of this conservative policy are somewhat less difficult to determine. There is some evidence of economies of scale in automobile distribution. In the long run, any representation policy which ignored this would be unsuccessful. If the large dealership has a cost advantage over the small dealership, a policy based on the use of many small dealerships rather than a few large dealerships is bound to fail. The incentive to grow is high. Once some dealers expand, the others would be at a cost disadvantage. In the long run, they would be less likely to survive. As will be shown, the largest percentage of reductions in Ford and Chevrolet franchises from 1937 to 1952 have taken place in towns with fewer than 1,000 inhabitants and cities with more than 100,000 inhabitants, that is, in the smallest and largest markets. In the smaller towns, because these dealers are at the greatest cost disadvantage due to their limited volume, and, in the cities, because of the greater price competition, a premium is placed on efficiency which tends to eliminate the smaller dealers. How long it takes for this process of elimination to work itself out is difficult to determine. Much depends on how soon the representation policy is changed so as to encourage the increase in dealership size.

A second reason for the change in representation policy has already been mentioned. The increase in the density of the population encourages an increase in the size of the dealership. However, the great diversity in market representation policies in the middle price class may indicate this is not critical.

A third reason for the increase in the size of the dealer is the use of the franchise system. The franchise system protects existing dealers by blocking entry. It lowers dealer turnover and encourages the establishment of consumer-dealer attachments. The franchise system fosters the growth of the large volume but, not necessarily, the low cost dealer. Dealers, who may for a variety of reasons be relatively inefficient (on higher cost schedules) and who would sustain losses with free entry, are protected by the system. However, this may be an optimal market representation policy if consumer-dealer attachments can be established at lower cost than by some other sales promotion policy.

Market Representation Policy in the Middle Price Class. There is greater diversity among market representation policies of producers of middle price automobiles. The relationship between franchises and new car registrations for each General Motors division producing a middle price class automobile is presented in Figure 5. A similar plot of each Chrysler Corporation division is presented in Figure 6.[9] In several respects, the policies adopted by the middle price class divisions are similar to the policies

---

[9] The data for Chrysler Corporation makes apparently underestimate total franchises of each make in 1927 and 1929. Data released by the Chrysler Corporation indicate there were more dealers in 1927 and 1929 than the Chilton data show.

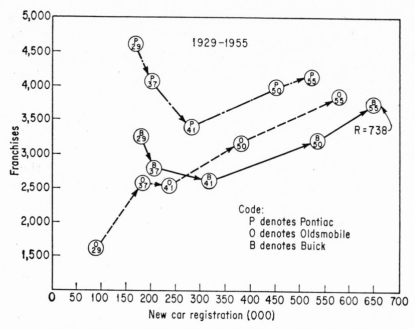

Fig. 5. Relationship between franchises and new car registrations, General Motors divisions in middle price class

adopted by Ford and Chevrolet. All divisions reduced franchises during the 1938–1941 period. In the postwar period, franchises have been more sensitive to changes in new car registrations than in the low price class. This is particularly true of General Motors divisions. There also seems to be more consistency in the market representation policies among General Motors divisions than among Chrysler Corporation divisions.[10]

Comparison of the Market Representation Policies of the Independents and the Big Three. By now the reader has undoubtedly wondered why there was a simultaneous reduction in franchises by all divisions during the 1938–1941 period. Is there oligopolistic interdependence in franchise policy? To discuss this question, it is desirable to begin by comparing the indepen-

---

[10] However, this result may be due entirely to the limitations of the data.

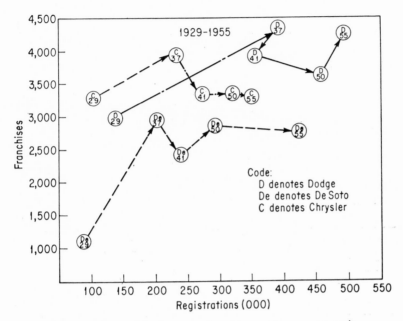

Fig. 6. Relationship between franchises and new car registrations, divisions of the Chrysler Corporation

dents' franchise policy with the franchise policy of the Big Three.
Consider three periods when total industry new car registrations
increased: 1927–1929, 1933–1937, and 1939–1941. During each
period each company or division had the option of increasing,
decreasing or holding constant its franchises. Did the independents react differently from the Big Three during any of these
periods?

Four independents have been selected for comparison with
the Big Three. They are Hudson, Nash, Studebaker, and Packard. Each division of the Big Three (except Cadillac and Lincoln) and each independent was classified according to whether
new car registrations increased or decreased during each period
(noted above). Then, each division or each company (as the
case may be) was classified as to whether franchises increased
or decreased. These data are reproduced in Table 15. This table
can be read as follows: in the 1927–1929 period two divisions of

TABLE 15. A COMPARISON OF THE MARKET REPRESENTATION POLICIES OF THE
BIG THREE AND THE INDEPENDENTS IN THREE GROWTH PERIODS

		Eight Divisions of Big Three		Four Independents	
		New Car Registrations		New Car Registrations	
		Increase +	Decrease −	Increase +	Decrease −
Franchises 1927–1929 ᵃ	Increase +	2	0	1	0
	Decrease −	3	2	1	2
Franchises 1933–1937	+	6	0	4	0
	−	2	0	0	0
Franchises 1939–1941	+	1	0	3	0
	−	7	0	1	0
Franchises 1937–1941	+	0	0	2	0
	−	6	2	0	2

ᵃ DeSoto division not yet formed.
The table should read as follows : Two divisions of the Big Three experienced an increase in registrations in the 1927–1929 period and increased their franchises ; three other
divisions experienced an increase in registrations but decreased their franchises, and
so on.
Source : See Table 13.

the Big Three experienced an increase in new car registrations
and increased their franchises, for three other divisions, new car
registrations increased but franchises decreased. Each matrix
can be read in a similar manner. Normally, all observations would
be expected to fall on the diagonals; that is, an increase in new car
registrations would be expected to increase franchises and vice
versa. Consequently, all off-diagonal elements represent departures from this policy. There are several departures in the 1927
and 1929 period. There is no significant difference between the
two groups in the 1933–1937 period. The story appears to be different in the 1939–1941 period. Seven of the eight divisions of the
Big Three simultaneously reduced franchises even though new car

registrations increased. In contrast, three of the four independents (the exception is Hudson) increased franchises as registrations increased. Because of the limited number of observations, a chi square test was not applied to the data to test the significance of these differences.

In summary, the independents did not adopt the 1938–1941 representation policies of the Big Three. There may be some interdependence in franchise policy among divisions of the Big Three. However, the independents' market position required them to practice independent representation policies. Because of their lower density of market coverage, the marginal value of each franchise was much higher for the independents than for the Big Three. They took full advantage of this when their new car registrations increased. With more franchises the Big Three had less of an incentive to increase franchises.

The extent of recognized interdependence among producers in franchise policy is difficult to judge. The simultaneous reduction in franchises in the 1938–1941 period lends support to the contention. However, evidence will be introduced in another section of this chapter which will show differences in the number of dealers of competing makes in the same market. This would indicate substantial variability in representation policies is possible. Whereas it may be true that Ford could not add a large number of dealers without forcing Chevrolet to counter, there is, within wide limits, substantial variability in the number of dealers. In other words, location is not that important a determinant of sales. In the early days of the industry, many of the metropolitan areas in the East had too many dealers. In part, this resulted from the failure of oligopolists to recognize their interdependence, as well as the belief that one successful way of increasing sales was to increase the number of dealers. Thus, markets in the East have often had too many dealers compared to markets in the West.

The simultaneous reduction of franchises in the late thirties may be explained in part by partial recognition of the interdependence of franchises. Having placed too many dealers in the past, there was a mutual recognition that a simultaneous reduction would be optimal for each producer. This seems to be the only consistent explanation.[11] An alternative explanation could attribute the reduction to a sudden increase in the optimal size of dealership during the late thirties. However, this view fails to explain why the independents increased their franchises during this period. If there was an increase in the optimum size of dealership, this should have applied to both the independents' dealers and the dealers of the Big Three. Consequently, the reduction in franchises cannot be attributed to this cause.

It would appear, therefore, that the change in franchise policy resulted from deliberate administrative policy adopted by each of the Big Three.[12] Whether each company's policy change was independent of the policy changes of the other two companies is, as of now, unknown.

4.3. Stability in the Number of Dealers

It has frequently been claimed that the independents' dealers are at a cost and product disadvantage. Their dealers have smaller volumes and therefore higher per unit costs. The effective margin between the retail and wholesale price of the independents' automobiles is said to be lower because of the larger discounts on their autos. Profit rates of the independents' dealers are said to be lower. Thus, a larger percentage of their dealers are marginal. If so, the independents' dealers would be more vulnerable to cyclical changes in new car registrations. The independents should experience a greater percentage decline in

---

[11] Not all firms carry out extensive market studies. The largest may and then decide to reduce franchises. The others may then copy the policies of the largest firm and thereby secure the benefits (if they exist) without incurring the research costs.

[12] The change in policy also implied that previous franchise policies, which encouraged the addition of franchises as new car registrations increased, were now considered inferior policies and, moreover, still are.

their franchises for any given percentage decline in new car registrations than do the Big Three.

Cyclical Variability in New Car Registrations. Do the sales of the independents fluctuate more than the sales of the Big Three? Do the sales of the independents decrease by a larger per cent in recessions than the sales of the Big Three? The 1926–1958 period has been divided into periods when industry new car registrations increased: 1927–1929, 1932–1937, 1938–1941, 1946–1950, and 1952–1955. It has also been divided into periods when industry new car registrations decreased. 1926–1927, 1929–1932, 1937–1938, 1950–1952, and 1955–1958. New car registrations have been grouped as follows: (1) the low price makes of the Big Three (Chevrolet, Ford, and Plymouth), (2) the middle and upper price makes of the Big Three, and (3) the independents. The percentage change in new car registrations for each of these groups in each period is shown in Table 16.

TABLE 16. CYCLICAL VARIABILITY IN NEW CAR REGISTRATIONS BY PRICE CLASS, 1926–1958

Period	Chevrolet, Plymouth, and Ford (Per cent)	Middle and Upper Price Makes of the Big Three (Per cent)	Independents (Per cent)
1926–1927	−36	−1	−2
1927–1929	+109	+1	+11
1929–1932	−68	−71	−80
1932–1937	+188	+406	+110
1937–1938	−44	−46	−54
1938–1941	+74	+142	+97
1946–1950	+261	+246	+213
1950–1952	−36	−35	−28
1952–1955	+91	+91	−43
1955–1958	−31	−54	+81

Source: R. L. Polk and Co.

Before the depression, there is no reason to believe the new car registrations of the independents varied more than the new car registrations of the Big Three. During the depression a reversal can be observed. The independents retailed automobiles which can best be considered middle price automobiles. For comparability, compare the middle and upper price makes of the Big Three with those of the independents. The independents experienced greater percentage declines in new car registrations in the 1929–1932 and 1937–1938 periods than did the middle and upper price makes of the Big Three. In the two recovery periods, 1933–1937 and 1938–1941, the independents experienced smaller percentage increases in new car registrations than did the middle and upper price makes of the Big Three. Consequently, the independents' share of the market decreased throughout this period. Also, the independents experienced greater percentage reductions in new car registrations in this decade.

In the postwar period, comparisons are more difficult to make. From 1946–1952, output was restricted by raw material shortages or output controls. From 1953 to 1958, the diverse movements in the independents' new car registrations and the new car registrations of the Big Three do not permit comparisons. The 1958 recession is the only other period during which the effects of a cyclical decline on new car registrations can be investigated. However, the emergence of the small car balks this inquiry.

Cyclical Variabilty in Franchises. Do the independents experience a greater percentage change in franchises than the Big Three for any given change in new car registrations? In other words, do the independents find their franchises decrease by a greater percentage than the Big Three during recessions? Then, during recovery, do they tend to recoup their previous losses by increasing franchises by a greater percentage than the Big Three do?

Before considering these questions, one other point must be considered. Do new car registrations determine the number of franchises, or do the number of franchises determine new car registrations? Clearly, there is no simple answer to this question.

However, it is probably a better approximation to consider the number of franchises as being determined by the number of new car registrations. For support of this view, note the reduction in franchises by the divisions of the Big Three throughout the thirties, even though new car registrations did not change appreciably. Apparently, franchises can differ appreciably without noticeably affecting new car registrations. Beyond a certain minimum number of franchises, which the low price makes of the Big Three have surpassed, the density of market coverage does not appear to be an important determinant of new car registrations. The independents were not and have not been in this advantageous position. In the absence of a comprehensive study it seems more accurate to consider the number of franchises as a function of new car registrations.

Franchise Policy of the Big Three and the Independents during the Nineteen-Thirties. Total new car registrations decreased in three periods; 1929–1932, 1937–1938, and 1955–1958. The maximum and minimum of new car registrations of each make do not coincide with these dates in all cases. Comparisons of maximum and minimum new car registrations of each make have been made, regardless of whether they coincide with the maximum and minimum of industry new car registrations in the years specified above. For example, new car registrations of most makes reached lows in 1932, but several recorded lows in 1933. In these cases, the 1933 figure was considered the minimum of new car registrations.

In Figure 7 the relationship between the percentage decline in franchises and the percentage decline in new car registrations in the three periods when new car registrations decreased have been plotted. During the 1929–1933 decline, the independents did experience a greater percentage decline in franchises. However, this was apparently due to the greater percentage decline in new car registrations experienced by them. Once an adjustment is made for this, it appears that the independents did not experience

Code:
C-Chrysler Ch-Chevrolet B-Buick N-Nash G-P-Graham Paige
De-De Soto P-Pontiac F-Ford S-Studebaker Am-American Motors
D-Dodge O-Oldsmobile H-Hudson Pk-Packard M-Mercury

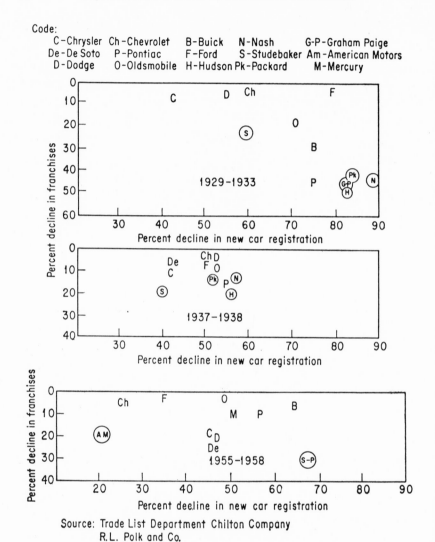

Source: Trade List Department Chilton Company
R.L. Polk and Co.

Fig. 7. Per cent decline in franchises and per cent of decline in new car registrations by make

a greater percentage decline in franchises. In this period there is little to suggest that a larger percentage of the independents' dealers were marginal, and, therefore, more vulnerable to a reduction in new car registrations. For an unknown reason, the independents experienced a greater percentage decline in new car registrations.

During the 1933–1937 recovery, franchises were added. Two of the independents, Studebaker and Hudson, added franchises by a greater percentage relative to the percentage increase in their new car registrations. These data are plotted in Figure 8.

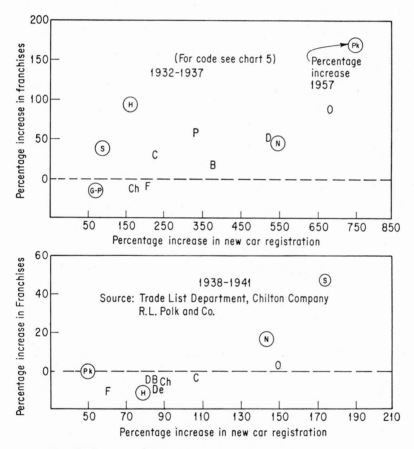

Fig. 8. Per cent of increase in franchise and per cent of increase in new car registrations by make

The 1937–1938 recession caused new car registrations and franchises to decrease. This time the story is different. In this recession, the independents and the Big Three experienced approximately equal percentage reductions in new car registrations. However, the percentage reductions in the independents' franchises were generally higher. It would appear that a larger percentage of the independents' dealers had become marginal and were, therefore, more vulnerable to a cyclical decline in new car registrations. Possibly, the independents lost many of their better dealers to the Big Three before or at this time. A larger percentage of the independents' dealers were marginal when the 1937–1938 recession arrived. Compared to the Big Three, a larger percentage of their dealers failed to survive the recession. Once again recovery began. As noted above, the Big Three reduced franchises. The independents, recovering from the last recession, added franchises. By the end of the thirties, the independents appeared to be more vulnerable to a cyclical decline in new car registrations.[13]

Since the late twenties, the independents have been subjected to greater cyclical variability in sales. Moreover, a given percentage change in the sales of the independents (increase or decrease) has caused a greater percentage change in the total franchises of the independents (increase or decrease). In the thirties the independents lost a larger percentage of their dealers, and in periods of growth they increased their franchises by a greater percentage, apparently to compensate for the loss in the preceding period. This suggests the time horizon of the independents is shorter. When the independents find their sales increase, they do not permit the existing dealers to expand in size but tend to expand the number of franchises. Consequently, when the

---

[13] It would appear that Chrysler Corporation dealers have become more vulnerable to a decline in sales. In the 1955–1958 period, the percentage decline in Chrysler Corporation franchises much exceeded the percentage decline of the franchises of the divisions of General Motors and Ford. This represents a substantial change from the 1937–1938 recession experience. For an equal percentage decline in new car registrations, the divisions of the Chrysler Corporation experienced a greater percentage decline in dealers than Ford or General Motors.

next decline in new car registrations occurs, it drives more of the independents' dealers out of business.[14]

Distribution Problems of the Independents. There has been a tendency for the sales of the independents to fluctuate more than the sales of the Big Three. In addition, there has been greater fluctuation in the franchises of the independents than in the franchises of the makes of the Big Three, even after an adjustment has been made for the greater variability in sales of the independents. The evidence tends to support the contention that the dealers of the independents are less profitable, and more are vulnerable to sales fluctuations. Most likely, this arises from the smaller sales volume of the independents' dealers and possibly because of the lower effective margins obtained by the independents' dealers.

The greater fluctuation of sales means that the risk of failure facing the new entrant in the automobile manufacturing industry is higher. Because the independents experience greater fluctuations in sales, the risk premium facing a potential dealer of an independent is also higher.

The greater risk would ordinarily be compensated for by a greater expected return. Since the expected volume of a potential dealer of an independent is lower, the expected rate of return is also probably lower. Thus, the independents obtain fewer dealers and probably less capable dealers. The opposite path open to the independents is to restrict the number of franchises and in this way increase their dealers earning rates. This would reduce the density of coverage and probably increase the profit

---

[14] It is possible that the large percentage change in franchises results from increases of franchises in single point markets as sales increase and corresponding decreases in franchises in these single point markets as sales decline. The independents may not expand the number of dealers in large markets as sales increase but allow these dealers to expand. This contention was tested and was rejected. The percentage change in franchises seems to be independent of size of town. The point is discussed at greater length in section 4.5.

rate of the remaining dealers. This policy has been adopted by the Big Three. It tends to decrease the turnover rate and protect the dealer from cyclical declines. The expected increase in sales due to the placement of another dealer is higher for the independents because of their lower density of coverage. In the short run, there is a constant pressure for them to expand dealers. In the long run, there may be advantages from a stable experienced dealer organization which has established consumer attachments. This can best be accomplished by restricting the number of dealers or being fortunate enough to experience a persistant increase in sales. When faced with this choice, the independents have frequently chosen the former course of action. Yet, this policy could only be successful in an expanding market. Needless to say, such a market did not exist in the thirties and is not likely to be observed in any future automobile market.

Nash adopted a restrictive policy in the postwar period. However, this policy apparently was not successful.

> During the days when you could sell any car you could build, and sign all the dealers you wanted to, we deliberately held our body down to 1,200 dealers, which is too small a dealer body, because at that time steel was short and other things were short, and we felt that we should not appoint dealers in excess of the production that we could see, so that they would have an adequate sales volume.
>
> I am very sorry to report, sir, that despite the fact that we pursued that policy for many years, very few of those big, fine dealers we built up are still with us. They have been raided and taken over by others, or they have been disloyal and gone to others or they have retired.[15]

Restricting the number of dealers in hopes of increasing the profit rates of the remaining dealers may not be a successful

---

[15] *Automobile Marketing Practices,* Hearings before the Subcommittee on Interstate and Foreign Commerce, U.S. Senate, 84th Congress, 2nd Session, pursuant to S. Res. 13, continued by S. Res. 163, Part 1, p. 44. For further information on the Nash program see "The Nash Tunes Up," *Fortune* (September 1945), p. 125.

policy. These dealers generally will switch to other makes at the first opportunity. This may be due to the fact that the profit rates of the independents' dealers may still be lower than the profit rates of the Big Three dealers which, in turn, may be because of their lower volume. Or, the lower profit rates of the independents' dealers may be caused by lower effective margins on the independents' autos. However, there seems to be no doubt that the independents lose dealers to the Big Three. Data showing intercorporate raiding is considered highly confidential by the automobile companies. However, some information is available. It has been reported that of the 1,225 exclusive dealers that Mercury had in 1951, 40 per cent were dealers from competing makes and most of these came from the independents.[16] Many of the initial group of Edsel dealers were from competitors, mostly from the independents and Chrysler. According to *Fortune*, Chrysler Corporation lost 175 dealers (out of 9,000), General Motors lost approximately 165 (out of 18,500) and the two independents lost 200 (out of 4,700). Moreover, Edsel deliberately turned down some of the independents' dealers.

This evidence suggests that the independents' dealers would prefer to retail Big Three automobiles. Most seem quite willing to transfer. Although it is difficult to document the case, it seems that General Motors franchises are generally preferred; then other middle price divisions of Ford and Chrysler are desired. Presumably, Ford and Chevrolet have little difficulty replacing dealers. Most dealers would welcome the opportunity to transfer.

In summary, the independents have great difficulty in holding capable dealers. Although the evidence is not entirely satisfactory, this difficulty cannot be traced *solely* to lower volume. Not only do the independents' dealers have lower volumes, but their realized margins are lower. The greater depreciation rates on the used cars of the independents indicates that (1) either the buyer of an independent's automobile realizes a loss when he trades

---

[16] "Lincoln-Mercury Moves Up," *Fortune* (March, 1952), p. 176.

it in on his next purchase, or (2) the independents' dealers give higher than market price quotations to the new car buyer on trade ins and then take a loss when the trade in is resold. In the latter case, the dealer absorbs the loss because the gross margin is less. Because of this, their profit rates will be less. In the latter case, the profit rates of the independents' dealers would be less, even if they sold the same volume as the Big Three dealers.

Under such conditions, a policy of restricting the number of dealers need not be optimal. As was just noted, even if the independents' dealers had comparable volumes with the Big Three dealers, their effective margins and profit rates would be lower. Under such circumstances, their dealers would be quite willing to replace Big Three dealers when the time and place arose. The independents would still be in the same position of continuously obtaining substitutes to replace dealers who have transferred to the Big Three. Consequently, as long as there is recognized interdependence in price policy so that list prices are approximately equal, the independents continually have distribution difficulties. The only alternative open to the independents was to increase the dealer's margin by lowering the wholesale price. However, this policy would only be successful if (1) the reduction in the wholesale price is passed along, so that the retail price falls; (2) the fall in the retail price increases the manufacturer's sales, so that total revenue of the manufacturer increases; and (3) the price reduction does cause competitors to reduce price and thereby nullify the initial price cut. It is important that the reduction in the wholesale price be passed along in the form of a retail price reduction. If the retail price does not fall, sales will not increase. The net effect of the reduction in the wholesale price would simply be a decrease in the manufacturer's profits and a corresponding rise in dealers' profits. Consequently, the manufacturer would not reduce the wholesale price under such circumstances. Moreover, it is not entirely clear whether a reduction in the wholesale price would cause a fall in the retail price. The independents have fewer dealers and most operate in markets where they have few competitors selling their make. Price rigidity may be expected. Even if the retail price did decrease, demand may be inelastic. Even if the demand curve were elastic, a price reduction would not be initiated if price reprisals were expected. The independents have seldom engaged in price cutting. Facing these alternatives the independents choose the former. Rather than restrict the number of dealers they added dealers. While this policy was not likely to solve the long run problem of establishing a stable group of dealers, it would meet the pressing short run problem of increasing sales.

Assuming this to be an accurate description of the independents' position, what alternatives can be proposed? There is some evidence which suggests the independents may be more vulnerable to cyclical fluctuations. Entry into the industry appears difficult. It is likely that a new firm, not already in the industry will face higher entry costs than an existing firm which has a small share of the market. Public policy should be different in industries of this kind where product differentiation is an important factor in determining industry structure. What policies, if any, can be adopted to insure more stability in the dealer organization of the independents? In particular, what advantages would the independents obtain from the use of multi-line dealerships, that is, dealerships which sell many makes? It seems that the independents' dealers retail fewer cars per dealer and are at a cost disadvantage. When sales decline, this cost disadvantage increases and forces many of the independents' dealers to leave the industry. Would multi-line dealers lessen this disadvantage? Under such a system, the independents' coverage would be more likely to be maintained in rural and small urban markets. However, it is not clear if this is of sufficient importance to improve the position of the independents. Consumers may not purchase the independents' autos because nearby dealers are not available. Or, consumers may not purchase the independents' autos even if their dealers are nearby. It is difficult to attribute the sudden failure of Studebaker, Packard, Hudson, and Nash in the 1953–1955 period to a sudden lack of dealers. More likely, changes in the tastes of the American public determined the fate of the independents. Frequent model changes favor the large firm.

Nevertheless, it seems clear that the cost disadvantage of the independents' dealers increases when sales decline. This disadvantage would be smaller under a multi-line system. The benefits derived by the independents from such a policy can be partially evaluated by determining whether the independents experience greater losses in franchises in the small markets than in the large markets when sales decline. If they experience greater losses in the small markets, then they are likely to find their vulnerability to cyclical change is reduced by the adoption of a multi-line system. This point will be investigated in section 4.5.

4.4. Distribution of Franchises by Size of Town

The Direct Mail Division of the Chilton Company tabulates data showing the number of franchises of each make by size of town. These data are available from 1927, although they are not available for each year.[17] These data can be used to show changes in franchise policy of a particular make over time. Have the manufacturers tended to concentrate franchises in the large cities? Are there differences in franchise policy between Chevrolet and Ford? Do the manufacturers copy each other? When Ford adds franchises in one town size class, does Chevrolet counter? Or, are there differences between the companies in the distribution of franchises by city size? These data will also help resolve the question left unanswered in the last section. Is the greater variability of the independents' franchises due to greater changes in their franchises in smaller markets than in the larger markets?

---

[17] These data are published in the annual review issues of *Automotive Industries*. Once again, the author would like to remind the reader of the tentative nature of the conclusions.

Ford Franchise Policy, 1927–1952. Data showing the distribution of Ford franchises by size of town are available from 1927 to 1952. Similar data for other makes are available from 1934 to 1952. The number of Ford franchises by size of town in 1927, 1934, 1941, and 1952 is presented in Table 17. The number

TABLE 17. FORD FRANCHISES BY SIZE OF TOWN

Town Size	1927 [a]	1933	1941	1952	Difference 1927–1952
0–1,000	3,594		1,933	1,478	−2,116
1,000–2,500	2,335		1,888	1,875	− 460
		} 6,190			
2,500–5,000	1,078		1,047	1,107	29
5,000–10,000	629		772	774	145
10,000–25,000	449		570	583	134
		} 666			
25,000–50,000	180		209	210	30
50,000–100,000		125	145	148	
	} 719				} − 120
Over 100,000		499	470	451	
Total	8,984	7,480	7,034	6,626	−2,358

		Per cent [b]			
0–1,000	40		27	22	
1,000–2,000	26		27	28	
	} = 85	} 83	80 =		} = 79
2,000–5,000	12		15	17	
5,000–10,000	7		11	12	
10,000–25,000	5		8	9	
	} = 7	} 9	11 =		} = 12
25,000–50,000	2		3	3	
50,000–100,000		2	2	2	
	} 8				
Over 100,000		7	7	7	
Total	100	100	100	100	

[a] Approximate figures.
[b] Columns may not add because of rounding.
Source: Trade List Department, Chilton Company.

of Ford franchises in each size class as a percentage of total Ford franchises is also presented. Note that there has been (1) a reduction in the number of franchises in cities with more than 50,000 inhabitants, (2) a larger reduction in towns with fewer than 2,500 inhabitants and (3) an increase in the number of franchises in towns with 2,500 to 50,000 inhabitants.[18] There has been a concentration of franchises into the medium size towns. Some, but not all, of these changes can be explained by changes in the distribution of population among towns and cities. The rural population has increased from 51.6 million in 1920 to 61.8 million in 1950 (old Census definition), and the urban population has increased from 54.2 million in 1920 to 88.9 million in 1950 (old Census definition). Therefore, the decline in the number of franchises in the two smallest population classes cannot be adequately explained by a depletion of the rural population. The rural population has slightly increased. The distribution of the population by size of place in 1930 and 1950 is presented in Table 18. The number of places by size of place in 1930 and 1950 is

TABLE 18. PER CENT DISTRIBUTION OF POPULATION BY SIZE OF PLACE, 1930 AND 1950

Place	1930	1950	Difference
Urban	56.2	59.0	2.8
1,000,000 or more	12.3	11.5	—.8
500,000–1,000,000	4.7	6.1	1.4
250,000–500,000	6.5	5.5	—1.0
100,000–250,000	6.1	6.4	.3
50,000–100,000	5.3	6.0	.7
25,000–50,000	5.2	6.3	1.1
10,000–25,000	7.4	8.3	.9
5,000–10,000	4.8	5.2	.4
2,500–5,000	3.8	3.7	—.1
Rural	43.8	41.0	—2.8
1,000–2,500	3.9	3.6	—.3
Under 1,000	3.6	2.7	—.9

Sources : 1930 *Census of Population.*
         1950 *Census of Population.*

[18] Because of the limitations of the data, the estimates of the change in the number of franchises by size of town cannot be considered accurate. However, it seems safe to say, and this is all that is needed for the moment, the largest declines occurred in the two *tails* of the distribution.

presented in Table 19. These data show the number of places with fewer than 1,000 inhabitants has declined by 519. The decrease in the number of Ford franchises in this class was 2,116,

TABLE 19. NUMBER OF PLACES BY SIZE OF PLACE, 1930 AND 1950 [a]

Place	Number of Places		
	1930	1950	Difference
Urban	3,165	4,023	858
1,000,000 or more	5	5	—
500,000–1,000,000	8	13	5
250,000–500,000	24	23	−1
100,000–250,000	56	66	10
50,000–100,000	98	128	30
25,000–50,000	185	271	86
10,000–25,000	606	814	208
5,000–10,000	851	1,133	282
2,500–5,000	1,332	1,570	238
Rural	13,433	13,235	−198
1,000–2,500	3,087	3,408	321
Under 1,000	10,346	9,827	−519

[a] Based on old Census definition
Sources : 1930 *Census of Population.*
1950 *Census of Population.*

four times as large and probably larger. It is clear that shifts in the rural population cannot solely explain the decrease in Ford franchises in this class. Moreover, this decrease in franchises was not offset by an increase in franchises elsewhere in rural areas. The number of places with 1,000 to 2,500 inhabitants increased by 321. The number of Ford franchises in towns of this size decreased by 461. In the larger markets, those with 50,000 or more inhabitants, a similar decline in franchises is observed, even though the number of places and the total population of this class increased. At the two ends of the distribution there has been a reduction in the number of Ford franchises.

These changes in market representation policy have also changed the market structure in local markets. This can be seen by making the following crude comparison. Compare the trend over time in the number of Ford dealers per place by size of place. For example, in 1927 there were 719 Ford dealers in places with 50,000 or more inhabitants and 191 such places. The average number of Ford franchises in such places in 1927 was about 3.8. In 1952 the average number of Ford franchises per place in places of this size was 2.5. In other words, there were about four Ford franchises in each city of this size in 1927. In 1952 the average number of Ford dealers in towns of this size was 2.5. The average number of Ford franchises per place by size of place in select years is presented in Table 20. Except for the smallest

TABLE 20. NUMBER OF FORD FRANCHISES PER PLACE BY SIZE OF PLACE,
1927, 1941 AND 1952

Size of Place	1927	1941	1952	Per cent Change 1927–1952
0–1,000	.35	.19	.15	−57
1,000–2,500	.76	.59	.55	−27
2,500–5,000	.81	.74	.71	−12
5,000–10,000	.74	.80	.68	− 8
10,000–25,000	.74	.86	.72	− 3
25,000–50,000	.97	.98	.77	−21
50,000–100,000	} 3.76	1.36	1.16	} −32
Over 100,000		5.11	4.21	

Source : See Tables 17 and 19.

size class, the greatest percentage reduction in the number of franchises per place has occurred in the largest markets. There has been a persistent long term decrease in the density of Ford dealerships in the larger markets. Quite likely, the increased mobility of the consumer has enlarged local markets and lessened the importance of dealership location.

Chevrolet Franchise Policy, 1933–1952. The number of Chevrolet franchises in each size of place in 1933, 1937, 1941, and 1952 is presented in Table 21. The percentage of total Chevrolet franchises in each class is also presented. Again, note that there has been a reduction in the number of franchises in (1) cities with 100,000 or more inhabitants, (2) in towns with fewer than 2,500

TABLE 21. CHEVROLET FRANCHISES BY SIZE OF TOWN

Town Size	1933	1937	1941	1952	Difference 1933–1952
0–1,000		3,366	2,430	1,941	
1,000–2,500		2,169	2,071	1,999	
	7,316				−1,454
2,500–5,000		1,092	1,136	1,136	
5,000–10,000		711	788	786	
10,000–25,000		589	589	592	
	704				99
25,000–50,000		176	216	211	
50,000–100,000	118	136	138	136	18
Over 100,000	447	513	427	415	−32
Total	8,585	8,752	7,795	7,216	−1,369

		Per cent [a]			
0–1,000		38	31	27	
1,000–2,500		25	26	28	
	85	= 83	= 82	= 82	
2,500–5,000		12	15	16	
5,000–10,000		8	10	11	
10,000–25,000		7	8	8	
	8	= 9	= 11	= 11	
25,000–50,000		2	3	3	
50,000–100,000	1	2	2	2	
Over 100,000	5	6	5	6	
Total	100	100	100	100	

[a] Columns may not add to 100 because of rounding.
Source: Trade List Department, Chilton Company.

inhabitants, and (3) an increase in towns with 10,000 to 50,000 inhabitants. These changes are similar to the changes noted above for Ford.

Differences between Ford and Chevrolet Franchise Policies.
Ford and Chevrolet distributions appear to be similar. Although

a chi square test would show that the Ford distribution does differ significantly from the Chevrolet distribution, this is solely due to the ability of Chevrolet to secure representations in the smallest size class. The reason for this is not absolutely clear. Possibly, Chevrolet has developed the service and parts market to a greater extent than Ford has and is able to maintain more franchises in these small markets. A second difference, which is of some interest, is the larger number of Ford franchises in the largest cities with over 100,000 inhabitants. Chevrolet has more franchises outstanding than Ford, but, in the largest markets, Chevrolet has *fewer* franchises. The author initially thought this difference in representation policy would enable Ford to obtain a larger percentage of its total registrations in the larger markets. A thorough test of this hypothesis is not possible because of inadequate data. However, the following test is possible. First of all, rank metropolitan areas by total new car registrations. Take the largest 60 which, by the way, include 151 counties. Determine the proportion of total new Ford registrations recorded in these 60 metropolitan areas. Then, repeat the process for Chevrolet. The reader would find the percentages were approximately equal, at least they were in 1956 and 1957. This would suggest that Ford's numerical advantage over Chevrolet in the number of franchises in the large markets is not sufficient for it to obtain a larger percentage of its total new car registrations in these markets. The author found this somewhat surprising. An even more surprising result is that the percentage total sales of middle price makes recorded in the largest 60 metropolitan markets is no different from the percentage of total sales of low price makes recorded in these same markets. The middle price makes have a larger percentage of their franchises in the large markets than the low price makes do. One would expect the middle price class to record a larger percentage of their total sales in the larger markets. Apparently, this is not so. This is further evidence in support of the contention that location of dealership is not an important determinant of automobile sales.

The number of Chevrolet franchises per place by size of place in 1933, 1941, and 1952 has been computed. These data are presented in Table 22 and can be compared with the comparable

TABLE 22. NUMBER OF CHEVROLET FRANCHISES PER PLACE BY SIZE OF PLACE, 1937, 1941, AND 1952

Place	1933	1941	1952
0–1,000		.24	.20
1,000–2,500		.65	.59
	.47		
2,500–5,000		.80	.72
5,000–10,000		.82	.69
10,000–25,000		.89	.73
	.89		
25,000–50,000		1.01	.78
50,000–100,000	1.20	1.29	1.06
Over 100,000	4.81	4.64	3.88

Source: See Tables 19 and 21.

Ford data presented in Table 19. As was noted above, there are fewer Chevrolet franchises per place than Ford franchises in the larger cities. For example, in 1952 the average number of Chevrolet franchises in cities with 100,000 or more inhabitants was 3.9. In the same cities the average number of Ford franchises was 4.2.

Middle Price Class, Big Three and the Independents. The number of franchises per place by size of place in 1937, 1941, and 1952 is presented in Tables 23 through 25 for all middle price makes. This is a convenient measure with which to compare franchise policies.

Consider Tables 24 and 25. There are several points of interest. First, each Chrysler Corporation division had more franchises in cities with more than 100,000 inhabitants than any of the General Motors divisions. Dodge had more than Pontiac; DeSoto had more than Oldsmobile; and Chrysler had more than

TABLE 23. NUMBER OF FRANCHISES PER PLACE BY SIZE OF PLACE, MIDDLE PRICE MAKES, 1937

Size of Place	Dodge	Pontiac	DeSoto	Olds-mobile	Buick	Chyrs-ler	Arith-metic Average (Big Three)
0–1,000	.09	.06	.06	.03	.03	.08	.06
1,000–2,500	.28	.29	.15	.15	.16	.26	.22
2,500–5,000	.52	.50	.29	.34	.37	.42	.41
5,000–10,000	.63	.61	.41	.44	.52	.52	.52
10,000–25,000	.76	.79	.62	.65	.73	.69	.71
25,000–50,000	.85	.92	.80	.76	.79	.83	.83
50,000–100,000	1.03	1.04	1.02	.93	.89	.93	.97
Over 100,000	4.08	3.59	3.68	2.75	1.98	3.61	3.28

Size of Place	Stude-baker	Hudson	Nash	Packard	Arithmetic Average (Independents)
0–1,000	.03	.06	.02	.01	.03
1,000–2,500	.10	.18	.07	.02	.09
2,500–5,000	.24	.36	.16	.11	.22
5,000–10,000	.38	.49	.27	.23	.34
10,000–25,000	.63	.69	.49	.49	.58
25,000–50,000	.87	.79	.70	.70	.77
50,000–100,000	1.07	1.16	1.01	.81	1.01
Over 100,000	3.33	4.99	2.80	2.40	3.38

Sources : 1940 *Census of Population;* Trade List Department, Chilton Company.

Buick. General Motors divisions generally have more new car registrations than Chrysler Corporation divisions (including Plymouth new car registrations). Therefore, the difference in the number of franchises cannot be explained by differences in the size of market. The reader may remember the same result was observed when Ford and Chevrolet franchise policies were compared. Chevrolet had fewer franchises than Ford in the large cities. It appears that General Motors deliberately lowers the number of franchises in the larger markets. Second, the independents have changed their franchise policy in the large mar-

TABLE 24. NUMBER OF FRANCHISES PER PLACE BY SIZE OF PLACE, MIDDLE PRICE MAKES, 1941

Size of Place	Dodge	Pontiac	DeSoto	Olds-mobile	Buick	Chyrs-ler	Arith-metic Average (Big Three)
0–1,000	.06	.04	.03	.02	.02	.05	.04
1,000–2,500	.24	.22	.12	.14	.13	.19	.17
2,500–5,000	.49	.45	.24	.34	.32	.39	.37
5,000–10,000	.65	.58	.37	.47	.56	.55	.53
10,000–25,000	.81	.73	.61	.64	.71	.74	.71
25,000–50,000	.96	.93	.94	.89	.83	.95	.92
50,000–100,000	1.04	1.12	1.11	.96	.91	1.01	1.03
Over 100,000	3.47	3.15	3.48	2.65	1.98	3.47	3.03

Size of Place	Stude-baker	Hudson	Nash	Packard	Arithmetic Average (Independents)
0–1,000	.04	.03	.02	.00	.02
1,000–2,500	.13	.09	.07	.02	.08
2,500–5,000	.28	.23	.16	.09	.19
5,000–10,000	.45	.37	.31	.22	.34
10,000–25,000	.66	.58	.50	.40	.54
25,000–50,000	.87	.85	.77	.71	.80
50,000–100,000	1.25	1.25	.98	.79	1.07
Over 100,000	3.62	3.92	2.77	1.91	3.06

Sources : 1940 *Census of Population*; Trade List Department, Chilton Company.

kets. In 1937 the average number of franchises per place for the independents was greater than the average number of franchises per place of the divisions of the Big Three in the two largest population groups. For example, Hudson had more franchises than Pontiac in these markets, even though Pontiac registrations were more than twice those of Hudson. By 1941 the number of franchises per place of the independents was approximately equal to the number of franchises per place of the divisions of the Big Three in the two largest population groups. For example, there were about three franchises of each middle price

TABLE 25. NUMBER OF FRANCHISES PER PLACE BY SIZE OF PLACE, MIDDLE PRICE MAKES, 1952

Size of Place	Dodge	Pon-tiac	De-soto	Olds.	Buick	Chrys-ler	Mer-cury	Arith-metic Average (Big Three)
0–1,000	.05	.03	.04	.02	.02	.05	.01	.03
1,000–2,500	.24	.25	.15	.18	.16	.18	.04	.17
2,500–5,000	.46	.49	.24	.43	.40	.36	.11	.36
5,000–10,000	.59	.59	.39	.50	.57	.46	.23	.48
10,000–25,000	.64	.66	.58	.64	.62	.62	.47	.60
25,000–50,000	.69	.76	.73	.72	.72	.68	.68	.71
50,000–100,000	.91	1.03	.88	.96	.93	.90	1.10	.96
Over 100,000	2.88	2.61	2.83	2.42	2.10	2.93	2.21	2.57

Size of Place	Stude-baker	Hudson	Nash	Packard	Arithmetic Average (Independents)
0–1,000	.08	.02	.00	.00	.03
1,000–2,500	.08	.07	.02	.02	.05
2,500–5,000	.23	.20	.06	.11	.15
5,000–10,000	.40	.31	.20	.24	.29
10,000–25,000	.57	.46	.47	.41	.48
25,000–50,000	.66	.52	.66	.54	.60
50,000–100,000	.91	.71	.86	.77	.81
Over 100,000	2.30	2.18	1.92	1.55	1.99

Sources : 1950 *Census of Population;* Trade List Department, Chilton Company.

make, whether independent or Big Three, in cities with more than 100,000 inhabitants. So, in 1941, the independents matched each division of the Big Three, franchise for franchise, in cities of this size. The same is true in towns with between 50,000 and 100,000 inhabitants. However, in the smaller markets, the independents were not able to secure representations in as many towns as the Big Three. The independents obtained much less coverage in the smaller markets.

By 1952 the number of franchises and the density of coverage had declined for all makes. General Motors divisions still had fewer franchises in the larger cities than Chrysler Corporation divisions. By 1952 independents had fewer franchises per place than the Big Three divisions in all population groups. To some extent, this reflects the early postwar policy of the independents to reduce their franchises. However, the difference was not large enough to increase the size of the independents' dealers to that of the dealers of the Big Three.

The independents may have attempted to secure an advantage over the Big Three by placing more franchises in the large cities and hoped to obtain a locational advantage. However, it appears this locational advantage was not as important as it was suspected it might be because this policy has been abandoned in favor of a policy which narrowed the difference between the average size of the independents' dealers and the average size of the Big Three dealers.

4.5. Stability in the Number of Franchises by Size of Town

In the 1937–1938 recession the independents and the Big Three experienced approximately equal percentage declines in new car registrations. Yet, the independents experienced a greater percentage decline in franchises. Is this because the Big Three experienced approximately equal percentage reductions in franchises in small and large markets, and, in contrast, the independents experienced greater percentage reductions in franchises in small markets than in large markets? Suppose the independents do experience comparatively greater losses in the smaller markets than the Big Three. This would support the contention that a multi-line policy would lessen the cyclical vulnerability of the independents.

A priori, it is not possible to say whether a reduction in sales would cause a greater percentage reduction in franchises in large or small markets. For one thing, dealers in small markets are less profitable because of their smaller volumes. In a severe recession they would be less likely to cover their variable costs.

This would lead one to expect a greater percentage reduction in franchises in small markets.

However, an opposite force is at work. In towns with fewer than 100,000 inhabitants there will be one dealer of each make, if the town is covered at all. In the larger markets, those with 100,000 or more inhabitants, there will be between two and six dealers, depending on the make. Some form of price agreement will have been established. However, all such agreements can be broken when the opportunity presents itself. A large decline in sales is likely to act as a catalyst. Price shading can be expected. In the large markets reductions in both prices and sales are therefore possible. In the smaller markets more price rigidity can be expected. One might expect a larger percentage decline in franchises in larger rather than in smaller markets.

Because these two effects operate in opposite directions, it is not possible to predict whether a decline in sales will cause a greater percentage decline in franchises in large or small markets.

Data showing the number of franchises by size of town are only available from 1933 to 1952. During this period there was only one recession, the 1937–1938 recession, which caused automobile sales to decline substantially. The percentage decline in franchises by size of town for each make was determined. These data are presented in Table 26. There is no unique pattern. The largest percentage decline occurred in the largest markets for six makes and in the smallest markets for five makes (Pontiac experienced the largest percentage decline in both the largest and smallest markets). Two of the independents, Hudson and Packard, experienced the largest percentage decline in the largest markets.

By now, the reader will probably have noted that the smallest declines occurred in cities with 50,000 to 100,000 inhabitants. In these markets, there is usually one dealer per make. With very few exceptions each town in this size class is represented by one franchise of each make; that is, there is one franchise per

TABLE 26. PERCENTAGE CHANGE IN FRANCHISES BY SIZE OF PLACE, 1937–1938

Size of Town	Low Price Class		
	Chevrolet	Ford	Arithmetic Average
0–10,000	−4	−5	−5
10,000–50,000	−2	−6	−4
50,000–100,000	1	−5	−2
Over 100,000	−8 [a]	−18 [a]	−13 [a]

	Middle Price Class (Big Three)						
	Dodge	Pontiac	DeSoto	Olds-mobile	Buick	Chrysler	Arith-metic Average
0–10,000	−8 [a]	−17 [a]	−11 [a]	−4	−3	−15 [a]	−10 [a]
10,000–50,000	1	−7	−3	−3	−4	−4	−3
50,000–100,000	—	−7	−5	2	4	−2	−1
Over 100,000	−7	−17 [a]	−1	−8 [a]	−5 [a]	−4	−7

	Independents				
	Studebaker	Hudson	Nash	Packard	Arithmetic Average
0–10,000	−24 [a]	−22	−15 [a]	−18	−20 [a]
10,000–50,000	−16	−14	−13	−11	−14
50,000–100,000	−11	−10	−14	−1	−9
Over 100,000	−12	−27 [a]	−3	−19 [a]	−15

[a] Indicates largest percentage decline for each make.
Source: Trade List Department, Chilton Company.

place, and all places are represented. This would suggest that these markets can invariably support a profitable dealer. Smaller markets have one franchise per place but a smaller percentage of these markets are covered.

Because of indivisibilities, an additional dealer cannot be added in these markets until the market size (say) doubles. It is likely, therefore, that these markets are profitable (1) because of the lack of competitors,[19] and (2) because the economies of scale are

---

[19] Even though they may be harassed by bootlegged sales.

fully realized. Because of these reasons, dealers in these markets can absorb large reductions in sales and still remain in operation.[20]

Now consider the independents' position. Two of the independents, Studebaker and Nash, experienced their largest percentage declines in the smallest markets. However, the independents did not differ in experience from the divisions of the Big Three. Three of the six Big Three divisions experienced the largest declines in the smallest markets. Two of the four independents also experienced the largest percentage decline in the smallest markets.

In review, the independents experienced greater percentage declines in franchises than the divisions of the Big Three. However, they experienced these losses throughout all size classes and roughly in the same proportions as the Big Three did. For example, the divisions of the Big Three experienced an average decline of 10 per cent in the smaller markets and an average decline of 7 per cent in the largest markets. The ratio of the latter to the former is .70. A similar computation for the independents indicates a ratio of .75. Thus, for every 1 per cent decline in Big Three franchises in the smaller markets, a .75 per cent decline in their franchises was experienced in the larger markets. For every 1 per cent decline of the independents' franchises in the smaller markets, the percentage decline in the independents' franchises in the larger markets was even higher than the Big Three experienced. By this test it cannot be claimed that the independents' dealers in the small markets are relatively more vulnerable to a decline in sales than their counterparts of the Big Three. This limited test does not support the contention. The independents experience greater percentage reductions in total franchises, but they appear to be at no more of a disadvantage in the smaller markets than in the larger markets.

---

[20] The author was not surprised to find that the dealers who cast the largest majority vote in favor of legislation establishing territorial security came from cities with 20,000 to 100,000 inhabitants. They have most to gain from the provision. See *Automobile Dealers Territorial Security,* Hearings before a Subcommittee of the Committee on Interstate and Foreign Commerce, House of Rep., 86th Cong., 2nd Sess., on H.R. 10201, p. 42.

4.6. Dualing Policy

At the beginning of this chapter market representation policy was defined to include (1) the determination of the number of dealers, (2) the distribution of dealers by size of town, and (3) the use of multi-line or dual dealerships. The first two points have been discussed. Now consider the use of dual dealerships.

Dual dealerships are generally used in those markets where volume of one make is inadequate to support a dealership. Thus, in small markets, dual dealerships will be frequently observed, for example, a Pontiac-Oldsmobile dual. Dualing also is popular during depressions or recessions. When volume declines, manufacturers encourage dualing.

However, dual dealerships have been discouraged as long-run policy. Separate dealer organizations were developed for Mercury and Edsel. The major exception is Plymouth which is dualed with other Chrysler Corporation dealers. Even in this instance, efforts are being made to establish exclusive Plymouth dealers.[21] On January 1, 1959, 176 exclusive Plymouth dealers, 292 exclusive Dodge dealers, 38 DeSoto dealers, and 60 Chrysler dealers had been established.[22] The process is slow, but soon Dodge dealers will discontinue retailing Plymouths, exchanging the Plymouth for the Dart.[23]

The standard argument used by the manufacturers to justify the use of single line dealerships is that it enables the dealer and his salesmen to concentrate on one line. The manufacturers claim more cars will be sold if exclusive dealers are used than if dual dealers are used. There is little theoretical support for this argument. If it pays for a Mercury dealer to sell a Mercury, it is not clear why it wouldn't pay for a Ford-Mercury dealer to sell the same Mercury. There may be some increase in costs

[21] *Automotive News* (January 14, 1957), p. 44.
[22] "1959 Almanac," *Automotive News* p. 185.
[23] *The New York Times* (June 7, 1959), p. 34.

in the handling of multiple lines but these additional costs do not appear to be very large.

Some claim a multi-line dealer with a capital constraint will allocate the use of capital toward the make where the net margin is highest. Consequently, other makes will not be promoted by the dealer.[24] This practice is claimed to have been followed by Chrysler Corporation dealers. It is said that they prefer to promote a higher margin auto, for example, Chrysler, rather than a low margin auto such as Plymouth. If there is a fixed capital budget, then this is rational policy. Usually, automobiles can be readily financed. Consequently, this may not be as convincing an argument as it sounds.

In the author's view, one reason for the manufacturers' preference for exclusive dealership is that it improves their bargaining position with the dealer. An exclusive dealer must rely on a single manufacturer or division for his entire output. A dual dealer may have greater freedom in bargaining with his suppliers. When it is in the interest of the manufacturer to dual, for example in small markets, dualing is permitted. In the larger markets, the manufacturer has little interest in dual dealerships, and it is not frequently observed.

Trends in the Use of Exclusive Dealers. Of late there has been much talk in the trade claiming the dealership of the future will be a large multi-make dealership. Proponents of this view may be confusing a recent short-run trend to multi-make dealerships, perhaps due to the decline in sales, for a long-term trend.

Has there been a long-term trend to exclusive dealers, or has more use been made of multi-line dealers? Banner studied the

---

[24] It has been argued that if a Pontiac is placed next to a Chevrolet in the same showroom the salesman will be successful in switching the buyer from the Chevrolet to Pontiac or vice versa. Carrying the argument a step further, presumably the buyer would make a different choice if the autos were in different showrooms even if they were next door to each other! The author finds it difficult to believe this is an important effect.

dualing policy of the automobile companies.[25] He showed exclusive dealers accounted for a declining per cent of total dealers, from 1928 to 1939. These data are presented in Table 27. Then he

TABLE 27. EXCLUSIVE DEALERS AS A PERCENTAGE OF TOTAL DEALERS AND REPRESENTATIONS PER MULTI-LINE DEALER

	All Dealers		All Dealers Except Chrysler Corporation Dealers	
	Per cent Exclusive	Representations Per Multiple Line Dealer	Per cent Exclusive	Representations Per Multiple Line Dealer
1927	82.1	2.0	79.5	2.05
1928	88.4	2.8	86.5	2.83
1929	79.1	2.1	75.7	2.12
1930	80.2	2.1	76.9	2.13
1931	72.2	2.2	85.3	2.42
1932	66.7	2.1	80.5	2.29
1933	65.6	2.2	78.6	2.33
1934	61.4	2.2	79.2	2.50
1935	60.2	2.2	81.9	2.70
1936	58.3	2.2	82.0	2.67
1937	61.2	2.1	83.6	2.41
1938	60.5	2.1	80.7	2.31
1939	58.9	2.0	79.1	2.11

Source: Paul F. Banner, *Competition in the Automobile Industry* (Unpublished doctoral dissertation, Harvard University, 1954), pp. 227–228.

showed this decline was partially caused by the dualing of Plymouth with other Chrysler Corporation dealers. By excluding Chrysler Corporation dealers, he was able to show that exclusive dealers accounted for a constant share of total non-Chrysler Corporation dealers. These data are also reproduced in Table 27. From 1933 to 1939 exclusive dealers accounted for a constant share of total dealers. General Motors depression dualing policy caused a slight decline in the number of exclusive dealers from 1932 to 1934. However, the dualing effort of General Motors was primarily directed at dealers who were already multiple line

---

[25] Paul F. Banner, *Competition in the Automobile Industry* (Unpublished doctoral dissertation, Harvard University, 1954), pp. 227–228.

dealers (generally dealers retailing higher price makes in small markets). Representations per multiple line dealer rose in 1934 and 1935 and then continued to decline. Thus, an effort was made to provide dealers in small markets with larger volumes through dualing.[26]

Have there been changes in dualing policy in the postwar period? Has the expansion in volume encouraged greater use of exclusive dealers? Several data problems must be solved before a comparison can be made. Fortunately, *Automotive News* has estimated the number of exclusive franchises, multi-line franchises, and total franchises by make as of January 1 of each year since 1957. The number of dealers of each corporation is also estimated.[27] The following adjustments must be made. Nash and Hudson franchises, many of which were considered by *Automotive News* as multi-line franchises, were changed to Rambler franchises in 1958, all of which were then classified by *Automotive News* as exclusive dealers. The same is true of Studebaker and Packard franchises, most of which were initially considered multi-line franchises, but in 1959 were classified as exclusive franchises (presumably because of the introduction of the Lark). These changes would cause an artificial increase in the percentage of exclusive dealers from 1957 to 1959. To avoid this, three series were developed. In the first, all dealers were combined and no adjustment was made. The second series excluded the independ-

---

[26] Incidentally, this type of marketing behavior can be used as further support for the contention that there are economies of scale in automobile distribution.

[27] The Ford data, as reported by *Automotive News* are accurate. *Automotive News* may underestimate the number of exclusive Chrysler Corporation dealers. President Colbert reported 85 per cent of Chrysler Corporation dealers were dualed in 1958. See *Detroit News* (September 17, 1959), p. 1. *Automotive News* reported 93 per cent of Chrysler Corporation dealers were dualed (excluding intercorporate dualing) as of January 1, 1959. *Automotive News* reported 74 per cent of General Motors car dealers were dualed with other General Motors dealers as of January 1, 1957. General Motors reported 75 per cent of its car and truck dealerships were dualed with other General Motors lines as of August 31, 1955. See *General Motors,* Hearings before the Subcommittee on Antitrust and Monopoly of the Committee on the Judiciary, U.S. Senate, 84th Cong., 1st Sess., pursuant to S. Res. 61, Part 8, p. 4381.

ents' dealers. The third series included General Motors Corporation and Ford Motor Company dealers. In each case, the percentage of exclusive dealers to the total was computed. Then, however, further problems arose. These data were now not comparable with the 1937–1939 data, since they excluded the independents' exclusive and multi-line dealers and the 1937–1939 data did not. The independents' exclusive and multi-line dealers had to be eliminated from the earlier data. Once this was done, a comparison could be made. The relevant data are presented in Table 28. It is clear that there have been no major changes. Of late,

TABLE 28. EXCLUSIVE DEALERS AS A PERCENTAGE OF TOTAL DEALERS

Year	(1) All Dealers Included	(2) Big Three Dealers	(3) Ford Motor Co. and General Motors Corporation Dealers[a]
1937	61.2	51.2[b]–55.7[c]	84.3
1939	58.9	49.1 –51.3[c]	74.8[d]
1957	50.4[e]	55.2	73.2
1958	56.6[e]	55.6	72.2
1959	61.6[e]	52.9	68.5[f]

[a] Estimated by subtracting exclusive and (estimated) multi-line dealers of the independents and Chrysler Corporation dealers from total dealers.
[b] Estimated by subtracting exclusive independent dealers from total dealers.
[c] Estimated by subtracting exclusive and (estimated) multi-line dealers of the independents from total dealers.
[d] Decrease due to the introduction of Mercury.
[e] Increase is spurious due to arbitrary classification of the independents' dealers as exclusive dealers.
[f] Decrease partially due to dualing of Edsel dealers.
Sources: Trade List Department, Chilton Company; Almanac Issues, *Automotive News*.

the percentage of exclusive dealers has declined, but this may be due to the 1958 recession.[28]

These data provide little support for the contention that

---

[28] The advent of the compact car has certainly confused the issue. There are few single line dealers left! The dualing of the compact with the established make does not appear to be a trend to large multi-line dealerships but rather reflected the difficulty of promoting and establishing a new dealer organization in an industry where there are scale economies in the distribution sector, a point which was either ignored or disputed by Edsel officials.

dealerships in the future will be large multi-line dealerships. Quite likely, the average size of dealership will continue to grow, but the dealership of the future is not likely to be a multi-line dealership. Several structural changes will have to occur before multi-line dealers will be commonly used. Perhaps the most important would be the lessening of brand loyalty. As the product becomes more homogeneous, the cost position of the dealer and, therefore, volume becomes more important. Under these conditions, there would be a greater incentive for dualing. This is especially true when there are significant economies of scale. A significant lessening of consumer attachments to existing brands is difficult to foresee. A second factor which would increase the use of multi-line dealerships would be an increase in the bargaining position of the dealer over the manufacturer. However, the superior position of the manufacturer is likely to persist as long as entry into manufacturing is difficult. Given present conditions, an increase in the use of multi-line dealership is not expected.

Although the independents might have been expected to use more dual dealers, they did not. Perhaps they did not because the independents could only dual with each other. Not many Ford Motor Company or General Motors Corporation dealers did retail an independent's make. This may have been tacitly discouraged.[29]

The number of exclusive franchises as a percentage of total franchises in 1931, 1935, 1939, 1957, and 1959 is presented in Table 29. Exclusive dealers accounted for a larger percentage of the independents' dealers. Even though they lacked volume, fewer of their dealers obtained it through dualing. Since the independents' dealers marketed middle price makes, they would have

---

[29] Between 1950 and 1955 the number of General Motors dealerships dualed with non-General Motors as a percentage of total General Motors passenger and truck dealerships varied between 7.6 and 6.4 per cent. See *General Motors*, Hearings before the Subcommittee on Antitrust and Monopoly of the Committee on the Judiciary, U.S. Senate, 84th Congress, First Session, pursuant to S. Res. 61, Part 8, p. 4381.

TABLE 29. EXCLUSIVE FRANCHISES AS A PERCENTAGE OF TOTAL FRANCHISES BY MAKE,
1931–1959

Make	1931	1935	1939	1957	1959
Ford	78.8	89.3	75.1	83.0	82.1
Chevrolet	82.8	82.1	83.1	77.0	71.7
Pontiac	62.7	33.4	67.5	50.7	45.8
Oldsmobile	57.6	37.5	48.1	45.7	37.6
Buick	58.9	17.7	50.0	61.1	51.0
Hudson	70.6	74.3	80.7	a	a
Nash	63.4	64.0	80.3	a	a
Studebaker	52.4	59.4	79.5	a	a
Packard	45.6	37.0	55.0	a	a

a Not included due to merger.
Sources: Trade List Department, Chilton Company, Almanac Issues, *Automotive News*.

desired to dual with a low price make. However, few were able to acquire a Plymouth, Ford or Chevrolet franchise.

A comparison of 1957 and 1959 data indicates there has been a decline in the number of exclusive franchises. As in the depression, when many Pontiac, Oldsmobile, and Buick dual franchises were established, greater use of dual franchises has been made during the latest recession.

It is perhaps best to consider the use of multi-line dealers as a short-run device for cushioning the effects of a sales decline. To a great extent, long-run policy is formulated independently of dualing policy. Dualing policy is an appropriate method of introducing flexibility in representation policy. When sales decline, some dealerships lose money and leave the industry. Others are encouraged to dual. The number of exclusives declines. As recovery begins and sales increase more exclusives are appointed; formerly dualed dealerships are changed to exclusive dealerships as one franchise is withdrawn. In this way the manufacturer obtains continuous representation. In the long run, however, changes in the use of dual dealerships will depend on changes in the structural factors noted above.

CHAPTER 5

Determinants of Dealer

Placement in Small and

Large Market Areas

5.1. Introduction

The purpose of this chapter is to specify and measure the importance of those independent variables which determine the number of dealers in a market. Much of the analysis consists of a cross-sectional study of local markets.

5.2. Entry Barriers in Automobile Distribution

Certain cost and demand conditions place broad restrictions on each company's market representation policy. On the supply side, the extent of dealership economies of scale and the size of the absolute capital requirements will partly determine the number of representations in a market. If large dealerships have a cost advantage over small dealerships, they are more likely to grow and survive. Under such conditions, a representation policy which is based on the use of many small dealerships, rather than a few large dealerships, is likely to fail. This is because the incentive to expand by a small dealership is high. Once one dealership increases its volume, it will force the others to grow or to fail. In short, certain minimum cost conditions must be satisfied to insure dealership survival.

On the demand side, the strength of consumer attachments to existing dealerships may also restrict the number of representations in a market. If these attachments to existing dealerships are strong enough, they are a barrier to entry which a new dealer can only overcome by persistently offering lower prices or engaging in higher sales promotion expenditures.

These are *possible* barriers to entry which a new dealership may face. They may or may not be important. A separate study of each barrier to entry is required to determine its importance.

Capital Requirements. The capital requirements necessary to establish and operate a dealership are difficult to estimate since they depend on the type of local construction, whether the dealer is to stress service operations, differences in regional construction costs and whether the dealer will lease the building. However, several estimates of their size and importance can be made. Two sources of data were used to estimate dealer capital requirements. Dealer investment requirements, as established by two automotive companies, are shown in Table 30. These investment requirements exclude investment in real estate and buildings. They are subject to alteration to meet local conditions. These data show the minimum capital required. They do not show whether capital requirements are high or low relative to other retailing industries. To determine this, an analysis of *Statistics of Income* data is necessary.[1] *Statistics of Income* data (*SI* hereafter) show the distribution of *corporations* by asset

---

[1] U.S., Treasury Department, Internal Revenue Service, *Statistics of Income, 1956–57*, Part II (Washington, D.C.: U.S. Government Printing Office, 1959).

TABLE 30. INVESTMENT REQUIREMENTS IN AUTOMOBILE DISTRIBUTION
(EXCLUDES INVESTMENT IN REAL ESTATE AND BUILDING)

Estimated Annual New Car Values (in units)	Company A [a] Estimated Investment	Company B Estimated Investment
100– 200	$ 80,000	$ 68,000
200– 300	90,000	
300– 400	100,000	129,000
400– 500	125,000	
500– 600	160,000 ⎫	176,000
600– 700	(180,000 ⎬ city	
700– 800	⎩ dealerships	210,000
800– 900	(200,000	
900–1,000		236,000
1,000–2,000	260,000	395,000

[a] These estimates apply to a dealership marketing a low price make. Investment requirements of a dealership marketing a middle price automobile would be 25 per cent higher. This would be caused by the higher price of vehicles in the used car inventory.
Source : Data supplied by two automobile companies.

size for each major retailing industry.[2] These industries can be ranked by asset size of corporation. Then, the asset size of corporation in the automobile retailing industry can be compared to the asset size of corporation in other retailing industries to determine if capital requirements for entry are relatively high or low in automobile retailing.

Two measures of asset size are presented in Table 31. One

---

[2] The use of *SI* data to measure capital requirements is not strictly correct because of inadequacies of the data. The percentage of total industry assets or sales accounted for by the corporate sector of each industry varies from industry to industry. Automobile distribution ranks second highest among retailing industries in the proportion of total industry sales accounted for by the corporate sector of the industry. In general, large firms are more likely to be incorporated. Hence, *SI* data probably miss a large number of small firms in most retailing industries but relatively more in industries other than automobile retailing. In these industries with many small unincorporated firms, *SI* data overstates the percentage of total industry assets accounted for by large corporations. Professor Niehans' measure of size of firm, to be explained shortly, will overstate the asset size of firms in these industries because of these data defects.

TABLE 31. ASSET SIZE OF CORPORATION IN SELECTED RETAIL AND SERVICE INDUSTRIES, 1956

Industry	Weighted Average ($000)	Rank	Unweighted Average ($000)	Rank
General merchandise	$258,398	1	$1,217	1
Food	115,065	2	433	2
Filling stations	14,514	3	123	8
Drug stores	6,219	4	119	10
Automotive repairs and service	6,092	5	135	7
Apparel and accessories	5,900	6	153	6
Furniture and house furnishings	2,244	7	162	5
Eating and drinking places	2,132	8	64	11
Other retail	1,478	9	120	9
Building materials and hardware	930	10	167	4
Automobile and truck dealers	810	11	227	3

Source: U.S. Treasury Department, Internal Revenue Service, *Statistics of Income, 1956–1957* Part II (Washington, D.C.: U.S. Government Printing Office, 1959).

measure is the unweighted or simple average. A second measure is the weighted average, originally proposed by Professor Jürg Niehans.[3] This measure weights the average asset size of corporation in each asset class by the share of total industry assets accounted for by firms in that class. Professor Niehans' measure of firm size can be obtained by repeating this computation for each asset class and, then, by summing cumulatively over each asset class. This measure is superior to the unweighted average because it is less sensitive to the large number of small firms which supply only a small share of industry output but which unduly affect the unweighted average.

Inspection of Table 31 will show that the capital requirements of automobile dealerships as measured by the weighted average, are relatively low. The unweighted asset size of automobile dealership ranks third among the eleven industries. This is a higher rank. Nevertheless, it does not appear that capital requirements are exceptionally high. Rather, capital requirements for

---

[3] Jürg Niehans, *Ein Messziffu Sür Betriebsgüssen*, Vol. III (Zeitschrift Sür die Gesamte Stuatswissenschaft), pp. 529–542.

entry into automobile retailing appear to be relatively low and are not likely to be an important barrier to entry.

Dealership Differentation: Shopping and Repeat Customers. The establishment of a new dealership may prove difficult if consumers are attached to existing dealerships. This is an important consideration in multi-point markets, that is in markets where more than one dealership of a given make exists. The available data originate from a single survey. Consequently, they should be treated with a healthy scepticism. These data do support the contention that shopping among dealerships is not prevalent. Less support can be given to the contention that existing dealerships are strongly differentiated in the eyes of consumers.

Consumer shopping data are presented in Table 32A. The Ford study found that 47 per cent of new car buyers purchased from the first dealer shopped.[4] Table 32B indicates shopping is

TABLE 32A. CONSUMER SHOPPING BEHAVIOR

Per cent of Buyers Who Approached the Dealer from Whom They Purchased:	Ford Study
And no other dealer	47
And other dealers of same make as purchased	20
And only dealers selling makes other than make purchased	
And dealers selling same and other makes	33
Total	100

Source: Ford study, Ford Motor Company, *A Basic Study of Automobile Retailing* (Detroit: Ford Motor Company, 1958), p. 9.

inversely related to price class. However, the difference in shopping behavior between buyers of autos in the low and middle price class is unexpectedly small. This may indicate that buyers of middle price automobiles are willing to allocate more time

---

[4] Results obtained from other surveys conducted by trade magazines indicate this percentage may be somewhat lower, in the neighborhood of 40 per cent.

TABLE 32B. NUMBER OF DEALERSHIPS VISITED BY NEW CAR BUYERS

	Buyers of Automobiles in		
Per cent of Buyers Who Shopped:	Low Price Class	Middle Price Class	High Price Class
One Dealership	44	51	70
Two or three dealerships	40	33	25
Four or more dealerships	16	16	5
Total	100	100	100

Source : Ford Motor Company, *A Basic Study of Automobile Retailing* (Detroit : Ford Motor Company, 1958), p. 9.

for shopping since dealers selling automobiles in the middle price class are more widely spaced than dealers selling automobiles in the lower price class.

The Ford study extended the analysis of consumer purchasing decisions somewhat further. The Ford study determined the per cent of all new car buyers who shopped only one dealer of the make purchased. These data are shown in Table 33. The

TABLE 33. NUMBER OF DEALERSHIPS VISITED OF MAKE PURCHASED

New Car Buyers Who:	Per Cent of Total New Car Buyers	
Visited only one dealer	47	66 per cent of all new car buyers visited only one dealer of make purchased
Visited two or more dealers but only one of make purchased	19	
Visited two or more dealers of make purchased	34	

Source : Ford Motor Company, *A Basic Study of Automobile Retailing* (Detroit : Ford Motor Company, 1958), p. 9.

Ford study found that 66 per cent of all new car buyers shopped only one dealer of the make bought. Limited as these data are, they indicate little shopping among dealers selling the make bought.

Unfortunately, few definitive inferences can be made about consumer attachments to dealerships solely from consumer shopping data. Conceivably, dealership repeat sales could be very low even though there was little shopping among dealers by buyers. The typical consumer may purchase from a different dealer (each selling the same make) each time he purchases an automobile, even though he continues to purchase the same make. The consumer may be indifferent as to which dealership he purchases his auto from. Hence, data which show little shopping among dealerships do not necessarily demonstrate that consumers are strongly attached to existing dealerships.

Repeat purchasing from the same dealership accounts for somewhat more than 50 per cent of those new car buyers who previously owned the same make as they currently purchased. These data are presented in Table 34. The reader may find this table somewhat difficult to read. Hence, several descriptive comments are in order. In any given year many of the buyers of a particular make will have previously purchased the same make; some others may be purchasing a car for the first time; still others

TABLE 34. REPEAT PURCHASING FROM DEALERSHIPS: 1957

Name of Make	Buyers Who Trade in Same Make as Car Purchased, Percentage Who Purchased Both Cars From Same Dealership	Survey Response Rate
Low price class		
Ford	46.6	67.6
Chevrolet	53.2	66.6
Plymouth	48.2	68.5
Rambler	51.0	n.a.
Middle price class		
Pontiac	58.8	63.3
Mercury	56.6	66.3
Dodge	62.4	68.1
Desoto	65.4	70.0
Oldsmobile	57.8	69.3
Buick	58.1	63.0
Chrysler	66.4	69.2
Studebaker	54.4	70.7
High price class		
Cadillac	76.4	60.5
Lincoln	58.9	64.6
Imperial	74.8	66.9

Source: *A Market Study of the People Buying New Automobiles,* conducted jointly by Market Research Division, Advertising Department, *U.S. News & World Report* and Benson & Benson, Inc. Princeton, New Jersey (New York: U.S. News and World Report, 1957). A separate report is presented for each make.

will have previously purchased other makes. Of those buyers who had previously purchased the same make as they currently purchased, some will repurchase from the same dealer. Clearly, the percentage of *total buyers* of this make who repurchase from the same dealership will depend on the number of buyers who have switched to this make for the first time. If many buyers switch to this make during the year, the percentage of *total buyers* of the make who will have repurchased from the same dealership in that year will be low. Therefore, to obtain an estimate of dealership repeat sales which is free from this switching of buyers from one make to another and which may distort the figures in any given year, it is necessary to consider only those buyers who trade in the same make as they purchase. Dealership repeat sales should be measured by observing the behavior of these buyers. The data in Table 34 apply to these buyers.[5] The data in Table 34 indicate dealership repeat sales account for about 50 per cent of these buyers in the low price class and are somewhat higher in the middle price class. Dealership repeat sales may be higher in the middle price class than the low price class partly because the density of dealers selling automobiles in the middle price class is lower than the density of dealers selling automobiles in the low price class. Also, this may be the reason why buyers who purchase automobiles in the middle price class tend to shop less than buyers who purchase automobiles in the low price class. However, differences between these two classes of buyers either in their shopping or purchasing behavior cannot be completely accounted for by differences in the density of dealers between the two price classes.

By themselves, these figures give no idea whether dealerships are differentiated or not. If dealerships are differentiated, consumers would tend to repurchase from the same dealership (assuming no differences in prices among dealers). An alternative assumption is that consumers choose dealerships at random once

---

[5] The author has inspected certain confidential data showing dealership repeat sales. These data suggested that dealership repeat sales may be somewhat higher than the figures in table 34 indicate.

they have selected the make to be purchased. A crude test of this hypothesis can be made. Suppose 50 per cent of the sales of a make are recorded in market areas where there is only one dealer of that make *per market area*. Each time a consumer in one of these market areas decided to purchase the same make as he purchased previously, he is likely to purchase from the same dealer. Hence, dealership repeat sales would equal 100 per cent in these markets. Suppose the remaining 50 per cent of total sales are recorded in market areas where there are five dealers of that make *per market area*. Further, suppose consumers in these market areas select their dealerships at random once they have selected the make. Then, the probability that consumer will repurchase an auto from the same dealership would be .20. Over time the company would find 20 per cent of its customers in these market areas would be repurchasing from the same dealership. Over all, the company would find its dealership repeat sales average 60 per cent; that is, all sales in the single dealer market areas, or 50 per cent of total sales, would be dealership repeat sales and 20 per cent of the sales in multi-dealer markets, or 10 per cent of total sales would be dealership repeat sales. Hence, dealership repeat sales of the company would average 60 per cent. Thus, dealership repeat sales would appear to be high even though consumers choose dealerships at random. To determine if dealership repeat sales are higher than can be attributed to random consumer selection, it is necessary to determine the distribution of sales by size of community and then to estimate the number of dealers the consumer may select from in each market area. The distribution of car sales by metropolitan area is shown in Table 35. The number of dealers the consumer is assumed to select from has been estimated. Three sets of estimates have been made: low, medium, and high. The low estimate assumes the consumer selects from a relatively small number of dealers, and so on. Although these estimates are arbitrary, they probably measure the number of dealers the consumer can choose from

TABLE 35. PREDICTED AND ACTUAL DEALERSHIP REPEAT SALES (LOW PRICE MAKE)

(Inhabitants) Size of Community (1)	Percentage Distribution of New Car Sales (2)	Estimated Number of Buyers from which Buyer Selects			Expected Repeat Sales per cent		
		Low (3)	Medium (4)	High (5)	Low (6)	Medium (7)	High (8)
Metropolitan areas							
2,000,000 and over:							
Central city	9	4	5	6	2.25	1.80	1.50
Outside central city	18	2	3	3	9.00	6.00	6.00
500,000–1,999,999:							
Central city	6	3	4	5	2.00	1.50	1.20
Outside central city	10	2	2	2	5.00	5.00	5.00
Under 500,000							
Central city	11	2	3	4	5.50	3.67	2.75
Outside central city	12	1	2	2	12.00	6.00	6.00
Non-metropolitan areas							
City, 10,000–49,999	10	1	1	2	10.00	10.00	5.00
City, 2,500– 9,999	5	1	1	2	5.00	5.00	2.50
Rural	20	1	1	1	20.00	20.00	20.00
	—						
Predicted dealership sales (before adjustment)					70.75	58.97	49.95
Adjustments for dealer Turnover (.85 × predicted repeat sales)					60.14	50.12	42.46
Adjustment for consumer mobility:							
1. Assume 7 per cent of population move from county to county from 1954–1957					55.93	46.61	39.49
2. Assume 14 per cent of population move from county to county from 1954–1957					51.72	43.10	36.52
Actual Dealership Repeat Sales							
Ford						46.6	
Chevrolet						53.2	

Source: Column 2, Board of Governors of the Federal Reserve System, *Financing New Car Purchases*, Part **IV**: *Consumer Installment Credit* (Washington, D.C.: U.S. Government Printing Office, 1957), p. 18.

without incurring a large transport cost. It should be noted that these estimates refer to a buyer of a low price auto. Predicted dealership sales range from a high of 71 per cent to a low of 50 per cent.

Two additional adjustments must be made. A consumer may find the dealer from whom he last purchased has gone out of business in the meantime. Obviously, the consumer will have to purchase from another dealership and, hence, will not be classified as a buyer repurchasing from the same dealer. Hence, the actual dealership repeat sales of Chevrolet and Ford are lower than the dealership repeat sales which would have been recorded if some Chevrolet and Ford dealers had not gone out of business. A downward adjustment should also be made in the predicted dealership repeat sales. In a study of the Cuyahoga County (Greater Cleveland), to be presented in the next chapter, the author found that Ford and Chevrolet dealers who were in business throughout the 1954–1958 period accounted for 69 and 72 per cent respectively of total Ford and Chevrolet sales made in Cuyahoga County in 1954. Hence, 31 and 28 per cent of Ford and Chevrolet buyers who purchased a Ford or a Chevrolet in 1954 would not be able to purchase from the same dealer when they re-entered the automobile market, in (say) 1957 or 1958. However, dealer turnover may be higher in metropolitan areas than small markets. So, the Cleveland data may overstate dealer turnover. A conservative estimate would be 15 per cent, that is 15 per cent of buyers who purchased low priced autos in (say) 1954 would find the dealer from whom they purchased in 1954 out of business when they next purchased in (say) 1957. Therefore, to determine the predicted dealership repeat sales, these consumers who represent 15 per cent of those buyers who purchase the same make as traded in must be eliminated from the calculations. Assume that 15 per cent of total purchasers in each market area are not able to repurchase from the same dealer because the dealer is out of business. Then predicted dealership repeat sales, after adjustment, would vary from a high of 60 per cent to a low of 42 per cent.

A second adjustment must be made. About 7 per cent of the United States population moves from one county to another each year. Anywhere from 7 to 21 per cent of the population would have moved from the county they lived in in 1954 by 1957. Two estimates of population mobility have been made. In the first case 7 per cent of the population is assumed to have moved from one county to another from 1954 to 1957, and in the second case 14 per cent of the population is assumed to have moved from one county to another during this period.

The final estimates of predicted dealership sales varies from a high of 52 per cent to a low of 37 per cent. Actual dealership repeat sales for Ford are 47 per cent and for Chevrolet are 53 per cent. So, actual repeat sales appear to be about 50 per cent. The estimates of predicted dealership sales were based on some conservative estimating techniques. Even so, predicted dealership repeat sales are either equal to (as in case of the low estimate) or less than (as in the case of the medium and high estimates) actual repeat sales. In the author's opinion the best estimate of the predicted dealership repeat sales would be either the medium or high estimate. Hence, these data can be used to support the view that new car buyers do not select dealerships at random. Rather, they show some evidence of repeating their purchases from the same dealership to a greater extent than would be predicted from a random selection of dealerships. The extent and strength of buyer attachments to dealerships is difficult to estimate. All that can be safely inferred is that some dealership differentiation appears to exist, and it could be considerable.

Are these consumer attachments to existing dealerships strong enough to make entry difficult for a new dealership? Dealer responses to a questionnaire designed to measure the importance of consumer attachments to existing dealerships suggested a new dealer would have to offer lower prices or engage in higher sales promotion expenditure to overcome these attachments.[6] Although no answer can be given to this question, the possibility can be raised that a new dealership may have to offer lower prices or undertake higher promotion costs for a short period in order to reach its sales potential. Thus, there may be a period where familiarity with customers will have to be established during which sales will be less than the long term sales objective.[7]

The most important barrier to entry is likely to be the extent of economies of scale in automobile retailing. This topic has not as yet been discussed, but several tentative remarks are appropriate. The probability of successful entry by a new dealership declines with an increase in the difference between the sales volume of the new entrant and the sales volume of existing dealerships. Size appears to be the most (but not only) important determinant of dealership success. The minimum sales volume necessary for survival for a new dealer will depend on the type of market, for example, metropolitan versus rural. This is likely to be the most important barrier the new dealer will face. Documentation of this point will be made shortly in this and then in subsequent chapters.

5.3. Market Representation Policy in Small Markets

In this section a study will be made of the market representation policies practiced by automobile manufacturers in small markets. Towns with 10,000 or fewer inhabitants will be considered small markets. Often, but not always, these towns are located in rural districts.

---

[6] See Appendix B. Dealers, who had recently opened a dealership and who may be best qualified to answer, thought consumer attachments were less important. Half of the responses from these dealers reported consumer attachments to existing dealerships to be an important barrier.

[7] I believe industry officials feel that dealership differentiation is more important than these results suggest.

Determinants of Dealer Placement in Small Markets. What determines whether a dealership will be established in a town of this size? Three hypotheses are to be tested. First, the larger the town size the greater the probability of a dealership being located in the town. Second, the placement of a dealer in a particular town will depend on the distance from that town to the nearest town with a dealership of that make. For instance, one would not expect a Ford dealership to be placed in a town of 3,000 inhabitants if there is another town of similar size with a Ford dealership within (say) two miles of the town. The economies to be derived from increasing size, which one dealer would obtain by serving both towns, are likely to more than offset the cost of consumer movement from one town to another. Third, the placement of a dealership in a town will depend on the size of the nearest town with a dealership. If there are economies of scale in automobile retailing, there should be a greater realization of these economies, the larger the nearest town which has a dealership is (given the distance between these towns). Hence, the more likely that consumers will be willing to travel from one town to the other in response to lower prices to purchase, and, therefore, the less likely a dealership will be placed in the town.

These three hypotheses are to be tested. Each hypothesis is tested in some form, although the last hypothesis could not be tested as extensively as might be desired.

The market representation policies of Ford and Buick in six states were studied. These states were Oregon, Colorado, Alabama, Indiana, New York, and Massachusetts. The states were chosen to obtain regional balance and to determine the importance of differences in population density among states. The makes were selected to observe differences in market representation policy among price classes. Towns in each state were classified into four population groups of 500 to 999 inhabitants, 1,000 to 2,499 inhabitants, 2,500 to 4,999 inhabitants, and 5,000 to 9,999 inhabitants. The list of towns was obtained from the *Rand McNally Road Atlas*.

The location of each Ford and Buick dealer was obtained from the 1956–1957 *Directory of American Automobile Dealers* published by B. Klein and Company.[8]

Each town with a Ford or Buick dealership was so denoted on a *Rand McNally Road Atlas*. The distance from each town in each population group, regardless of whether a dealership was located in the town or not, and the nearest town with a dealership of the particular make under study was then determined. Then, for each population group, towns were further classified into two groups: those with dealerships of that make and those without dealerships of that make. For each population group, a frequency distribution of the distance between each town and the nearest town with a dealership of the same make was developed. An example is given below. Towns in Alabama with 2,500 to 5,000 inhabitants with or without Ford dealerships along with the distance between the town and the nearest town of any size with a Ford dealership are shown below.

TOWNS WITH 2,500–5,000 INHABITANTS

ALABAMA—FORD

Miles from Nearest Town with a Ford dealer	Number of Towns with Ford Dealerships	Number of Towns without Ford Dealerships
0– 5	—	8
5–10	1	5
10–15	3	4
15–20	2	1
20–25	7	1
25–	7	—
Total	20	19

These data indicate that most towns which have Ford dealerships generally are more than 15 miles from the nearest town

---

[8] It is difficult to obtain an independent check of the accuracy of these data. The safest assumption is that the list understates the number of dealers since it is difficult to obtain a complete enumeration of dealers in these small markets. This understatement is probably less likely in the larger markets.

with a Ford dealership; for example, seven are between 20 and 25 miles from the nearest town with a Ford dealership. Conversely, most towns without Ford dealerships are within 15 miles of a Ford dealership; for example, eight towns without a Ford dealership are within five miles of a town with a Ford dealership.

These frequency distributions contain all the relevant information obtained from this study, but these distributions are difficult to work with. It is desirable to specify a minimum distance from one town to the nearest town with a Ford (Buick) dealership beyond which a Ford (Buick) dealership will be established. By using all of the information contained in each frequency distribution, an estimate of this distance can be made. As may be expected, this minimum distance will depend on the size of town, becoming shorter as the size of town increases. Dealerships in larger towns need less protection from nearby competing dealerships.

What would be an improved distribution of *these* dealerships among *these* towns? Suppose the one dealership in the town which is between five and ten miles of another town with a Ford dealership was placed in the town (of similar size) which does not have a Ford dealership and which is 20 to 25 miles from the nearest town with a Ford dealership. Would total Ford sales increase? Ford buyers in the town which had a Ford dealership would now have to travel five to ten miles to the nearest town with a Ford dealership. However, Ford buyers in the town which did not have a Ford dealership would now have one and, therefore, would not have to travel between 20 to 25 miles to the nearest town with a Ford dealership. All other things equal, it can be assumed Ford sales would increase since the aggregate distance traveled by Ford purchasers located in these two towns would decrease. This process of substitution of Ford dealerships among these towns could continue. One of the three dealerships located in towns within 10 to 15 miles of towns with Ford dealerships could be placed in the town which does not have a Ford dealer and is 15 to 20 miles of the nearest town with a Ford dealership.

If these hypothetical substitutions were made, the distribution of Ford dealerships in towns in Alabama with 2,500 to 5,000 inhabitants would appear as:

AFTER ADJUSTMENT TOWNS WITH 2,500–5,000 INHABITANTS
ALABAMA—FORD

Miles from Nearest Town with a Ford dealer	Number of Towns with Ford Dealerships	Number of Towns without Ford Dealerships
0– 5	—	8
5–10	—	6
10–15	2	5
15–20	3	—
20–25	8	—
25–	7	—
Total	20	19

No further advantage would be obtained from further substitutions.

An estimate of the minimum distance required between towns before Ford dealerships can be placed in both towns would be, in this case, between ten and 15 miles. Thus, a town with 2,500 to 5,000 inhabitants located in Alabama would have to be between ten and 15 miles from the nearest town with a Ford dealership before a Ford dealership could be placed in that town. Given the shopping behavior of consumers and the extent of economies of scale, attempts to place Ford dealers in towns closer than this distance are likely to be unsuccessful.[9]

In practice, some Ford dealerships are placed closer to other Ford dealerships because size of town is such an imperfect measure of new car sales. Furthermore, there are differences in the

---

[9] It should be noted that this distance is only an approximation to the actual minimum distance required for dealer survival. Each time a dealership is substituted among towns, some other town would now be closer or further than before from the nearest town with a Ford dealer. The rearrangement cannot be referred to as an optimal rearrangement.

populations surrounding these towns, and per capita income differs among towns of the same size.[10]

It should be noted that this distance is not a measure of the market area. True, most buyers do not in fact travel more than this distance to purchase an auto, because if they did travel longer distances to purchase cars (say to larger cities), they would have forced some of these Ford dealers out of business.

As noted above, the analysis was restricted to Ford and Buick and was completed for four sizes of town in each of six states. The frequency distributions of the distance between each town and the nearest town with a Ford (Buick) dealership are presented in Tables 36 and 37. The percentage of towns in each population group with Ford (Buick) dealerships is shown in Table 38. The minimum distance from a town to the nearest town with a Ford (Buick) dealership before which a Ford (Buick) dealership can be placed in the town is shown in Table 39. As would be expected, there is an inverse relationship between the size of town and the minimum distance. In other words, as the size of the town decreases, the dealership in the town needs greater protection from other dealerships selling the same make in order to survive. This protection is obtained by placing competing dealerships a greater distance from the town. For example, a high percentage of towns with 5,000 to 10,000 inhabitants have Ford dealerships. This percentage decreases as the size of town decreases. In order to place a Ford dealership in a town with 1,000 to 2,500 inhabitants in Massachusetts, the nearest town with a Ford dealership must be at least ten miles away and somewhat farther in other states.[11]

---

10 Many other reasons could be cited.

11 Most consumers do not in fact travel more than the distances listed in Table 39. For, if they did, they would force some of the existing dealerships out of business, and a different set of distances would be determined. If those consumers in Massachusetts living in towns with 1,000 to 2,500 inhabitants did in fact travel more than ten miles in response to lower prices, they would force some existing dealers who are now ten miles from the nearest town with a Ford dealership out of business.

TABLE 36. PLACEMENT OF FORD DEALERSHIPS IN SMALL TOWNS—TOWNS CLASSIFIED
BY DISTANCE FROM NEAREST TOWN WITH FORD DEALERSHIP

Distance from Nearest Ford Dealership	Alabama W.ᵃ W.O.ᵇ		Colorado W. W.O.		Oregon W. W.O.		Indiana W. W.O.		New York W. W.O.		Massachussets W. W.O.	
Number of Towns with 5,000–10,000 inhabitants												
0– 5	—	1	1	—	—	2	—	6	14	22	7	12
5–10	1	2	2	1	3	—	8	—	21	5	6	3
10–15	6	—	2	—	1	—	11	1	8	—	6	—
15–20	5	1	2	—	5	—	8	1	3	—	—	—
20–25	3	—	1	—	—	—	2	—	2	—	—	1
25–	4	—	3	—	3	—	—	—	—	—	—	—
Number of Towns with 2,500–5,000 inhabitants												
0– 5	—	8	—	5	1	1	1	5	5	35	5	22
5–10	1	5	1	1	3	3	8	4	17	18	4	4
10–15	3	4	3	—	4	2	9	1	16	6	3	—
15–20	2	1	1	—	3	—	8	—	3	1	—	—
20–25	7	1	4	—	3	—	2	—	1	—	2	—
25–	7	—	2	—	4	1	2	—	1	—	2	—
Number of Towns with 1,000–2,500 inhabitants												
0– 5	—	9	—	3	—	6	1	12	n.c.ᶜ		2	36
5–10	2	19	2	—	2	8	14	36			4	36
10–15	4	15	3	3	3	6	26	12			1	3
15–20	6	13	—	5	6	7	6	9			1	3
20–25	7	4	2	1	1	1	1	—			—	—
25–	5	4	14	9	5	6	—	—			2	—
Number of Towns with 500–1,000 inhabitants												
0– 5	—	11	—	8	1	7	—	32	n.c.		—	6
5–10	—	23	—	10	—	22	6	82			—	7
10–15	2	32	2	13	1	17	5	46			—	1
15–20	—	23	1	10	—	7	1	12			—	2
20–25	—	9	2	3	1	8	2	1			—	—
25–	5	3	5	9	1	13	—	—			—	—

ᵃ W. denotes town with Ford dealership.
ᵇ W.O. denotes town without Ford dealership.
ᶜ n.c. denotes not compiled.
Sources: Data developed by author. Dealer data was taken from 1956–1957 *Directory of American Automobile Dealers*, Vols. 1 and 2 (New York: B. Klein & Company, 1957).

TABLE 37. PLACEMENT OF BUICK DEALERSHIP IN SMALL TOWNS—TOWNS CLASSIFIED
BY DISTANCE FROM NEAREST TOWN WITH BUICK DEALERSHIP

Distance from Nearest Buick Dealership	Alabama W.[a] W.O.[b]		Colorado W. W.O.		Oregon W. W.O.		Indiana W. W.O.		New York W. W.O.		Massachussets W. W.O.	
			Number of Towns with 5,000–10,000 inhabitants									
0– 5	1	2	—	1	2	2	—	3	1	21	—	10
5–10	—	1	—	—	—	1	1	5	9	20	4	11
10–15	—	2	2	—	3	—	5	2	9	4	—	7
15–20	—	1	1	—	2	—	10	1	2	1	—	—
20–25	1	1	1	—	1	—	5	1	7	—	—	—
25–	7	7	6	—	2	1	4	—	1	—	—	—
			Number of Towns with 2,500–5,000 inhabitants									
0– 5	—	7	—	5	—	2	—	4	1	30	1	21
5–10	—	3	—	2	2	2	2	5	4	25	—	9
10–15	—	4	—	1	3	3	1	11	10	13	2	2
15–20	—	4	—	2	2	1	8	3	6	5	1	2
20–25	—	5	2	—	1	—	5	—	5	1	2	—
25–	2	14	3	2	8	1	—	1	3	—	—	2
			Number of Towns with 1,000–2,500 inhabitants									
0– 5	—	n.c.[c]	—	2	—	4	—	12	n.c.		1	21
5–10	—		—	4	—	6	—	33			—	41
10–15	—		1	3	1	9	4	43			—	14
15–20	—		—	2	1	9	5	10			—	3
20–25	—		1	5	—	6	3	4			—	3
25–	—		5	19	3	12	—	3			1	4

[a] W. denotes towns with Buick dealerships.
[b] W.O. denotes towns without Buick dealerships.
[c] n.c. denotes not computed.
Source: See Table 36.

To determine the separate influence of the variables which determine whether or not a dealership will be placed in a town, two regression analyses were completed. These analyses were restricted to Ford dealerships and to towns with 2,500 to 5,000 and 5,000 to 10,000 inhabitants in the state of New York. The probability that a town will have a Ford dealership Y is assumed

TABLE 38. PERCENTAGE OF TOWNS IN POPULATION CLASS WITH DEALERSHIPS

Size of Town (Inhabitants)	Alabama	Colorado	Oregon	Indiana	New York	Massa- chusetts
Ford						
5,000–10,000	83	92	86	78	64	54
2,500– 5,000	39	65	72	75	42	38
1,000– 2,500	29	50	33	41	n.c.[a]	11
500– 1,000	6	16	5	7	n.c.	0
Buick						
5,000–10,000	39	90	71	68	45	25
2,500– 5,000	5	29	64	40	28	14
1,000– 2,500	0	17	10	10	n.c.	2
500– 1,000	n.c.	n.c.	n.c.	n.c.	n.c.	n.c.

[a] n.c. denotes not computed.
Source: See Tables 36 and 37.

TABLE 39. MINIMUM REQUIRED DISTANCE IN MILES FROM TOWN TO NEAREST TOWN WITH COMPETING DEALERSHIP BEFORE DEALERSHIP CAN BE PLACED IN TOWN

Size of Town (Inhabitants)	Alabama	Colorado	Oregon	Indiana	New York	Massa- chusetts
Ford						
5,000–10,000	10	5	5	5–10	5	0– 5
2,500– 5,000	10–15	5–10	5–10	5–10	5–10	0– 5
1,000– 2,500	15–20	25+	15–20	10–15	n.c.	10
500– 1,000	25+	25+	25+	15–20	n.c.	25+
Buick						
5,000–10,000	25+	5	0– 5	10–15	5–10	10–15
2,500– 5,000	25+	25	10–15	15–20	10–15	15
1,000– 2,500	25+	25+	25+	15–20	n.c.	25+
500– 1,000	n.c.[a]	n.c.	n.c.	n.c.	n.c.	n.c.

[a] n.c. denotes not computed.
Source: Tables 36 and 37.

to be related (1) to the distance from that town to the nearest town with a Ford dealership, x_1 and (2) to the size of the nearest town with a Ford dealership, x_2.

If the town had a Ford dealership, the dependent variable was given $a + 1$ value. Otherwise, the dependent variable was given a zero value. The regression equations took the form:

$$Y = a + bx_1 + cx_2$$

where b is assumed to be greater than zero and c is assumed to be less than zero. The regression equations are:[12]

(Towns with 5,000 to 10,000
  inhabitants) $Y_F = .9422 + .0484x_1 - .0020x_2$
  $(.0100) (.0013)$
  $R = .561$

(Towns with 2,500 to 5,000
  inhabitants) $Y_F = .7302 + .0551x_1 - .0027x_2$
  $(.0084) (.0008)$
  $R = .600$

The multiple correlation coefficients, the regression coefficients of x_1 and the regression coefficient of x_2 in the second equation are significant at the 1 per cent probability level.[13]

These equations suggest that the distance variable, that is, x_1, and the variable denoting the size of nearest town with a Ford dealer, that is, x_2, become more important as the size of town decreases. The regression coefficient of x_2 becomes significant at the 1 per cent level as the size of town decreases. Apparently, the placement of a dealership in a town with 5,000 to 10,000 inhabitants is not significantly affected by the size of the nearest town. This variable does become important in the placement of dealerships in towns with 2,500 to 5,000 inhabitants.

---

[12] The dependent variable was given the discrete values of $+1$ or zero. Hence, the multiple correlation coefficient can not equal 1. This can be seen by considering the following example. Suppose there is a critical distance between towns. If the distance between towns was greater than this critical distance, a dealership would be established in the town. If the distance between towns was less than this critical distance, a dealership would not be established in the town. Then, suppose data were collected showing (1) whether a dealership was or was not established in the town and (2) the distance to the nearest town with a dealership. These data could then be used to complete a regression analysis. The multiple correlation coefficient would always be less than one because the dependent variable only assumes discrete values. The maximum of the correlation coefficient would depend on the distribution of observations of the distance variable. Hence, the correlation coefficients of .561 and .600 are not necessarily low.

[13] The Beta coefficients are .9274 for x_1 and $-.3418$ for x_2 in the first equation and .5241 for x_1 and $-.2848$ for x_2 in the second equation. Thus, the size of the nearest town with a Ford dealership becomes relatively more important in the second equation, that is, as the size of town decreases.

Summary. The density of dealership coverage differs by price class. In the low price class, dealerships are established with regularity in towns with 2,500 to 5,000 inhabitants and less frequently in smaller towns. Dealerships selling middle priced automobiles are often established in towns with 5,000 to 10,000 inhabitants.

The placement of a dealership in a town is related to the size of town, the distance between the town and the nearest town with a dealership of the same make, and the size of the nearest town with a competing dealership. The latter two variables become more important as the size of town diminishes.

The importance of volume in determining the density of dealer coverage should also be noted. The independents, with volumes much less than those of most makes in the middle price class, have not been able to match the density of dealer coverage of most of these makes in these smaller markets. The reader may remember a similar conclusion was reached in the last chapter.

In general, this study suggests that the market representation policies practiced by the auto companies in small local markets are influenced, in part, by dealership cost conditions. It appears that the market representation policies of the companies are designed with these cost conditions in mind. This can only be considered a preliminary conclusion since the study has been limited in scope. Subsequent studies may reach an opposite conclusion. However, the results of this study suggest there is a certain order in the placement of dealers in these markets. The results of the regression analyses tend to support this view.

5.4. Consumer Mobility in Large Markets

The analysis has been restricted so far to a study of small and generally rural towns. Attention is now shifted to large city markets.

Little data of consumer purchasing behavior in large city

markets are publicly available. In particular, data showing the distances buyers travel to purchase automobiles are virtually non-existent. In the next chapter a study will be made of the distances travelled by car buyers located in Greater Cleveland to purchase an automobile. Fortunately, certain data showing consumer mobility were kindly made available by an automobile manufacturer. For selected cities, new car registration data showing both buyer and dealer location were used to determine the extent of consumer mobility. The percentage of all buyers located in selected cities purchasing (1) from dealers within their own city, and (2) from dealers in their own metropolitan area are shown in Table 40. In the central cities approximately 70 to 80 per cent of all buyers located in central cities purchased from dealers in the central city and 85 to 95 per cent purchased from dealers within their own metropolitan area. These data would suggest few buyers located in central cities leave the city to purchase an auto. Whether one would care to define the market area as the metropolitan area or the central city is more difficult to determine. Clearly, there is support for both definitions.

A better way of specifying a market area is to determine the drawing power of the large city in attracting customers from surrounding small towns. The percentage of buyers who purchased from the dealer in the town in which they live is shown in Table 41. The percentage of buyers who purchase from dealers in the metropolitan area in which their town is located is also shown in this table. In some areas there is substantial movement of buyers from the small towns into the central city.[14] The percentage of buyers who are located in small towns and purchase locally tends to decrease as the size of the central city increases and as the distance between the town and the central city de-

---

[14] Strictly speaking, these data do not show this. A buyer who does not purchase from the dealer in his own town does not necessarily purchase from a dealer in the central city; that is, the buyer could purchase elsewhere in the metropolitan area, for example in another nearby small town. However, most buyers would probably purchase in the central city if they do not purchase from dealers in the towns where they are located.

TABLE 40. MOBILITY OF BUYERS LOCATED IN CENTRAL CITIES

City Where Buyer is Located (1)	City Where Dealer is Located (2)	Per cent of Buyers Located in City Purchasing from Dealers Specified in Column 2 (3)	Per cent of Buyers Located in City Purchasing from Dealers in Own Metropolitan Area (4)
San Francisco-Oakland Metropolitan Area			
San Francisco	Central City	79	91
Oakland	Central City	n.a.	93
Sacramento Metropolitan Area			
Sacramento	Central City	74	79
Stockton Metropolitan Area			
Stockton	Central City	84	86 [a]
Springfield-Decatur Metropolitan Area			
Decatur	Central City	81	85
Johnstown, Pa., Metropolitan Area			
Johnstown	Central City	73	91
Enid, Oklahoma Metropolitan Area			
Enid	Central City	84	89 [b]
St. Louis Metropolitan Area			
St. Louis	Central City	79	86

[a] Purchased from dealers in own county.
[b] Purchased from dealers in own and adjoining counties.
Source : Data supplied by an automobile manufacturer.

creases. The number of metropolitan areas included in the sample is limited. However, these data indicate there is some movement of buyers from small surrounding towns into the central city. It appears that 10 to 20 per cent of buyers in small surrounding towns will travel as much as 20 miles to purchase in the central city.

TABLE 41. CONSUMER MOBILITY FROM SMALL CITIES OR TOWNS TO NEARBY CENTRAL CITIES

City or County where Buyer is Located (1)	City where Dealer is Located (2)	Distance between Buyer and Central City (3)	Per cent of Buyers Located in City or County Purchasing from Dealers Specified in Column 2 (4)	Per cent of Buyers Located in City or County Purchasing from Dealers in Own Metropolitan Area (5)	Difference (5)–(4) (6)
San Francisco-Oakland Metropolitan Area					
Berkeley	Suburb adjoining Oakland	5-10 miles approximately miles	48	89	41
Marin County	Dealers in Rafael and Mill Valley	20 approximately miles	59	92	33
Sacramento Metropolitan Area					
Sacramento County	Smaller towns outside central city's environs	Approximately 20 miles	47	70 [a]	23
Yola County	Smaller towns outside central city's environs (excludes West Sacramento)	Approximately 20 miles	69	89	20
Stockton Metropolitan Area					
San Joaquin	Smaller towns outside central city's environs	Approximately 20 miles	66	86 [a]	20

149

TABLE 41—(*Continued*)

City or County where Buyer is Located (1)	City where Dealer is Located (2)	Distance Between Buyer and Central City (3)	Per cent of Buyers Located in City or County Purchasing from Dealers Specified in Column 2 (4)	Per cent of Buyers Located in City or County Purchasing from Dealers in Own Metropolitan Area (5)	Difference (5)-(4) (6)
Springfield-Decatur Metropolitan Area					
Lincoln	County seat	30 miles to Springfield	76	n.a.	n.a.
Clinton	County seat	22 miles to Decatur	72	n.a.	n.a.
Taylorville	County seat	27 miles to Springfield	75	n.a.	n.a.
9 small towns	Dealers in Sanagumar, Menard and Christian	unknown	47	95	48
Enid, Oklahoma Metropolitan Area					
Noble County	(Various Towns)	20-30 miles	84	89 b, c	5
St. Louis Metropolitan Area					
East St. Louis Belleville	two suburbs	10-15 miles	63	92	29
St. Louis County	various suburbs n.a.		n.a.	66	n.a.

a Purchased from dealers in own county.
b Purchased from dealers in own and adjoining counties.
c Only 1 per cent purchased in Enid.
Source: Data supplied by an automobile manufacturer.

5.5. Market Representation Policy in Large Markets

As the sales in a market area increase, a decision must be made which either allows the existing dealership to grow in size or allows for the establishment of another dealership in the market area. The decision to establish another dealer will depend on the extent of economies of scale experienced by the existing dealership as well as the distribution in space of new consumers. If there are further economies with increasing size of dealership, there are incentives to allow expansion by the dealership now serving the market. As the sales of the market area continue to grow, these cost economies may be exhausted. At this point there may be incentives to increase the number of dealers.[15]

Size of Dealership in Large Markets. As the sales in the market area increase, the existing dealer may find a per unit cost increase because of the difficulty of serving outlying consumers or because there are internal diseconomies of scale. At some point, a second dealer and then a third, and then more will be placed in the market area. A second dealer cannot be placed in the market area until the total sales in the market area are large enough so that both dealerships can operate in the market area without their per unit costs differing significantly. Suppose two dealerships were placed in the market area, even though total sales were only large enough to support one dealership. Over time, both could not persist. One would tend to grow and, in the process of growth, realize further cost economies. The other dealership would be subjected to continuous price competition

---

[15] The long run cost function may exhibit cost economies over initial sales volumes and then level out. In this case the manufacturer may permit the existing dealers to grow even when no further cost economies are realized. Sales may change greatly from year to year. Optimum policy would dictate the growth of the existing dealership. However, lower prices and more dealer sales promotion expenditures can be expected as the number of dealers is increased. Thus, if further real economies are not realized, the manufacturer may add an additional dealer as sales in the market area increase.

and would, therefore, be more likely to fail. Hence, it is in the interest of the manufacturer to allow the existing dealer to grow and realize the economies from increasing size. If this is so, the sales of the dealer in a single point market can be used as an estimate of the optimum size of dealership.[16] Actually, an average of the sales of dealers in single point markets will be used as an estimate of the optimum size of dealership. For example, a sample of cities, each with one Ford dealer, could be selected. Then, the average of the sales of these Ford dealers could be determined and used as an estimate of the optimum size of dealership.

An independent test of the accuracy of this estimate can be made by observing the relationship between the number of (say) Ford dealers in the market area and the total Ford sales in the market area. If the average number of new units retailed per dealer is constant as total market sales increase, it would indicate a dealership selling fewer cars than this average would be at a cost disadvantage. Because of this, the manufacturer has not added another dealership since smaller dealerships are at a cost disadvantage. Otherwise, more dealerships would be added. Therefore, if the average number of Fords sold by Ford dealers is the same in small city markets as in large city markets, it indicates that Ford dealerships selling fewer cars would be at a cost disadvantage. If more dealers could persist in these markets, why were they not placed by the manufacturer?

In summary, there are two points of interest:

1. What is the average number of new cars sold per dealer in single dealer city markets?

2. Does the average number of new cars sold per dealer remain constant as market sales increase? Or does the average number decline as market sales increase? If so, does this reflect

---

[16] An adjustment should be made for discontinuities in dealership size. Some dealerships in single point markets will be less than the optimal size because of the limited size of market. Some other dealerships in single point markets will be larger than the optimal size because the market is not yet large enough to sustain two dealers.

an attempt by the automobile manufacturer to obtain greater sales promotion outlay and/or greater density of market coverage in the larger markets?

Size of Sample. *Sales Management* lists metropolitan areas by number of families (as of January, 1957). These areas were grouped into size classes. In each size class a random selection of areas was made.[17] For those metropolitan areas where the total number of families exceeded 175,000, a complete enumeration was made.[18]

The number of metropolitan areas in each family size class included in the sample and the total number of metropolitan areas in each family size class are shown in Table 42. The market area was defined to be the city limits of the central city in the metropolitan area. This narrows the definition of the market area somewhat since, as has been shown, the central city at-

TABLE 42. TOTAL NUMBER OF METROPOLITAN AREAS IN SAMPLE

Total Number of Families in Metropolitan Area	Total Number of Metropolitan Areas in Class	Number of Metropolitan Areas Included in Sample
25– 50	94	14
50– 75	36	11
75–100	20	9
100–125	11	7
125–175	19	8
175 or more	25[a]	25
Total	205	74

[a] Excludes Tampa, Washington, D.C., San Bernardino, Kansas City, Cleveland, Boston, New York, Los Angeles, Chicago and Philadelphia.
Source: "Families Ranking of Metropolitan County Areas," *Sales Management* (May 10, 1957), p. 168.

---

[17] The size of sample was determined by letting the standard deviation of the sample means equal one quarter of the standard deviation of the population variable.

[18] Tampa, Washington, D.C., Miami, San Bernardino, Cleveland, and Boston were excluded because of one or more of the following reasons: (1) large number of tourists, (2) difficulty in obtaining an accurate enumeration of dealers, and (3) difficulty in obtaining an accurate estimate of total sales, and (4) difficulty in defining a market area. In addition, the four largest metropolitan areas were excluded for the last reason. Kansas City was also excluded through an omission.

tracts consumers from outlying communities. The total number of dealers of each make in each city was obtained from the 1956–1957 *Directory of American Automobile Dealers,* Vols. 1 through 4. New car registration data by make and by city are not publicly available. New car registration data for many cities were obtained from research departments of newspapers located in these cities. Where new car registration data were not publicly available, they were estimated by assuming that the ratio of new car registrations of a given make in the city to the total number of families in the city was equal to the ratio of total new car registration of the same make in the state to the total number of families in the state. At a later date Ford and Chevrolet new car registrations for selected metropolitan areas were made available by an automobile manufacturer and they were used to check the accuracy of these estimates.[19] The purpose of this analysis is to determine the relationship between total sales in a market and the number of dealers in the market. Unfortunately, this may not be possible because the data are subject to measurement errors. Total sales are underestimated because of two reasons. First, the estimating procedure generally underestimates new car registrations in large cities. Second, consumers enter the large city to purchase an automobile, but the automobile may be registered at the place of residence. Thus, new car registrations underestimate total sales. However, an independent check of these estimates is made in Chapter 8. This check indicates that the estimates of new units sold per dealer may not be subject to large error.

The analysis was restricted to four makes: Ford, Chevrolet, Buick, and Chrysler-Plymouth. All data used in the following

---

[19] The usefulness of this procedure was checked by comparing the estimated new car registrations with actual new car registrations. Generally it was found the estimated new car registrations were 10 per cent lower than the actual new car registrations in the low price class and 15 per cent lower in the middle price class, indicating greater new car purchases per family in the large cities than in the smaller cities and the rural community. This is one reason to believe the estimated new car registrations underestimate the actual new car registrations, which should be continually kept in mind.

analysis apply to 1956. These four makes were selected to observe differences in representation policy between the low and medium price class and among the three largest automobile companies.

For each make, the number of dealers in the market area and the number of new car registrations were determined. Markets were then grouped by the number of dealers located in the market area. For each group, the arithmetic mean of the estimated new car registrations in the markets of that group was computed. These data are shown for each make in Tables 43 through 46.

TABLE 43. MARKET REPRESENTATION POLICIES OF FORD IN LARGE CITY MARKETS

Number of Ford Dealers in Each Market Area (1)	Number of Markets with Ford Dealers as Specified in Column 1 (2)	Average of Ford Registrations Per Market Area (3)	Average Number of New Units Retailed Per Ford Dealer in Market Area, Column (3) ÷ (1) (4)
1	26	827	827
2	12	1,578	789
3	7	2,078	693
4	6	3,078	770
5	5	3,736	747
6	4	3,861	644
7	2	7,652	1,093
8	2	6,396	800
9	1	5,045	561
10	—	—	—
11	—	—	—
12	4	5,484	457
13	—	—	—
14	2	15,081	539
15	—	—	—
16	—	—	—
17	1	9,505	559
18	—	—	—
19	1	13,495	710
20	—	—	—
21	—	—	—
22	—	—	—
23	—	—	—
24	—	—	—
25	—	—	—
26	1	26,193	1,007

TABLE 44. MARKET REPRESENTATION POLICIES OF CHEVROLET IN LARGE CITY MARKETS

Number of Chevrolet Dealers in Each Market Area (1)	Number of Markets with Chevrolet Dealers as Specified in Column 1 (2)	Average of Chevrolet Registrations Per Market Area (3)	Average Number of New Units Retailed Per Chevrolet Dealer in Market Area, Column (3) ÷ (1) (4)
1	22	840	840
2	19	1,719	860
3	10	3,071	1,024
4	3	4,080	1,040
5	2	6,738	1,348
6	4	4,265	711
7	3	5,779	826
8	3	5,713	714
9	2	8,660	962
10	1	11,482	1,148
11	1	10,004	909
12	—	—	—
13	1	6,179	475
14	—	—	—
15	1	12,202	813
16	1	15,686	980
17	—	—	—
18	—	—	—
19	—	—	—
20	—	—	—
21	—	—	—
22	—	—	—
23	—	—	—
24	—	—	—
25	—	—	—
26	—	—	—
27	1	27,623	1,023

They show the volume advantage Ford and Chevrolet dealers have over Chrysler-Plymouth dealers. This advantage is not as large as the differences in volume suggest since the markup on Chrysler sales is higher. In 1956 Buick dealers seem to have had twice the volume of Chrysler-Plymouth.

Chevrolet and Ford. Inspection of Table 43 indicates the number of new units retailed per Ford dealership tends to de-

TABLE 45. MARKET REPRESENTATION POLICIES OF BUICK IN LARGE CITY MARKETS

Number of Buick Dealers in Each Market Area (1)	Number of Markets with Buick Dealers as Specified in Column 1 (2)	Average of Buick Registrations Per Market Area (3)	Average Number of New Units Retailed Per Buick Dealer in Market Area, Column (3) ÷ (1) (4)
1	38	343	343
2	16	1,006	501
3	8	1,667	556
4	4	2,185	546
5	1	2,641	528
6	1	2,474	412
7	2	2,965	423
8	1	4,440	555
9	—	—	—
10	1	2,266	227
11	1	4,414	401
12	—	—	—
13	—	—	—
14	1	8,685	620

TABLE 46. MARKET REPRESENTATION POLICIES OF CHRYSLER-PLYMOUTH IN LARGE CITY MARKETS

Number of Chrysler-Plymouth Dealers in Each Market Area (1)	Number of Markets with Chrysler-Plymouth Dealers as Specified in Column 1 (2)	Average of Chrysler-Plymouth Registrations Per Market Area (3)	Average Number of New Units Retailed Per Chrysler-Plymouth Dealer in Market Area, Column (3) ÷ (1) (4)
1	44	189	189
2	9	594	297
3	5	709	236
4	3	786	197
5	—	—	—
6	4	1,061	177
7	3	1,364	195
8	2	1,882	235
9	—	—	—
10	—	—	—
11	2	3,228	294
12	1	1,693	141
13	—	—	—
14	1	5,281	306

cline as the size of market increases. A simple regression analysis was completed, and the following results were obtained:

$$Y_F = .847 + 1.143x \qquad r = .899$$
$$(.208)$$

where Y_F represents the number of Ford dealers in the market area, and x represents Ford new car registrations (in thousands) in the market area. The correlation coefficient and the regression coefficient are significant at the 1 per cent probability level.[20]

Inspection of Table 44 shows no significant increase or decrease in the average number of new units retailed per Chevrolet dealer as the size of market increases. Again, a simple regression analysis was completed, and the following results were obtained:

$$Y_c = .647 + .950x \qquad r = .953$$
$$(.114)$$

where Y_c represents the number of Chevrolet dealers in the market area, and x represents Chevrolet new car registrations (in thousands) in the market area. The correlation coefficient and the regression coefficient are significant at the 1 per cent probability level.[21]

This study of the placement policies of Ford and Chevrolet indicates the number of dealers in a market area can be accurately predicted by knowing the sales in the market area. The study of Ford's placement policy indicated (1) the average of the number of new cars retailed per Ford dealer is between 600 to 800 units, (2) the number of new cars retailed per Ford dealer tended to decline as market sales increased, and (3) the regression analysis indicated another Ford dealer is added to the market area for every increase in Ford sales of 875 units. The study of Chevrolet's placement policy indicated (1) the average of the number of new cars retailed per Chevrolet dealer is between 800 to 900

---

[20] The slope of the regression equation is 1.143, indicating an additional dealer is added for every increase of 875 new Fords sold in the market area.

[21] The slope of the regression equation is .950, indicating an additional dealer is added for every increase of 1,050 new Chevrolets sold in the market area.

units, (2) the number of new cars retailed per Chevrolet dealer remained constant as market sales increased, and (3) the regression analysis indicated another Chevrolet dealer is added to the market area for every increase in Chevrolet sales of 1,050 units. Thus, the evidence is not altogether consistent. It is possible that a dealership retailing as few as 600 new units is at no significant cost disadvantage. However, it may be that a dealership of this size is at some small cost disadvantage compared to a dealership selling 800 units. In review, a dealership selling as few as 600 units in a city market is not likely to be at a large cost disadvantage compared to larger dealerships. A dealership selling as many as 800 units is likely to be at even less of a cost disadvantage.

While the author was developing this study, he made several regional comparisons of placement policies. In general, these comparisons indicated that the average number of new units retailed by Ford or Chevrolet dealerships was lowest in cities located in the East. This may be due to greater traffic congestion which increases the cost of consumer movement in these cities.

More likely, this results from the market representation policies practiced during the pre-war period. Also, examples can be given where there are large differences between the number of Ford and Chevrolet dealers in the same market area which cannot be accounted for by differences in sales. The number of new units retailed by Ford or Chevrolet dealers appeared to be highest in cities located in Texas. In these cities there are fewer dealers relative to the size of market than in other cities located in other sections of the country. The author was not able to determine why this is so.

The author was somewhat surprised at the extent of regional variation in market representation policies. Clearly, there is a certain measure of consistency in the practice of market representation policies. The high simple correlation coefficients show this. However, there were some cities where unexplained variations in representation policy were observed. Whether these are merely reflections of decisions made in the past which now cannot be quickly reversed, or whether they are due to particular adjustments to peculiar local market situations, cannot be fully determined. This is an area which deserves further work.

Bain found an excessive allocation of resources into the distribution sector of the oil industry.[22] While the evidence is not altogether one-sided, it suggests this is not a uniform characteristic of local automobile markets. The automobile companies appear to act with considerable restraint. There may be some excess of dealerships in the East, relative to the number placed in the West in markets with comparable sales. However, on the whole, the companies do not saturate a market area with an excess of dealerships.[23] This behavior appears to be consistent with the use of the franchise system.

Buick and Chrysler-Plymouth. The average number of new units retailed per Buick dealer does not appear to change as the size of market increases. A regression analysis was completed, and the following results were obtained:

$$Y_b = .69 + 1.810x_1 - .007x_2 \qquad R^2 = .83$$
$$(1.27) \qquad (.004)$$

where Y_b represents the number of Buick dealers in the market, x_1 represents Buick new car registrations (in thousands) in the market, and x_2 represents the square miles of the city.[24]

The average number of new units retailed per Chrysler-Plymouth dealer does not show any marked tendency to decline

---

[22] Joe S. Bain, *The Economics of Pacific Coast Petroleum Industry,* Vol. III, Chapter V (Berkeley: University of California Press, 1944).

[23] This view is not shared by all segments of the industry. Some dealers would disagree with this conclusion.

[24] The partial and simple correlation coefficients are

$$r_{Y1.2} = .88 \quad r_{Y2.1} = -.28 \quad r_{Y1} = .90 \quad r_{Y2} = .59 \quad r_{12} = .75$$

The negative signs of the regression and correlation coefficients of x_2 were not expected. The high correlation between x_1 and x_2 makes any statement about the significance of the regression coefficients rather dubious.

as the size of market increases. Again, a regression analysis was completed, and the following results were obtained:

$$Y_c = .78 + 3.17x_1 - .001x_2 \qquad R^2 = .85$$
$$\quad\;\; (.20) \quad\; (.004)$$

where Y_c represents the number of Chrysler-Plymouth dealers in the market, x_1 represents Chrysler and Plymouth new car registrations attributed to Chrysler-Plymouth dealers (in thousands) in the market, and x_2 represents the square miles of the city.[25]

A Buick dealer is added to the market area for every increase of 555 in Buick sales. A Chrysler-Plymouth dealer is added to the market area for every increase of 315 in sales. As was noted above, it is evident that Buick and Chrysler-Plymouth dealerships retail many fewer units than Ford or Chevrolet dealerships. Furthermore, the evidence does not support the contention that the automobile companies place more dealerships in the large markets relative to the sales in the smaller markets.[26]

---

[25] The partial and simple correlation coefficients are
$$r_{Y1.2} = .88 \quad r_{Y2.1} = -.03 \quad r_{Y1} = .92 \quad r_{Y2} = .57 \quad r_{12} = .63$$
[26] The discrepancy between the market representation policies of Chevrolet and Ford in the low price class and Buick and Chrysler-Plymouth in the middle price class has been left unexplained. The discrepancy between the "optimum" size of dealership in low price and the "optimum" size of dealership in the middle price class may be explained by a different distribution in space of middle price car buyers. Middle price buyers may be spread out in many small self-contained areas. To a great extent, this point has been left unexplored by the author. Also, the author has not conducted any systematic tests to determine whether the scale estimates derived from the placement policies in large city markets are consistent with the observed placement policies in the small markets. Preliminary tests suggest that the placement policies in small markets may not be easily reconciled with the scale estimates.

CHAPTER 6

An Analysis of the Retail Automobile Market in Greater Cleveland (Cuyahoga County)

6.1. Introduction

Much time and money is spent by the auto companies to determine the optimal placement of dealers in local markets. How many dealerships should be placed in the local market? Where should the dealerships be placed in the market area? Will the dealer succeed once placed? The market studies conducted by the companies are, of course, designed to supply answers to these questions. How accurately can these predictions be made?

The purpose of this chapter is to study the Greater Cleveland area to determine if it is possible to estimate the sales volume of each dealership and to predict the likely success of each dealership. The Cleveland market was selected because the relevant data are available.

Since 1954, the *Cleveland Plain Dealer* has published an annual analysis of new car sales in Cuyahoga County.[1] For each

---

[1] *Cleveland Plain Dealer, 1958 New Car Sales in Greater Cleveland,* a report compiled and reported by the Market Research Department (Cleveland: *Cleveland Plain Dealer,* 1959).

make, new car sales (in units), of every dealer and new car registrations for each make in each census tract are available. As far
as the author knows, similar data are not readily available for
other local markets. These data could be obtained for other local
markets, but this would require the services of local dealer organizations and the auto companies.[2]

Is the probability of dealership survival a function of dealership size? In the first part of this chapter a test will be applied
to determine if such a relationship exists. Suppose there are
economies of scale in automobile retailing. Then, the probability
of dealership survival should be higher, the larger the dealership.
Consumer purchasing behavior will be studied next. A hypothesis about consumer purchasing habits will be formulated and
used to predict the sales of each dealer. The chapter will end
with a discussion of the effectiveness of price and/or service
policy in encouraging consumers to travel to purchase from a
distant dealer.

6.2. Some Economic Characteristics of Greater Cleveland (Cuya-
hoga County)

The metropolitan area of Cleveland is composed of two counties, the largest being Cuyahoga County in which 95 per cent of
the metropolitan area's inhabitants are located. In 1956 over
90 per cent of the metropolitan area's new car registrations of
Fords and Chevrolets were recorded in Cuyahoga County. Thus,
most of the automobile market in the metropolitan area is located there, and over 90 per cent of the sales by dealers located
in the county are made to buyers located in the county.[3] While

---

[2] This study is severely limited in scope by the unavailability of dealer financial data.

[3] In 1958 sales by dealers located in Cuyahoga County to buyers located in
Cuyahoga County as a per cent of total sales of these dealers were

(Per cent)

Chevrolet	93
Ford	91
Buick	94
Chrysler	92
Mercury	93

some buyers live outside the county and purchase from a dealer located in it, they represent a small fraction of total buyers. Hence, there is some justification in considering the county as a market area.

The city of Cleveland faces Lake Erie. The central business district is just off the Lake. In the central business district of the city there are several large dealerships, any one of which will sell over 1,200 new units in a normal year. Beyond the heart of the city there is a low income area which forms a semi-circle around the business district. This area extends from three to four miles beyond the business district. Beyond this, population density declines while per capita income rises. Several small suburban communities ring the city. Generally these communities are large enough to support a dealership of each make in the low price class. This summary hardly does justice to the actual population distribution, but these minimum essentials are necessary background information since the size distribution of dealerships is partially determined by the population distribution within Cuyahoga County.

6.3. The Interest of the Manufacturer in the Placement of the Dealership

Why is the placement of a dealer important to the manufacturer? Why does the manufacturer not allow the dealer to select the location? Is it not in the interest of the dealer to select a location which will maximize his profits? With free entry, those dealers who select inferior locations would, in time, be forced to move to better locations or be forced out of business because of losses. However, the adjustment process may be long. Then, there is no assurance the errors would not be repeated. Furthermore, this assumes the dealer is able to secure and use market information to select the optimum location. Although the competitive process does sort out inefficient dealers, it does not necessarily assure the optimal location of dealerships. The dealer seldom has as much market information as the manufacturer who can conduct market studies and recommend locations to dealers. Many potential errors in dealership location can be eliminated by the manufacturer by pooling experiences from many local markets. Those policies which have been successful in certain markets can be selected and applied to other markets.

The selection of dealership locations is an important function undertaken by the manufacturer. Under a franchise system, errors in the selection of locations are likely to mean lower sales for a longer period. Because entry is blocked, the corrective market forces will probably act slowly. For this reason, one would expect even greater emphasis by the manufacturer on optimum dealership location. Inefficient locations also mean lower profits and the need for greater supervision by the staff at the zone offices. The anticipated benefits of these services will be lost if the dealer is subsequently forced out of business because of a poor location.

6.4. Dealer Turnover and Dealership Size

If larger dealerships have lower unit costs, they should also have a higher probability of survival than a small dealership. The large dealership is more likely to earn profits when margins are squeezed. The low cost dealership has a better chance of surviving even if poor business decisions are made. The high cost dealership cannot afford to make errors. The low volume, high cost dealer may offset his cost disadvantage by charging, if possible, higher prices. However, the profit rates of small dealerships will be lower if prices are relatively uniform from one dealership to another. If so, during times of price shading, small volume dealerships are under price pressure and are more likely to experience losses. Greater management turnover of small dealerships can be expected.

Measurement of Variables and Limitations of the Data. As
noted above, the sales of each dealer in Cuyahoga County
in each year from 1954 to 1958 are available. It is also possible
to determine which dealers were operating a dealership at the
beginning of the period but did not operate the dealership
continuously throughout the period. Management turnover was
measured by noting changes in the name of the dealership. Turnover can be caused by reasons other than actual or expected unprofitable operations, for example retirement. However, this will
not bias results unless there is a systematic relationship between
dealership size and these other variables which cause dealer turnover. There is no reason to believe retirements are more likely
to occur in small dealerships or large dealerships. Turnover may
be caused by errors in the selection of dealership locations or high
rents. These may be related to dealership size. Dealers operating
small dealerships may be more likely to make errors in business judgment. However, the author did not find many instances
where a dealer replaced another dealer and then selected a different location. In most cases, the dealer selected the same location.
Presumably, the new dealer would have selected a different location if the rent was relatively high at the old location. Furthermore, the manufacturer provides advice and suggestions to new
dealers. Hence, fewer errors are made than otherwise would be
by small or large dealers. Therefore, it is less likely that turnover
results from obvious errors in business judgment and more likely
from differences in costs.

Size was measured by determining the median of the annual
sales of each dealer from 1954 to 1958.[4] If a dealer did not operate
continuously throughout the period, the median sales of the
dealer during the period of operation was determined. Hence, it
is possible to specify for each dealer (1) median of annual sales
during the period of operation, and (2) whether the dealer oper-

---

[4] Perhaps, the mean rather than the median should have been selected. The
median was selected because the 1955 data would bias the results.

ated the dealership throughout the 1954–1958 period; that is, whether there was turnover in management.[5]

Initially, each make was studied separately. In each case, dealers were subdivided into two groups. The first group includes all dealerships located in distant communities surrounding the city. These communities are South Euclid, Chagrin Falls, Bedford, Independence, Berea, North Olmstead, Westlake, Lyndhurst, Breaksville, and Strongsville. The dealerships in this group of communities are somewhat protected from the price competition of city dealerships because of their locations. Their turnover experience may differ from the turnover experience of dealerships located in the city. The second group (referred to as the city group) includes all other dealerships in Cuyahoga County. Within each of these groups, dealerships were further subdivided into two classes: (1) that class where turnover in management had been noted, and (2) that class where it had not. Thus, it was possible to construct frequency distributions showing the turnover experience of dealerships of different sizes. The next step was to compare the properties of these distributions. Before reviewing the results, three points warrant mention.

The 1954–1958 period may and may not be an appropriate one in which to test the relationship between dealership size and turnover. By 1954 the excess demand for automobiles had disappeared. Price competition has been experienced since then. Since 1956 the share of the total market represented by the middle price class has declined.[6] One would expect that each of these factors would place a premium on economic efficiency.

What if entrepreneurial ability is related to dealership size?

---

[5] Included in the turnover counts are dealer terminations for which there were no replacements.

[6] The large decline in sales in 1958 may have caused a dealership which was optimal for a specific sales volume to leave the industry. However, a dealership with a more flexible cost structure could survive, even though there was a large decline in sales. There is some support for the view that a test of the size-turnover relationship should be made during an interval when sales expectations are not disappointed.

The relationship between turnover and size can not be measured. A third variable, entrepreneurial ability, will distort the relationship. Some dealers begin by managing a small dealership and then, if successful, purchase a larger dealership, perhaps in the same city or in another. The smaller dealers in the Cleveland sample may simply be mediocre dealers. This is possible. However, a small dealership could have superior management. There has been little turnover in management of the larger dealerships until lately. Consequently, the opportunity to purchase a larger dealership may not have presented itself to a dealer who operated a small dealership. Beyond this little can be said.

Differences in price competition between makes may also distort the results. Of two dealerships, selling different makes but with the *same* sales volume, one may obtain competitive or greater returns because price competition is less severe for that make. The other dealer may not be able to survive because price competition is greater. There is some evidence which suggests that the extent of price discounting differs among makes. It is well known that depreciation experience differs among makes. However, the scarcity of data preclude any adjustment of the data for this factor.

Results: Chevrolet and Ford Dealers. The frequency distributions of dealership size of Chevrolet and Ford dealers classified by frequency of management turnover are presented in Table 47. This table and the ones to follow can be read in the following manner. There were 12 Chevrolet dealerships, each with the median of their sales from 1954 to 1958 between 400 and 800 units. Of these 12, five did not operate continuously throughout this period (turnover). The other seven operated throughout this period with no management turnover. Each row can be read in the same way. There is no significant difference between turnover rates of the two makes. Turnover rates appear to be inversely related with size. This can be determined by inspecting Table 48. In this table, Ford and Chevrolet observations are combined. In the city group, turnover rates decline with increasing size, and reach a

TABLE 47. RELATIONSHIP BETWEEN SALES OF DEALERSHIP AND TURNOVER RATE, FORD
AND CHEVROLET DEALERS 1954–1958

City Dealers [a]

Median of Annual Volume of Dealership, 1954–1958 [b]	Chevrolet			Ford		
	(1)	(2)	(3)	(4)	(5)	(6)
	Total	Turnover [c]	Ratio of (2) to (1)	Total	Turnover [c]	Ratio of (5) to (4)
0– 400	—	—	—	2	1	.50
400– 800	12	5	.42	7	2	.29
800–1,200	6	0	.00	7	2	.29
1,200–	3	1	.33	4	1	.25
Total	21	6	.29	20	6	.30

Dealers in Surrounding Communities [a]

0–400	4	1	.25	8	2	.25
400–600	3	2	.67	1	0	.00
600–	1	0	.00	—	—	—
Total	8	3	.38	9	2	.22

[a] *City Dealers* includes all dealerships located in Cuyahoga County with the exception of dealerships located in South Euclid, Chagrin Falls, Bedford, Independence, Berea, North Olmstead, Westlake, Lyndhurst, Breaksville, and Strongsville. *Dealers in Surrounding Communities* includes all dealerships in the communities listed above.
[b] Includes sales to individuals and business.
[c] Dealerships where there were changes in management between 1954 and 1958.
Source: "New Car Sales in Greater Cleveland," annual volumes for 1954–1958, compiled and reported by the Market Research Department of the *Cleveland Plain Dealer.*

TABLE 48. RELATIONSHIP BETWEEN SALES OF DEALERSHIP AND TURNOVER RATES FORD
AND CHEVROLET COMBINED, 1954–1958

Median of Annual Volume of Dealership, 1954–1958	City Dealers			Dealers in Surrounding Communities			Combined		
	Total (1)	Turn-over (2)	Ratio of (2) to (1) (3)	Total (4)	Turn-over (5)	Ratio of (5) to (4) (6)	Total (7)	Turn-over (8)	Ratio of (8) to (7) (9)
0– 400	2	1	.50	12	3	.25	16	6	.38
400– 800	19	7	.37	4	2	.50	23	9	.39
800–1,200	13	2	.15	1	0	.00	14	2	.14
1,200–	7	2	.29	—	—	—	7	2	.29
Total	41	12	.29	17	5	.29	60	19	.32

[a] Totals do not add because the address of two dealers could not be located.
Source: See Table 47.

minimum in the 800–1,200 class; then they rise. If the 1958 data are excluded, the relationship is even more pronounced. In 1958 there were management changes in several large dealerships.[7] This can be seen by inspecting Table 49. Dealers were classi-

TABLE 49. RELATIONSHIP BETWEEN SALES OF DEALERSHIP AND TURNOVER RATE ALL FORD AND CHEVROLET DEALERS COMBINED, 1954–1957

Median of Annual Volume of Dealership, 1954–1957	Total Number of Dealers (1)	Number of Dealers with Management Turnover (0) (2)	Ratio of (2) to (1) (3)
0–800	36	14	.39
800 or greater	23	2	.09
Total	59	16	.27
1954–1958			
0–800	39	15	.38
800 or greater	21	4	.19
Total	60	19	.32

Source : See Tables 47 and 48.

fied into two groups: (1) those with annual sales of less than 800 units and (2) those with more than 800 annual units. These data show the increase in the turnover of large dealerships which took place in 1958. From 1954–1957 there appears to have been a pronounced inverse relationship between dealership size and dealership turnover.

Other independent evidence indicates smaller dealerships cannot offset their higher per unit cost by charging significantly higher prices.[8]

---

[7] It appears that the 1958 recession affected large dealerships more than small dealerships. One of these large dealerships belongs to a chain which closed the Cleveland branch.

[8] Dealer responses to the questionnaire suggest that prices do not differ significantly from dealership to dealership within large metropolitan markets. Dealers claimed a better service reputation does not allow the dealer to charge significantly higher prices. However, substantial price discrimination is observed.

Results: Middle and Upper Middle Price Class. The frequency distributions of Buick, Pontiac, and Oldsmobile dealers classified by frequency of management turnover are presented in Table 50.

TABLE 50. RELATIONSHIP BETWEEN SALES OF DEALERSHIP AND TURNOVER RATES MIDDLE
AND UPPER MIDDLE PRICE CLASS, GENERAL MOTORS DEALERS [a], 1954–1958
City Dealers

Median of Annual Volume of Dealership, 1954–1958	Buick			Oldsmobile			Pontiac		
	Total (1)	Turn-over (2)	Ratio of (2) to (1) (3)	Total (4)	Turn-over (5)	Ratio of (5) to (4) (6)	Total (7)	Turn-over (8)	Ratio of (8) to (9) (9)
0–200	—	—	—	—	—	—	—	—	—
200–400	4	0	.00	—	—	—	5	2	.40
400–600	6	3	.50	4	1	.25	5	1	.20
600–800	1	0	.00	2	1	.50	—	—	—
800–	1	1	1.00	2	1	.50	—	—	—
Total	12	4	.33	8	3	.38	10	3	.30

Dealers in Surrounding Communities

0–200	1	0	.00	4	1	.25	1	0	.00
200–400	1	0	.00	—	—	—	3	3	1.00
400–	1	0	.00	—	—	—	1	—	.00
Total	3	0	.00	4	1	.25	5	3	.60

[a] Excludes single line Cadillac dealers.
Source: See Table 47.

Similar distributions of Dodge, DeSoto, and Chrysler dealers are presented in Table 51 and of Mercury dealers in Table 52.

These data indicate turnover rates differ among makes, with DeSoto and Mercury having the highest turnover rates. It is also interesting to note that these two makes generally have the lowest average sales per dealer.[9] These data also indicate there

---

[9] In 1956 the average sales per dealer were:

General Motors Dealers	Chrysler Corporation Dealers	Ford Motor Dealers
Buick—545.5	Chrysler-Plymouth—366.9	Mercury—317.8
Oldsmobile—466.8	DeSoto-Plymouth—299.1	(excludes Lincoln-
Pontiac—367.0	Dodge-Plymouth—545.1	Mercury dealers)

TABLE 51. RELATIONSHIP BETWEEN SALES OF DEALERSHIP AND TURNOVER RATE, MIDDLE
AND UPPER MIDDLE PRICE CLASS, CHRYSLER CORPORATION DEALERS [a], 1954–1958
City Dealers

Median of Annual Volume of Dealership, 1954–1958	Dodge			DeSoto			Chrysler [b]		
	Total (1)	Turn-over (2)	Ratio of (2) to (1) (3)	Total (4)	Turn-over (5)	Ratio of (5) to (4) (6)	Total (7)	Turn-over (8)	Ratio of (8) to (9) (9)
0–200	3	3	1.00	4	2	.50	2	1	.50
200–400	9	3	.33	8	5	.63	5	0	.00
400–600	4	0	.00	1	1	1.00	2	1	.50
600–800	—	—	—	1	0	.00	—	—	—
800–	1	0	.00	—	—	—	1	0	.00
Total	17	6	.35	14	8	.57	10	2	.20

Dealers in Surrounding Communities

	Total (1)	Turn-over (2)	Ratio (3)	Total (4)	Turn-over (5)	Ratio (6)	Total (7)	Turn-over (8)	Ratio (9)
0–200	—	—	—	1	1	1.00	4	1	.25
200–400	1	0	.00	—	—	—	—	—	—
400–	1	0	.00	—	—	—	—	—	—
Total	2	0	.00	1	1	1.00	4	1	.25

[a] Includes Plymouth sales by each dealer.
[b] Does not include Imperial Sales of each dealer.
Source: See Table 47.

is less variability in size among dealers in the middle and upper middle price classes than among dealers in the low price class. Indeed, there are very few dealers with annual sales of greater than 800 units.

These combined frequency distributions of all middle and upper middle price class dealers are presented in Table 53. Except for the smallest size class, dealers with annual sales between 0–200 units, there are no significant differences in turnover rates.[10]

---

[10] In general, the author has found it consistently more difficult to make accurate predictions in any analysis of the middle price class.

TABLE 52. RELATIONSHIP BETWEEN SALES OF DEALERSHIP AND TURNOVER RATE, MIDDLE
AND UPPER PRICE CLASS, MERCURY DEALERS, 1954–1958

City Dealers

Median of Annual Volume of Dealership, 1954–1958 [a]	Total (1)	Turnover (2)	Ratio of (2) to (1) (3)
0–200	3	1	.33
200–400	8	5	.63
400–600	5	3	.60
600–800	1	1	1.00
Total	17	10	.58

Dealers in Surrounding Communities

0–200	—	—	—
200–400	2	0	.00
Total	2	0	.00

[a] Includes Lincoln sales of each dealer.
Source : See Table 47.

TABLE 53. RELATIONSHIP BETWEEN SALES OF DEALERSHIP AND TURNOVER RATE, MIDDLE
AND UPPER PRICE CLASS, ALL DEALERS COMBINED, 1954–1958

Median of Annual Volume of Dealership, 1954–1958	City Dealers			Dealers in Surrounding Communities			All Middle and Upper Middle Price Class Dealers Combined [a]		
	Total (1)	Turn-over (2)	Ratio of (2) to (1) (3)	Total (4)	Turn-over (5)	Ratio of(5) to (4) (6)	Total (7)	Turn-over (8)	Ratio of (8) to (7) (9)
0–200	12	7	.58	11	3	.27	29	16	.55
200–400	39	15	.38	8	3	.38	51	20	.39
400–600	27	10	.37	2	0	.00	29	10	.34
600–800	5	2	.40	—	—	—	5	2	.40
800–	6	2	.33	—	—	—	6	2	.33
Total	89	36	.40	21	6	.29	120	50	.42

[b] Rows do not add because several dealers whose addresses could not be located were
included in this tabulation.
Source : See Tables 50 through 52.

6.5 Survival Rates

A franchise system may maintain stability in the number of dealers and lower dealer turnover by protecting dealers in some degree from the rigors of price competition. The manufacturer benefits if consumer-dealer attachments are established; for example, the dealer is advertised as a reputable businessman who has been and will be in business and in whom the consumer can have confidence to service the product. Whether this works out as it should is a different matter.

What has been the survival experience of dealers in the Cleveland market? What per cent of the dealers selling automobiles in 1954 were still selling the same make in 1958? For each make the number of dealers selling automobiles in 1954 was determined. Then, the number of these dealers who were still operating at the end of 1958 was determined. In other words, what per cent of the dealers who were selling a particular make at the beginning of the period were still selling that make at the end of the period?

Raw survival figures do not indicate the relative importance of the group of dealers who survive. Perhaps many small dealers dropped from the market. Their combined share of the market may be small and therefore unimportant. How important were those dealers who survived? The sales in 1954 of those dealers who survived as a percentage of total 1954 sales was determined. This procedure was applied to each make. These percentages indicate the relative importance of these dealers in 1954.

The dealers who survived may account for a large per cent of 1954 sales. This would indicate many relatively small dealers did not survive. This would be perfectly consistent with the use of the franchise system. The franchise system is not designed to protect all dealers. In contrast, the dealers who survived may account for a small share of 1954 sales. Then, the anticipated benefits of the franchise system would not have been realized.

The advantages of the franchise system may not be realized

because of prediction errors. For example, suppose sales have increased over a period of time, while the number of dealers has been restricted. There will be an excess demand for entry because profits are high in automobile distribution. Entry is blocked because franchises are not issued. Then, suppose sales decline unexpectedly as they did in the middle price class from 1955 to 1958. Profits fall and some dealers leave the market. The demand for entry declines or disappears. If sales decline by an unexpectedly large percentage, many dealers, who had established consumer attachments, will leave the market. The benefits the manufacturer had hoped to obtain from the use of a franchise system are not realized.

In fact, sales of middle price cars declined by 54 per cent nationally and 49 per cent in Cleveland from 1955 to 1958. A percentage decline of this magnitude was last experienced in the 1937–1938 recession. In this case, the 1955–1958 decline occurred in a relatively prosperous period. A decline of this magnitude was not anticipated in 1955. In fact, a greater percentage decline was only experienced once before, from 1929 to 1932. In the low price class, sales declined by 31 per cent nationally and by 34 per cent in Cleveland. Sales in this price class had declined by a greater percentage four times before. The decline experienced in the low price class from 1955 to 1958 had been preceded by four larger declines. Consequently, it is possible to infer that a decline of this magnitude was more likely in the low price class than in the middle price class.

This point is important. The benefits of the franchise system may be lost because of an unexpected large decline in new car registrations. As dealers leave the industry, established consumer attachments are weakened. However, it cannot then be argued that the manufacturers obtained no benefits from the franchise system and, therefore, should abandon the system. The potential benefits of the franchise system, that is, the development of consumer-dealer attachments, are not realized because of dealer turnover. The costs are incurred by the manufacturer before the benefits of the system can be obtained. The costs to the manufacturer of the franchise system may be higher prices and, hence, lower sales. Retail prices may be higher because there will be fewer dealers than otherwise under a franchise system. However, one cannot conclude that the manufacturers should, therefore, discard the franchise system. Rather, it only means that in those periods when sales decline unexpectedly, the benefits of the franchise system are less likely to be realized. In other periods the manufacturers obtain the benefits of the system.

In summary, one would expect the recent survival rates in the middle price class will differ from the survival rates in the low price class. Also, one might expect the benefits of the franchise system are more likely to be realized when accurate sales predictions are possible.

Results. The number of dealers of each make in business in 1954 and still in business in 1958 as a percentage of the total number of dealers of that make in business in 1954 is presented in Table 54. The 1954 sales of those dealers who were operating in 1954 and at the end of 1958, separated by make, as a percentage

TABLE 54. SURVIVAL RATES BY MAKE IN THE CLEVELAND AUTOMOBILE MARKET, 1954–1958

Make of Car	Percentage of Dealers in Business in 1954 still in Business in 1958 [a] (per cent)	Share of 1954 Sales of those Dealers still in Business in 1958 [b]
Ford	73	.69
Chevrolet	64	.72
Buick	85	.77
Oldsmobile	64	.54
Pontiac	42	.49
Dodge-Plymouth	47	.69
DeSoto-Plymouth	27	.38
Chrysler-Plymouth	69	.76
Mercury	25	.24

[a] Column should be read 73 per cent of the Ford dealers operating in 1954 were still operating at the end of 1958, etc.
[b] Column should be read those Ford dealers who were operating in 1954 and at the end of 1958 accounted for 69 per cent of total Ford sales made by Ford dealers in 1954, etc.
Source: See Table 47.

of total sales of each make in 1954 is also presented in this table. It is clear there is greater turnover among DeSoto and Mercury dealers. What is surprising is that there has been no appreciable difference between the low price makes and several middle price makes in the share of 1954 sales which were accounted for by those dealers who survived. In particular, note the ratios for Ford, Chevrolet, Buick, Dodge, and Chrysler. However, in the other cases, the percentage of 1954 purchasers who will purchase from the same dealer when they re-purchase will be less than 50 per cent since many dealers have long since gone out of business.

6.6. Predicting Dealer Sales

In an earlier section of this chapter turnover rates were found to be inversely related to the size of the dealer. The probability of dealership survival was directly related to the size of dealer. This relationship is one of several which restricts the number of dealers in the market area. For example, in the low price class one would expect dealers to be located such that they would be able to retail at least 600 and preferably 800 or more units per year. These requirements would be scaled down for dealerships located in the surrounding communities.

In most cases these requirements would satisfy minimum cost requirements. However, it is not possible to formulate rules for the location of dealers until some information about consumer shopping and purchasing behavior is known.

How difficult is it to predict the sales of a dealer? Information which shows the extent of consumer shopping and mobility is not publicly available. Most dealers claim substantial shopping. Many claim any attempt to increase prices above the market price would mean a large decline in sales. This suggests substantial consumer mobility. The study by Ford indicated relatively little shopping.[11] This does not mean that prices differ substantially between dealers selling the same make. A few mar-

---

[11] The Ford report indicated 66 per cent of all new car buyers shopped only one dealer of the make purchased.

ginal buyers who shop and make this known to each dealer are sufficient to wipe out differentials. It has been reported that salesmen quote artificially low prices so as to encourage the buyer to return to the dealership after shopping at other dealerships.

The available evidence, meager as it is, suggests that on average price differentials among dealers selling the same make are small. If this is so, there would be savings to the consumer in time and transport expense if he purchased from the nearest dealer selling the make selected. The hypothesis to be tested is that consumers *tend* to purchase from the closest dealer selling the make the consumer desires to purchase.

Suppose this hypothesis is correct. The sales of each dealer should be predictable from the number of purchasing units located nearest the dealer. The sales of a dealership should be higher the larger the number of purchasing units located nearest the dealership. A market area for each dealer must be determined.[12] This area can be determined by marking off equal distances between a given dealer and all surrounding dealers selling the same make and then by connecting these points to form the outer boundaries of a market area.[13]

Definition and Construction of Market Areas. The analysis is restricted to four makes: Chevrolet, Ford, Buick, and Mercury. The address of each dealer was determined, and the dealer's location was plotted on a map of Cleveland and vicinity. To avoid short term variation in sales, the median of the annual sales of each dealer in the 1954–1956 period was used as the dependent variable. This period was chosen because several changes in the number and location of dealers occurred in 1957. The size of

---

[12] The term "market area" is usually used to denote an area where price or product policy of one seller can substantially affect the sales of other sellers. The term as used in this chapter does not have this meaning.

[13] It is assumed that the consumer pre-selects the make before shopping. This is consistent with the results of the Ford study. Furthermore, each dealer is assumed to compete only with other dealers selling his make. One major difficulty is that purchasers will be influenced by the proximity of the dealer to place of work.

several market areas would have changed. Each make was studied separately. In each case, the market areas were determined such that

(1) only one dealer of *that* make was included in each market area.

(2) once having selected the make to be purchased, the consumer living in the area would find the dealer in that area closer than any other dealer selling that make.

It should be clearly understood that *a separate set of market areas were determined for each make.* As the reader might suspect, the density of dealer coverage differs between makes, being highest in the low price class. Hence, market areas are smaller for Ford and Chevrolet dealers than for Buick and Mercury dealers.

First, the outer boundaries of the market area were determined. This, in turn, determined which census tracts would be included in each market area. The number of families in each census tract in 1956 was determined by the *Cleveland Real Property Inventory* which makes an actual physical count of occupied family units in each census tract in Cuyahoga County. The number of families located in each market area was then determined. Family income distributions in each census tract, as recorded in the 1950 *Census of Population,* were also used even though these data are dated.

Limitations of the Study. In Cleveland, as in most cities, several large dealers are located in the central business district of Cleveland where few families reside. No attempt was made to specify the determinants of the sales of these dealers. These dealers obtain a large volume of sales primarily because of their proximity to places of work. A second difficulty arises from sales to business by dealers. There is no way of excluding sales to business from the analysis. It can be a major distorting factor.[14]

---

[14] In 1958, 19 per cent of total passenger car sales in Cuyahoga County were sales to business. See *Cleveland Plain Dealer, 1958 New Car Sales in Greater Cleveland,* a report compiled and reported by the Market Research Department (Cleveland: *Cleveland Plain Dealer,* 1959), p. 17.

Specification of Variables. Throughout the following discussion, Y represents the median of annual sales from 1954 to 1956 of the dealership, X_1 represents the number of families in the market area of the dealership (in thousands), and X_2 represents the weighted average income per family (in thousands of dollars) in 1950. As will be explained later, X_1' represents the number of families with real income in 1956 comparable to 1950 family income of $3,500 or greater.

Analysis of Results, Low Price Class.

Chevrolet. The regression analysis was based on the sales performance of 18 Chevrolet dealerships. The sales of the dealerships in the sample varied from 149 units to 1,677 units. Basic regression data are presented in Table 55. The regression equation and the standard errors of the coefficients are [15]

TABLE 55. SIMPLE AND PARTIAL CORRELATION COEFFICIENTS, MULTIPLE REGRESSION ANALYSIS

	Chevrolet Dealers	Ford Dealers
Means:		
Y = units	766.4	690.2
X_1 = 1000's of families	23.0	20.5
X_2 = average family income in market area (000s)	$4.362	$4.480
Simple Correlation Coefficients:		
r_{Y1}	.679	.656
r_{Y2}	−.388	.005
r_{12}	−.051	−.195
Partial Correlation Coefficients:		
$r_{Y1.2}$	.716	.670
$r_{Y2.1}$	−.482	.179
Multiple Correlation Coefficient:		
$r_{Y.12}$	.765	.670

(1) $Y_c = 1,083.8 + 20.22X_1 - 179.60X_2$ $R = .765$
          (5.10)   (84.43)

[15] Through an omission, one dealer was placed incorrectly. If the correction were made, the multiple correlation coefficient would increase slightly.

The regression coefficient of X_1 is significant at the 1 per cent probability level and the regression coefficient of X_2 is significant at the 5 per cent probability level. The multiple correlation coefficient is significant at the 1 per cent probability level. The negative sign of the coefficient of X_2 was unexpected. One criticism of the equation is the size of the intercept. This is caused by the negative net relation between X_2 and Y.[16]

Ford. The regression analysis was based on the sales performance of 19 Ford dealerships whose sales varied from 46 to 1,508 units. Basic regression data are presented in Table 55. The regression equation and the standard errors of the regression coefficients are [17]

$$(2) \quad Y_F = -274.89 + 28.77X_1 + 84.03X_2 \quad R = .670$$
$$(7.97) \quad (115.33)$$

The multiple correlation coefficient is significant at the 1 per cent probability level. The coefficient of X_1 is significant at the 1 per cent probability level. The coefficient of X_2 is not significant at the 5 per cent probability level.[18]

Analysis of Results, Middle Price Class.

Buick. The regression analysis was based on the sales performance of 13 Buick dealerships whose sales varied from 80 to 1,077 units. Basic regression data are presented in Table 56.

---

[16] A simple regression equation was also determined and is shown below:
$$(1a) \quad Y_C = 287.5 + 20.79X_1 \quad R = .679$$
$$(5.62)$$
The regression coefficient of X_1 and the correlation coefficient are significant at the 1 per cent probability level. The negative sign of the coefficient of the income variable in (1) is puzzling and suggests the model and the data should be studied in greater detail.

[17] One dealer was incorrectly placed. The multiple correlation coefficient would increase slightly if a correction was made.

[18] A simple regression equation was also determined and is shown below:
$$(2a) \quad Y_F = 124.7 + 27.63X_1 \quad R = .656$$
$$(7.71)$$
The regression coefficient of X_1 is also significant at the 1 per cent level as is the simple correlation coefficient. The similarity between equations (2a) and (1a) and their respective correlation coefficients should be noted.

TABLE 56. SIMPLE AND PARTIAL CORRELATION COEFFICIENT, MULTIPLE
REGRESSION ANALYSIS

	Buick Dealers	Mercury Dealers
Means:		
Y = units	490.6	365.4
X_1 = thousands of families	31.1	35.9
X_2 = average family income (in thousands of dollars)	4.358	4.256
X_3 = number of dealers located within ½ mile of dealer	3.54	3.50
Simple Correlation Coefficients		
r_{Y1}	.268	.178
r_{Y2}	−.314	.354
r_{Y3}	.010	.356
r_{12}	.195	.122
r_{23}	−.429	.485
Partial Correlation Coefficients		
$r_{Y1.2}$	.354	.146
$r_{Y2.1}$	−.388	.340
$r_{Y2.3}$	−.356	.222
$r_{Y3.2}$	−.139	.225
Multiple Correlation Coefficients		
$R_{Y.12}$	.460	.380
$R_{Y.23}$	.422	.412

The regression equation is

$$(3) \quad Y_B = 1{,}009.4 + 5.65X_1 - 159.40X_2 \qquad R = .460$$
$$\phantom{(3) \quad Y_B = 1{,}009.4 + } (4.73) \quad\;\; (119.66)$$

The multiple regression coefficient is not significant at the 5 per cent probability level. Neither of the regression coefficients is significant at the 5 per cent probability level. These results are strikingly different from those obtained in the analysis of Chevrolet or Ford. To improve the results, the analysis was extended. Trade officials frequently suggest a dealer should be located on an "automobile row," that is, near other dealers. There are two offsetting effects. On the one hand, the dealership can lower its sales-promotion expense. On the other hand, the dealership will be competing with more dealerships. To determine if the placement of a dealership on "automobile row" is an important determinant of dealer sales, an additional variable was added to the analysis. X_3, the number of dealers (of all makes) located within one-half mile of the dealership was added to the analysis, and X_1, the number of families in the market area, was dropped as an independent variable. Basic regression data are presented in Table 56. The regression equation is

(3a) $\quad Y_B = 1{,}268.31 - 158.92X_2 - 24.05X_3 \qquad R = .422$
$\qquad\qquad\quad (137.31) \quad\ (51.51)$

The multiple correlation coefficient is not significant at the 5 per cent probability level, and the regression coefficients of X_2 and X_3 are not significant at the 5 per cent probability level. The negative sign of X_3 was unexpected.

In equation (3) income and number of families were both explicitly introduced as independent variables. If middle priced autos are primarily purchased by families with income above (say) average family income, this would have been reflected in the size of the partial correlation coefficient $r_{Y1.2}$. Yet, the partial correlation coefficient is low ($r_{Y1.2} = .354$), and is lower than the comparable coefficients obtained in the Ford and Chevrolet analyses. Thus, even if family income is held constant, the number of families in the dealers market area does not seem to predict the sales of individual Buick dealerships accurately.

Another method can be used to measure the importance of the number of families in a market as a determinant of sales of each Buick dealer. Rather than consider all families in the market area, consider only those families with incomes high enough above a specified value to purchase a middle price auto. The distribution of families by income class and by census trace is available from 1950 *Census of Population*. The percentage of families in each census tract with incomes greater than $3,500 in 1950 was computed. This percentage times the number of families in 1956 was used as a crude estimate of the total number of families with real incomes in 1956 equal to a 1950 income of $3,500 or more. This variable will be denoted as X_1^1.

By regressing X_1^1 on Y, another measure of the relationship between the number of families in the market area and the sales of the dealership, independent of income, can be obtained.

A simple regression between dealership sales and the number of families with real incomes equal to or greater than a 1950 income of \$3,500, X_1^1, was completed. The regression equation is

$$(3b) \qquad Y_B = 436.53 + 2.83X_1^1 \qquad R = .114$$
$$(2.45)$$

The simple correlation coefficient is not significant at the 5 per cent probability level. The regression coefficient of X_1^1 is not significant at the 5 per cent probability level. Hence, no improvement in results is observed.

In summary, this analysis suggests that predicting sales of Buick dealers is much more difficult than predicting the sales of Ford or Chevrolet dealers. This difficulty, as the results for Mercury will show, may be characteristic of the middle price class.

Mercury. The regression analysis was based on the sales performance of 12 Mercury dealerships whose sales varied from 167 to 552 units. Basic regression data are presented in Table 56. The regression equation and the standard errors of the regression coefficients are

$$(4) \qquad Y_M = 97.7 + 1.18X_1 + 52.95X_2 \qquad R = .380$$
$$(2.67) \qquad (48.77)$$

The multiple correlation coefficient and the coefficients of X_1 and X_2 are not significant at the 5 per cent probability level. Both the Mercury and Buick analyses indicate that the total number of families in the dealer's market area is not an important determinant of the sales of the dealership.

To determine the effect of dealer location relative to other dealers, X_3, the number of dealers within one-half mile of the dealer, was added to the analysis and X_1, the number of families in the dealer's market area, was dropped as an independent variable. The regression data are presented in Table 56. The regression equation and the standard errors of the regression coefficients are

(4a) $Y_M = 143.2 + 37.29X_2 + 18.16X_3$ $R = .412$
         (54.50)   (26.21)

Again, the multiple correlation coefficient and the regression coefficients of the independent variables are not significant at the 5 per cent probability level.

Finally, as an alternative method of measuring the net effect of the number of families in the market area on sales of a dealership, X_1^1, the number of families with real income in 1956 equal to or greater than incomes greater than a 1950 income of $3,500, was determined for each market area. A simple regression analysis, with X_1^1 as the independent variable, was completed. This is an alternative way of holding income constant and measuring the effect of the number of families in a market area on the sales of the dealership in the market area. The regression equation is

(4b) $Y_M = 238.0 + 5.72X_1^1$ $R = .414$
              (3.97)

Once again, the simple correlation coefficient and the regression coefficient of the independent variable are not significant at the 5 per cent level.[19]

Predicting Dealership Sales from New Car Registrations in the Market Area. In the preceding section an attempt was made to predict dealership sales from the number of families in the market area. This is an acceptable procedure if there is no variation between market areas in the preference for a particular automobile. An example will make this clear. It is possible that Fords are preferred over Chevrolets in certain parts of the city and Chevrolets over Fords in other parts of the city. Thus, there may be a large number of families in a market area. The sales of the dealership may be low because only a small proportion of the families prefer that make. At the other extreme, there may be a small number of families in a market area but the sales of the

---

[19] Possibly, these capricious results are due to the limited range of variation of the independent variables. A more detailed analysis of the data than the author has been able to make would be desirable.

dealership in the area may be relatively high because a large proportion of those families prefer that make. In other words, the penetration of the make may differ from market area to market area. This could have produced the low correlation coefficients. However, a correction can be made.

An automobile registration indicates the location of the purchaser. A second and perhaps superior method of predicting the sales of a dealership is to determine the new car registrations of the make in the market area and use this as an independent variable to predict the sales of the dealership. This method avoids the problem mentioned above, i.e., differences in penetration between market areas.[20]

For each make, new car registrations in each dealer's market area were computed. Hereafter, new car registrations will be denoted as R. Thus, for each market area two observations are available, dealership sales, Y, and new car registrations of the make, R. If, for example, each consumer purchased a Ford from the nearest Ford dealer, new car registrations would equal dealership sales. There would be no consumer mobility. This is not quite true. Consumers in one market area could cross over to another area and these could be just offset by other consumers traveling in the opposite direction. New car registrations would be equal to dealership sales. One would conclude there was little consumer mobility, even though there was considerable mobility. Some "cross hauling" by consumers occurs, but it is probably small relative to the movement by consumers from one market area to another in response to price differentials. Consumer movement is likely to flow in one direction, towards the low price areas. This point will soon be documented.

Four simple regression analyses were completed, one each for Chevrolet, Ford, Buick, and Mercury. In each case new car registrations in the dealer's market area, R, was used as an inde-

---

[20] Ordinarily, one does not wish to correlate one variable with itself or to correlate two variables with each other if there is a common element in each variable. In this case the test of the hypothesis is whether the two variables are identical.

pendent variable to predict the dealer's sales, Y. The regression equations and the simple correlation coefficients are presented below.

(5)   Chevrolet: $Y_C = 347.9 + .549R_C$ $R = .537$
(6)   Ford: $Y_F = 141.6 + .928R_F$ $R = .735$
(7)   Buick: $Y_B = 542.8 - .017R_B$ $R = -.026$
(8)   Mercury: $Y_M = 84.6 + .793R_M$ $R = .633$

Several points should be mentioned. Except for Mercury, the results are similar to those obtained in the previous analysis. However, new car registrations are a better predictor of dealership sales than the number of families for Mercury. Registrations do not predict as well as the number of families in the case of Chevrolet. For Buick, neither predicts well. Therefore, it is not unambiguously clear that new car registrations are a superior predictor of dealership sales than the number of families.

These regression studies were designed to determine the difficulty (or ease) of predicting the sales of a dealership. The accuracy of these predictions apparently depends on price class under investigation. In the low price class the regression analyses indicate the number of families in the market area was a significant determinant in explaining the sales of the dealership. This result, together with the relationship between management turnover and dealership size, should permit an evaluation, within limits, of whether a new dealer is likely to succeed once he is placed in the Cleveland market. However, it is more difficult to predict the sales of Buick or Mercury dealerships. The number of families in the market area failed to explain the observed variation in the sales of Buick or Mercury dealerships.

The introduction of new car registrations as an independent variable improved the correlation coefficient for Mercury but not for Buick. For an unknown reason, it is difficult to predict the sales of Buick dealerships.

Although the data are not completely consistent, they would suggest there is greater difficulty in predicting the sales of dealerships selling middle price autos. It is also more difficult to predict the success of dealers retailing middle price automobiles once the dealer's volume is estimated. These conclusions apply to the Cleveland market. It is not known whether these results can be generalized to other local markets. Perhaps, these results justify a healthy scepticism about the predictability of dealership sales.

6.7. Consumer Mobility

The difficulty of predicting dealership sales arises from consumer mobility from one market area to another. Can the discrepancy between the sales of the dealership and new car registrations in the market area be explained? Do consumers travel from one market area to another in order to obtain lower prices or superior service?

Those dealers who were known for their service reputations or their propensity to accept special prices were identified.[21] It should be noted that only those dealers who were known for their service excellence or for their propensity to accept special prices were identified. Many dealers were not so identified.

Consumers might be expected to travel outside their market area if they anticipate a lower price or if they expect to obtain superior service. This hypothesis can be tested. The difference between the dealer's sales and the new car registrations in the dealer's market area can be used as an index of out-of-market sales. A dealer with a service or price reputation should record an excess of sales over new car registrations of the dealer's make within his market area. Conversely, a dealer without a service and price reputation should operate in a deficit area; that is, new car registration of the dealer's make should exceed the dealer's sales. Residuals, that is, the excess of dealer sales over new car registrations of the dealer's make in the dealer's market area,

---

[21] These evaluations were made by an individual familiar with the Cleveland automobile market. There is no independent way to test the accuracy of these evaluations.

were computed. The next step was to determine whether those dealers who had service or price reputations had positive residuals.[22]

The results are presented in Table 57. This table can be read as follows. Of the 12 Ford dealers without a price or service reputation, the sales of three were greater than the new car registrations of Fords in their respective market areas. Seven Ford dealers had price or service reputations. Six of these recorded sales which were greater than the new car registrations of Fords in their respective market areas. Similar interpretations can be made for the other two makes. For Chevrolet and Ford, those dealers who had service or price reputations were drawing sales away from other dealers. The sales of each dealer in this group exceeded the new car registrations of his make in his market area. For Buick, the results are more debatable. There is less evidence that those dealers who have service or price reputations operate in surplus areas, that is, where the dealer's sales exceed new car registrations of the dealer's make.

The observations for the three makes have been combined and a chi square test was applied. There are significant differences between the two groups of dealers.

Effect of Price or Service Policy on Buyers Shopping Behavior. In a previous section an attempt was made to predict dealership sales from new car registrations in the market area of the dealership. If consumers purchased from the nearest dealer, new car registrations would predict dealer sales perfectly. This was not observed. Correlation coefficients varied from $-.026$ to $.735$. Why were the correlation coefficients not higher? One reason for the low coefficients is that the price or service policy of certain dealers is an important factor which draws buyers from other

---

22 The dealers were evaluated in late 1958. The data used to compute residuals were applicable to the 1954–1956 period. Between these dates, there had been a large turnover in Mercury dealers. Very few Mercury dealers who had been operating in the 1954–1956 period were still operating in 1958. Therefore Mercury was not included in the analysis.

TABLE 57. RELATIVE SALES PERFORMANCE OF DEALERS KNOWN FOR PRICE OR SERVICE
REPUTATIONS COMPARED TO RELATIVE SALES PERFORMANCE OF DEALERS
WITHOUT PRICE OR SERVICE REPUTATIONS

Make	Sales of Dealership Greater than New Car Registrations of Same Make in the Market Area of Dealership	Sales of Dealership Less than New Car Registrations of Same Make in the Market Area of Dealership
Ford		
Dealers *without* price or service reputations	3	9
Dealers *with* . . .	6	1
Chevrolet		
Dealers *without* price or service reputations	3	9
Dealers *with* . . .	5	1
Buick		
Dealers *without* price or service reputations	3	6
Dealers *with* . . .	2	2

Chi Square Test. All Dealers Combined

	Total Number of Dealers	Dealers with Sales Greater than New Car Registrations in Dealer's Market Area (O)	Expected Number (E)	(O-E)	(O-E)²	$\frac{(O-E)^2}{E}$
Dealers without price or service reputations	33	9	14.52	5.52	30.47	2.10
Dealers with price or service reputations	17	13	7.48	5.52	30.47	4.07
Total	50	22	22.00			$\chi^2 =$ 6.17

Results $n = 1$ χ^2 of 5.412 corresponds to $P = .02$
χ^2 of 6.635 corresponds to $P = .01$

areas. In particular, there is a group of price sensitive buyers who travel across market areas.[23] The evidence suggests that the correlation coefficients could be materially improved by introducing this variable explicitly into the analysis.

There is no reason to believe these results, which are applicable to the Cleveland automobile market, can be generalized to apply to other local markets. Even in the Cleveland market there is little uniformity in results. Greater success can be expected in the prediction of sales of dealerships retailing low price autos. However, even here, the error in the prediction of dealer's sales will be large. Predictions of the sales of dealers selling middle price makes are still less accurate. Since it is difficult to predict the sales of a dealer selling a middle priced auto, it is likely most dealer placements are made with great uncertainty as to the success of the dealer. In the low price class there is more regularity in results, and, therefore, the manufacturer is more likely to predict the success of a dealer, once the dealer is placed.

Information on consumer shopping and purchasing behavior is meager. In general, data are lacking, and few hypotheses can be thoroughly tested. The author can offer several conjectures of how prices are determined in local markets, but, at this stage, these can only be considered conjectures with meager empirical support.

It appears that a larger proportion of buyers of low price autos are shoppers who are willing to travel for small differences in price quotations. It is probably true that this proportion has been growing of late. Consequently, price shading by one dealer forces nearby dealers to counter with similar cuts. Otherwise, they would face a large percentage loss in sales. Thus, price

---

[23] This type of analysis can be extended to determine the relationship between distance traveled and income position of purchaser. That is, do buyers with low incomes travel farther than buyers with higher incomes? It would also be possible to estimate the number of sales a dealer would lose to other dealers who sell his make and who engage in price cutting. In the author's opinion future research in automobile distribution should be directed in this direction.

shading on the part of one dealer is likely to spread throughout the total market. In the middle price class there is greater variability in buyers purchasing behavior, some of whom are sensitive to price differentials, while others are less sensitive because of attachments to a particular dealer, and so on. Price shading by one dealer will attract some, but not all, buyers from other dealers. Nearby dealers need not counter with similar cuts since they lose only their price sensitive buyers who make up a smaller percentage of total buyers in this price class. Thus, price shading on the part of one dealer need not spread throughout the market, or, if it does, it will spread at a slower rate.

Distance Consumers Travel to Purchase. How far are consumers willing to travel to purchase an automobile? Do most consumers travel four, eight, or 12 miles?

A special tabulation of dealer sales by census tract for the six months period from November, 1955 to and including April, 1956 had been previously made. These data show for each dealer the location by census tract of each individual or business who purchased a new car from the dealer.[24] By using these data, it is possible to determine how far consumers travel to purchase new cars.

A complete analysis of the data would require the services of a computer. For this reason, the analysis must be limited to selected Ford dealers.[25] In particular, the analysis was almost wholly restricted to those Ford dealers who have service or price reputations. For each dealership, the number of sales made to individuals and businesses located within four miles, between four and eight miles, between eight and 12 miles, and more than 12

---

[24] These data were kindly made available by Mr. T. M. Murphy, Director of Marketing Research, *Cleveland Plain Dealer.*

[25] The analysis could be extended to show (1) distance-purchasing-behavior of consumers by make of car purchased, (2) distance-purchasing-behavior by income class of consumer, (3) distance-purchasing-behavior of consumers in response to lower prices, and (4) differences in distance-purchasing-behavior of consumers of dealers with service reputations versus dealers with price reputations.

miles of the dealership was determined. Each total was then expressed as a percentage of total dealership sales.

The percentage of dealership sales which are made to purchasers located (say) within four miles of the dealership will depend on (1) price or service policy of the dealership, and (2) the distribution of the population around the dealership. Consider a dealership located in a central business district. Because few purchasers are located in the central business district, a small percentage of the sales of the dealership will be made to purchasers located within four miles of the dealership. Now, consider a dealership located in the suburbs. Suppose it is known that the purchaser is more likely to obtain a lower price at this dealership, and this attracts many purchasers from the city. Because of this, a small percentage of the sales of the dealership will be made to purchasers located within four miles of the dealership. In contrast to the previous example, this is because of the price policy of the dealership rather than its location. Therefore, before dealerships can be compared, they should be classified by location within the county.

Dealerships were classified into three groups: those located in the central business district, those located in other parts of the city, and those located in surrounding communities. For each dealership, the percentage of total sales of the dealerships made to purchasers located within selected distances from the dealership was also determined. Each dealership was also classified as to whether or not it had a price reputation (P) and/or a service reputation (S). Also shown is the number of Ford dealerships within four miles of the dealership. These data are presented in Table 58.

As noted above, the distribution of the sales of the dealership by distance from the dealership will depend on the location of the dealership. Approximately 70 per cent of total sales of those dealerships located in the city but not in the central business district was to purchasers located within four miles of the dealership. Of dealerships located in the central business district a smaller per cent of their total sales was to purchasers located within four miles of the dealership. The exact proportion apparently depends on the dealership's price or service policy. Note

TABLE 58. PER CENT OF TOTAL SALES OF DEALERSHIP MADE TO PURCHASERS LOCATED AT
SELECTED DISTANCES FROM DEALERSHIP (SELECTED FORD DEALERS)

	Number of Dealerships of Same Make within Four Miles of Dealership	Location of Purchaser, Miles from Dealership			
		0–4	4–8	8–12	Over 12
Dealerships Located in Central Business District					
Dealership A (P)	(4)	34	30	17	18
Dealership B (S)	(6)	64	25	9	2
Dealerships located in city but not in Suburbs					
Dealership C (P)	(3)	61	25	6	7
Dealership D (P)	(4)	63	21	7	8
Dealership E (S)	(4)	65	23	5	7
Dealership F (P)	(2)	69	22	5	3
Dealership G (P)	(6)	75	16	4	6
Dealership H (P–S)	(3)	78	18	2	2
Dealerships Located in Surrounding Communities					
Dealership I (P)	(1)	31	14	28	26
Dealership J [a]	(0)	48	29	13	10
Dealership K [a]	(0)	84	12	—	4

[a] Dealer not classified as having service or price reputation.
Source: Unpublished data supplied by the market research department of the *Cleveland Plain Dealer*.

that the dealer with the price reputation attracts a large percentage of its purchasers from a greater distance than the dealer with the service reputation. Further analysis would probably support this result.

A large percentage of the sales of most Ford dealers is to purchasers located within four miles of the dealership. However, it should not be inferred that consumers do not shop. In the city there are usually three or four Ford dealerships located within four miles of the purchaser (see Table 58). Thus, the consumer is able to obtain several quotations without traveling very far. Whether consumers do in fact shop is a different question. The Ford study suggests they do not. However, purchasing behavior may be quite different in Cleveland than nationally.

If the results of the Ford study are applicable to the Cleveland market, it would suggest most consumers do not travel more than four miles to purchase an automobile and, moreover, do not obtain many quotations from other dealers located nearby.

CHAPTER 7

The Relationship Between Dealership Size and Profitability

7.1. Introduction

The purpose of this chapter is to investigate the profit performance of automobile dealerships from 1940 to 1956. The relationship between size and profitability is of primary interest. Also, a time series study of profit rates shows the extent of the fluctuations in profit rates and reflects the time lags necessary before resources can be introduced into and withdrawn from the distribution sector.

7.2. Sources of Data

The Internal Revenue Service publishes profit data for selected retail industries. For the 1938–1947 period, financial data are available for the major group "automobile dealers, retail," which is composed of the minor groups, "automobiles and trucks, retail," and "parts, accessories, tires, batteries, retail." For the 1948–1956 period, financial data are available for the major group "automotive dealers and filling stations, retail" and the minor groups "automobiles and trucks, retail"; "parts accessories, tires, batteries, retail" and "filling stations, retail."

For the purposes of this study, financial data presented for the years 1940–1947 cover the major group "automotive dealers," which includes some corporations primarily engaged in the distribution of parts, accessories, tires, and batteries. For the years 1948–1951 and 1953–1956 financial data cover the minor group "automobiles and trucks, retail." This minor group includes all corporations primarily engaged in the sale of new and used automobiles as well as retail dealers with a subsidiary amount of wholesale sales.[1]

Other data showing dealer profit performance are available. The profit performance of General Motors Corporation car dealers and Ford Motor Company dealers has been released by these companies for selected years. Whitney has also calculated profit rates.[2]

7.3. Measurement of Size and Limitations of the Data

The Internal Revenue Service classifies corporations by asset size. Assets may not be the best measure of dealership size. Assets are related to automobile sales, but they are also related to service volume. In any particular asset class two dealerships may be found with the same sales volume. One may obtain x per cent of its total sales from car and truck sales. The other could obtain a smaller portion of its total sales from car and truck sales and a larger portion from service sales even though it is of the same assets size. There is the possibility that the product mix of dealerships is a function of asset size, and thus some of the variation in profitability of dealerships is due to

---

[1] Personal letter dated January 23, 1958 from Mr. E. J. Engquist, Jr., Director, Statistics Division, U.S. Treasury Department.

[2] Simon N. Whitney, *Antitrust Policies* (New York: Twentieth Century Fund, 1958) I, 513.

changes in product mix and not due to differences in size alone. In particular, the larger dealerships are more likely to provide a broader range of repair services. The dollar output of a dollar input is lower for service sales than for car and truck sales. Also, in the smaller markets investment requirements, as established by the manufacturers, are likely to be relaxed so that the dealer has smaller dollar input for every dollar of sales. Thus, one difficulty of using *Statistics of Income* data to determine the relation between size and profitability is the difficulty of holding the dealership product mix constant throughout the asset range.

Some dealers lease their facilities, whereas others own their plants. Thus, two dealerships retailing the same number of new units could be in different asset classes. This is another defect of asset data.

The profit rate-size relationship may also be distorted by the relationship between dealership size and dealership location. Price competition differs greatly from market to market. In particular, large dealerships are likely to be in city markets where there is a greater degree of price and service competition. The profit rates of these dealerships are likely to be unduly depressed compared to the profit rates of dealerships in smaller markets because of this. A superior method of determining the relation between profitability and size, would be to consider only dealerships in a given metropolitan area. In this way each dealership in the market would face similar demand characteristics. Unfortunately, profit data for dealerships within a given local market are not available. Although this may be one limitation of the data, it need not be serious. In Chapter 5 the number of units retailed per dealership in city markets was shown to be independent of the size of market. Generally, the number of units sold by a dealership in a small city market did not differ significantly from the number of units sold by a dealership in a large city market. Thus, some of the dealerships in the larger asset classes are located in markets where price competition is less likely. Hence it should not be assumed that all dealerships in the larger asset classes are located in large markets in which price competition is common.

7.4. Comparison of Statistics of Income with Census Data

The *Statistics of Income* data from 1940–1947 include corporate returns of new car dealers; used car dealers; and parts, accessories, tires, and battery dealers. From 1948–1956, *Statistics of Income* data were obtained from the *Source Book, Statistics of Income* and include corporate returns by new car dealers, used car dealers, and dealers with a subsidiary number of wholesale sales. To determine the extent of bias due to the inclusion of used car dealers, total receipts of new car (franchised) dealers, as reported by the Census, can be compared with the corporate receipts, as reported by *Statistics of Income*. In Table 59 total receipts in 1948 and 1954 of corporations in the minor group "automobiles and trucks" are compared with total receipts of corporations in the "new and used" (franchise) and the "used" (non-franchised) Census categories. Because a small percentage of used car dealers are incorporated, the bias which will be introduced by their inclusion in the *Statistics of Income* minor group "automobiles and trucks" is small. Incorporated used car dealers accounted for 6.0 per cent in 1948 and 3.6 per cent in 1954 of total sales by incorporated new car dealers and incorporated used car dealers. Census data indicate that incorporated new car dealers accounted for 60.0 per cent of total sales by all new car dealers in 1948 and 66.0 per cent of such sales in 1954. It would appear, therefore, that *Statistics of Income* data account for 60 to 66 per cent of total sales by new car dealers in these two years.

7.5. Profit Rates Over Time, 1940–1956

The total number of corporate returns, the total assets, and total receipts of these corporations from 1940 to 1956 are presented in Table 60. The rate of return (before income tax) on

TABLE 59. COMPARISON OF STATISTICS OF INCOME DATA WITH CENSUS DATA ($ MILLIONS)

	New and Used Dealers^a		Used Car Dealers		Total		Statistic of Income^b		Ratio of Census to Statistics of Income	
	Number	Receipts	Number	Receipts	Number	Receipts	Number	Receipts	Number	Receipts
1948:										
Corporations	14,339	9,579	1,850	615	16,189	10,193	16,393	11,096	.988	.919
All legal forms of ownership	43,999	15,953	16,874	2,441	60,873	18,394				
Receipts of corporations as a per cent of total receipts		60.0		25.3		55.4				
Corporations as a per cent of all legal forms of ownership	32.6		11.0		26.6					
1954:										
Corporations	15,869	16,571	2,029	639	17,898	17,195	18,380	17,476	.974	.984
All legal forms of ownership	41,407	25,108	20,140	2,424	61,547	27,532				
Receipts of corporations as a per cent of total receipts		66.0		25.6		62.6				
Corporations as a per cent of all legal forms of ownership	38.3		10.1		29.1					

a "New and used" Census category was changed to "franchise" category and the "used" Census category was changed to "non-franchise" category for the 1954 U.S. Census of Business.
b Includes corporate returns of new and used car dealers as well as dealers with a subsidiary amount of wholesale sales.
Sources: U.S. Bureau of the Census, Census of Business, 1948 and 1954; U.S. Treasury Department, Internal Revenue Service Source Book, Statistics of Income, 1948 and 1954.

TABLE 60. TOTAL NUMBER OF CORPORATIONS, TOTAL ASSETS, AND TOTAL RECEIPTS
1940–1952: 1953–1956, AUTOMOBILE DEALERS

Year	Total Corporations Reporting	Total Assets ($ millions	Total Receipts ($ millions)
1940	9,954	766	3,776
1941	9,964	856	4,452
1942	8,233	703	1,388
1943	7,295	590	1,231
1944	6,869	563	1,195
1945	7,506	661	1,391
1946	11,401	1,380	4,390
1947	15,119	2,348	8,586
1948	16,393	2,955	11,096
1949	17,181	3,080	12,793
1950	17,855	3,784	15,949
1951	18,150	3,965	15,655
1952	n.a.	n.a.	n.a.
1953	18,076	4,042	17,523
1954	18,380	3,977	17,476
1955	20,352	5,120	25,194
1956	20,489	4,668	21,652

Sources : U.S. Treasury Department, Internal Revenue Service, *Statistics of Income,* Part II, 1940 through 1947 ; U.S. Treasury Department, Internal Revenue Service, *Source Book, Statistics of Income,* 1948 through 1956.

equity, assets, and sales as well as average receipts per corporation from 1940–1956 are presented in Table 61.

Year-to-year changes in profit rates are large relative to changes in sales. The increase in profit rates from 1940–1941, 1949–1950, and 1954–1955 suggest most dealership costs are of a fixed or semi-fixed nature. Increases in demand permit better utilization of capacity. Additional resources cannot easily enter the industry in response to the change in profits. The franchise system prevents this. Profit rates cannot be quickly reduced through increased competition from new competitors.

The profit rates of automobile dealers during the 1942–1945 period are of interest for they give some indication of the profitability of dealer service operations. Since dealers were not retailing new automobiles during the war, their profits were primarily obtained from the sale of used cars, replacement parts, and service. There is no indication that dealers were losing money on their service operations during the war period. Moreover, their profits were higher than those of corporations classified in the

TABLE 61. PROFIT RATES OF AUTOMOBILE DEALERS, 1940–1956, ALL CORPORATIONS

Year	Return on Equity (before tax)	Return on Assets (before tax)	Average Receipts per Corporation ($ millions)	Return on Sales (before tax)
1940	10.8	4.6	379	.9
1941	24.8	11.0	466	2.1
1942	11.6	5.8	169	3.0
1943	17.0	10.2	169	4.9
1944	16.7	10.9	174	5.2
1945	16.4	10.2	184	4.8
1946	49.3	28.4	385	8.9
1947	55.4	33.8	568	9.2
1948	45.3	28.7	677	7.7
1949	23.4	15.8	745	3.8
1950	31.0	20.2	893	4.8
1951	19.3	12.7	863	3.2
1952	n.a.	n.a.	n.a.	n.a.
1953	7.5	4.7	969	1.1
1954	3.1	1.9	951	.4
1955	9.2	5.0	1,238	1.0
1956	4.7	2.6	1,057	.6

Source : See Table 60.

automotive repair services and garage category. The rates of return on equity of corporations in this category were 8.6 per cent in 1942, 12.0 per cent in 1943, 14.1 per cent in 1944, and 15.9 per cent in 1945. Thus the profit rates of auto dealers were persistently higher than the profit rates of independent repair corporations during the war period. There is little evidence that dealers have lost money in service operations. Service was profitable during the war, and there is no reason to believe it is not so now. Little support can be given to the argument that large volume dealers, who, it is claimed, do not offer service, and consequently do not lose money on service operations, can offer lower car prices than the service dealerships can. Furthermore, empirical verification cannot be mustered in support of the contention.

7.6. Number of New Units Retailed per Dealership of Dealerships in Each Asset Class

Returns from corporations with assets of less than $50,000 probably represent returns submitted by small repair shops and gas stations which also sell automobiles. These firms are probably located in small markets. A dealership with less than $50,000 in assets can hardly be considered a full-time automobile operation. Hence, attention will primarily be directed at dealerships with assets of greater than $50,000.

The average number of new units retailed per corporation of corporations classified in each asset class can be estimated, though the estimates are probably not very precise. In this way it is possible to relate the two measures of size, that is, assets and new units retailed.

From National Automobile Dealers Association data it is possible to estimate total receipts per dealership and total receipts per new unit retailed of dealerships retailing 1–149, 150–399, 400–749 and 750 or more new cars and trucks annually.[3] From *Statistics of Income* data, the total receipts per corporation of corporations in each asset class can be determined. Then, these corporations can be compared with those dealerships with equal total receipts, as reported by the N.A.D.A. An example will make this clear. In 1956 *Statistics of Income* corporations with assets between $250,000 and $500,000 averaged $1,801,000 in total receipts per corporation. The N.A.D.A. reported those dealerships which retailed between 150 to 399 new units in 1956 averaged $1,408,000 in total receipts, which is slightly less but close to the receipts per corporation of corporations with assets between $250,000 and $500,000 in assets. The N.A.D.A. reported these same dealerships received $5,120 per new unit retailed (in total receipts, that is, parts, labor, used cars, and so on). The receipts per corporation computed from the *Statistics of Income*

---

[3] See *Operating Averages for the Automobile Retailing Industry* (Washington, D.C.: National Automobile Dealers Association), reports for entire years 1954, 1955, and 1956.

data are approximately equal to the receipts per dealership computed from N.A.D.A. data. By dividing the total receipts per *Statistics of Income* corporation, that is, $1,408,000, by the N.A.D.A. figure of total receipts per new unit retailed, or $5,120, one can determine the average number of new units sold by a dealership in this asset class. In this case, it is 163 units. This process can be repeated for each asset class. The estimated number of new units retailed per corporation in each asset class in each year from 1954 to 1956 is shown in Table 62. Dealerships

TABLE 62. ESTIMATED NUMBER OF NEW UNITS RETAILED PER DEALERSHIP IN EACH
ASSET CLASS, 1954–1956

Asset Size Class (in $1,000)

Year	100–250	250–500	500–1,000	1,000–5,000	2,500–5,000
1954	173	423	882	1,562	n.a.
1955	181	430	1,055	1,336	2,542
1956	163	352	895	1,590	2,783

Sources : U.S. Treasury Department, Internal Revenue Service, *Source Book, Statistics of Income; Operating Averages for the Automobile Retailing Industry*, prepared by National Automobile Dealers (Washington : National Automobile Dealers Association), reports for entire year 1954, 1955 and 1956.

with assets of less than $500,000 are generally small dealerships, that is, they sell fewer than 500 new units. Dealerships selling over 1,000 units have more than $1,000,000 in assets. Thus large volume dealerships are in the larger asset classes. It is entirely possible that large volume dealerships are also service dealerships.

7.7. Relationship Between Profitability and Size

Unadjusted compiled net profit as a percentage of net worth is presented in Table 63 for each asset class, all corporations included. In the 1940–1941 period corporations in the $250,000–$500,000, $1,000,000–$5,000,000, and the $10,000,000–$50,000,000 asset class exhibited higher earning rates. In the 1946–50 period the rates of return of firms in the $500,000–$1,000,000 asset class exhibited the highest rates of return, and in the 1951–1956 period

TABLE 63. RATE OF RETURN ON EQUITY BY ASSET CLASS ALL CORPORATIONS, AUTOMOBILE DEALERS

Asset Size Class (in $1,000)

	Total	Under 50	50 100	100 250	250 500	500 1,000	1,000 5,000	5,000 10,000	10,000 50,000
N[a]	9,954	5,823	2,418	1,372	236	67	31	4	3
1940	10.8	(.9)	9.6	12.5	15.4	12.1	19.6	6.6	19.7
N	9,964	5,305	2,268	1,558	298	88	38	6	3
1941	24.8	12.8	22.6	26.1	28.2	23.9	35.7	13.8	43.6
N	11,401	4,327	3,231	2,809	767	208	47	10	2
1946	49.3	34.2	43.5	50.9	59.0	55.2	47.6	50.8	39.3
N	15,119	4,101	4,206	4,539	1,605	542	117	8	1
1947	55.4	31.0	42.3	54.7	64.9	68.1	55.1	41.2	25.1
N	16,393	3,331	4,290	5,589	2,175	796	204	7	1
1948	45.3	21.6	34.2	43.0	50.9	52.9	47.6	17.4	29.5
N	17,181	3,431	4,510	5,979	2,207	824	223	7	
1949	23.4	(8.1)	14.6	20.5	26.7	30.1	29.5	7.5	
N	17,855	2,813	4,355	6,474	2,694	1,137	372	9	1
1950	31.0	9.0	21.4	26.3	33.9	36.6	35.4	28.1	11.3
N	18,150	2,557	4,462	6,665	2,814	1,235	409	8	
1951	19.3	.1	12.3	15.9	20.3	22.6	24.1	18.8	
N	18,076	2,915	3,929	6,806	2,738	1,237	438	11	2
1953	7.5	(35.6)	(4.3)	3.2	7.6	12.1	14.3	13.3	19.4
N	18,380	3,185	4,190	6,654	2,696	1,229	416	9	1
1954	3.1	(40.8)	(8.9)	(.9)	4.3	7.0	10.6	3.6	(9.0)
N	20,352	3,309	3,827	7,315	3,459	1,790	640	88	4
1955	9.2	(35.7)	(1.1)	5.1	9.5	12.9	14.6	10.1	8.0
N	20,489	3,710	4,211	7,351	3,158	1,539	505	12	3
1956	4.7	(43.3)	(6.2)	1.9	5.2	7.3	10.1	4.3	15.2

[a] N denotes number of corporations in asset class.

Source: See Table 60.

the firms in the $1,000,000–$5,000,000 asset class exhibited the highest rates of return.[4] Throughout the period under study, profit rates increase with asset size and reach a maximum in the $500,000–$5,000,000 asset range. Then they decline with a further increase in asset size. Thus, the profit rate function is hump-shaped.[5]

Is there a relationship between stability in profit rates and asset size? Do larger dealerships find their profit rates to be more stable than the profit rates of smaller dealerships? Two measures of stability have been used. The first measures the percentage point change in profit rates from one year to another. The second measures the absolute value of the percentage point change in profit rates from the first period to the next period divided by the profit rate in the first period. Suppose the profit rate was 20.0 per cent in the first period and −10.0 per cent in the second period, an absolute difference of 30.0 percentage points. The percentage change in profit rates would be 30.0 divided by 20.0, or 150.0 per cent.

The percentage point change and the percentage change in profit rates in each asset class are shown in Table 64. In general, there appears to be more stability in the profit rates of large dealerships than in the profit rates of small dealerships. Possibly, this results from a greater emphasis on service by the dealerships in the larger asset classes.

Profit Rates of Income Corporations. There are few non-income corporations in the larger asset classes. There are many non-income corporations in the smaller asset classes. A comparison of the profit rates of corporations in the larger asset classes with the profit rates of corporations in the smaller asset classes

---

[4] A similar conclusion is reached if profits are expressed as a per cent of total assets. The peak in profit rates is reached in the $500,000–$5,000,000 asset range throughout the 1940–1956 period.

[5] The returns in the largest asset class may represent consolidated returns of several dealerships.

consists of a comparison of the profit rates of income corporations in the large asset classes with the profit rates of income and non-income corporations in the smaller asset classes.

TABLE 64. STABILITY IN PROFIT RATES AND ASSET SIZE, ALL CORPORATIONS,
AUTOMOBILE DEALERS

Asset Size Class (in $1,000)

	Total	Under 50	50 100	100 250	250 500	500 1,000	1,000 5,000	5,000 10,000	10,000 50,000
Percentage Point Change in Profit Rates									
1947–1949	−32.0	−39.1	−27.7	−34.2	−38.2	−38.0	−25.6	−33.7	
1950–1954	−27.9	−31.8	−30.3	−27.2	−29.6	−29.6	−24.8	−24.5	+7.2
Percentage Change in Profit Rates [a]									
1947–1949	57.8	126.1	65.5	63.4	58.9	55.9	46.5	81.8	
1950–1954	90.0	553.3	141.6	103.4	87.3	80.9	71.8	87.2	

[a] Absolute difference in profit rates from the beginning of the period to the end of the period divided by profit rate at beginning of the period.
Source : See Table 60.

A more stringent test for determining the existence of differential profit rates can be applied only by considering income corporations. There is some question of whether or not one should analyze income and non-income corporations when attempting to determine the existence of cost economies. If differences in profits rates result from differences in costs, with similar demand conditions given, then these differences in costs are better approximated by only considering income corporations. It can be argued that one reason for the increase in rates of return with increasing size is due to greater variability in demand conditions facing smaller dealerships. These dealerships may not have made adjustments to changes in demand conditions and are not in long-run equilibrium. They are therefore more likely to experience losses. As such, the static cost-size relation is better measured by considering the profit performance of income corporations.

Profits as a per cent of net worth by asset class for *income* corporations are presented in Table 65. In general, the maximum profit rates fall in the same asset classes as the maximum profit

TABLE 65. UNADJUSTED AND ADJUSTED PROFIT RATES OF AUTOMOBILE DEALERS, 1940–1956
Asset Size Class (in $1,000)

	Under 50	50 100	100 250	250 500	500 1,000	1,000 5,000	5,000 10,000	10,000 50,000
1940 U *a*	13.4	15.6	15.9	17.3	13.9	28.3	6.6	25.6
A *b*								
1941 U	22.2	25.6	27.6	29.1	25.5	42.5	13.8	43.6
A								
1946 U	41.5	45.9	52.2	60.0	56.3	47.6	50.8	39.3
A								
1947 U	38.6	44.0	55.6	65.3	68.6	55.2	41.2	25.1
A								
1948 U	33.8	36.6	43.9	51.3	53.1	48.2	17.4	29.5
A	38.5	45.6	52.8	58.2				
1949 U	20.7	22.2	24.3	28.5	31.0	30.0	11.0	—
A	26.8	27.0	29.3	32.9	33.3			
1950 U	25.7	24.9	27.7	34.2	36.8	35.5	23.7	11.3
A	33.6	34.5	36.2	41.6				
1951 U	19.9	17.9	17.8	21.5	23.2	24.5	18.8	—
A	20.3	23.4	20.4	25.5	26.9			
1953 U	14.8	11.2	10.6	12.7	14.7	16.0	16.4	19.4
A	21.5	16.7	14.1	16.2	16.8	18.0		
1954 U	18.1	9.8	9.8	11.1	11.0	13.5	5.8	—
A	25.4	13.6	12.7	13.1	12.5	14.5		
1955 U	22.9	12.7	11.9	13.6	15.5	15.6	10.1	10.2
A	26.7	19.5	16.2	17.2	18.5	18.0		
E *c*	(33.8)	3.0	8.2	12.5	15.5	16.9		
1956 U	19.0	11.3	10.4	10.5	11.7	12.6	8.1	15.2
A	31.9	14.7	14.7	13.4	13.6	14.6		
E	(37.5)	(4.2)	4.8	7.4	8.7	11.8		

a U denotes unadjusted profit rates of income corporations.
b A denotes adjusted profit rates, of income corporations, no adjustments made between 1940–1947.
c E denotes adjusted profits of income corporations plus deficit of non-income corporations as a percentage of net worth of income and non-income corporations.
Source: See Table 60.

rates computed from all returns. However, differences in profit rates between asset classes of income corporations are smaller. This is particularly true of late.

In review, an historical comparison of unadjusted profit rates of income corporations indicates the corporations in the $500,000–$5,000,000 asset grouping have persistently earned higher rates of return. However, differences in earning rates between asset classes have narrowed in the last few years. From 1951 to 1956 the profit rates of income corporations with assets between $1,000,000–$5,000,000 have persistently exceeded the profit rates of income corporations in the $250,000–$500,000 asset class by two to three percentage points.

Adjustment of Profit Rates for Officers' Compensation. Another test can be made to determine if profit rates differ between asset classes.

A comparison of the profit rates of income corporations in the smaller asset classes with the profit rates of income corporations in the larger asset classes is subject to another criticism. Income corporations may underestimate profits by overcompensating their officer-owners. A closely held corporation can lower its total tax liability by increasing salaries rather than paying higher dividends. Corporations of this type are more likely to be found in the smaller asset classes. Alexander has suggested that the dollar compensation per thousand dollars of assets of *non-income* corporations be used to approximate the market value of officers' and owners' services of *income* corporations.[6] Any excess of dollar compensation per thousand dollars of assets that income corporations pay their officers over that paid to officers by non-income corporations is considered a part of the profits of income corporations. This adjustment was made. Adjusted profit rates on net worth by asset class were computed for the 1948–1956 period. In several cases there were few non-income corporations and no adjustment could be made. Adjusted profits as a per cent of net worth by asset class are presented in Table 65. These figures are denoted by the letter A.

---

[6] Sidney Alexander, "The Effect of Size of Manufacturing Corporation on the Distribution of the Rate of Return," *Review of Economics and Statistics,* Vol. 31 (August, 1949), pp. 229–235.

There were few non-income corporations in the late forties. Hence little use can be made of the data for this period. In the 1953–1956 period the adjusted profit rate tends to rise slightly from the $100,000–$250,000 asset class to the $1,000,000–$5,000,-000 asset class. However, the differences, though persistent, are small and at no time are greater than two percentage points.

The conventional procedure is to combine the adjusted profits of income corporations with the deficits of non-income corporations and then to express this total as a percentage of the net worth of income and non-income corporations. The justification for this procedure is that small corporations are non-income corporations because there are economies of scale. The correct method of measuring these scale effects is to include the deficits of non-income corporations with the adjusted profits of income corporations and then to observe the relationship between size of firm and profit rate. These computations have been completed for two years, 1955 and 1956. They are shown in Table 65. In each year there is persistent rise in the profit rate until the $1,000,000–$5,000,000 asset class is reached. However, the increase in the profit rates from the $250,000–$500,000 asset class to the $1,000,000–$5,000,000 asset class appears to be modest. These data do support the contention that there are economies of scale in automobile retailing. However, they suggest that further economies appear to be modest once a firm has reached the asset size of about $500,000 which would be equivalent to a new car volume of about 600 new units annually. Further economies may be experienced as the size of firm increases, but they do not appear to be significant.

7.8. Summary of Statistics of Income Data

Several comparisons of the relationship between dealership size and profitability have been made. The unadjusted profit data indicated corporations in the $500,000–$5,000,000 asset category have persistently exhibited higher profit rates throughout the

1940–1956 period. A similar conclusion is reached if income corporations are considered. Large corporations have also shown an ability to avoid losses and have experienced less variability in profit rates than small corporations. In sum, these data are consistent with the contention that a dealership continues to realize economies until it reaches an asset size of $500,000 or retails 800 or more new units annually.

A somewhat different conclusion is reached if adjusted profit rate data of income corporations are considered. This is the most stringent test which can be applied to these data. Differences in adjusted profit rates exist, although they are small.[7] Hence a different conclusion must be reached if adjusted profit rate data are considered. These data offer weak support for the contention that there are economies of scale in automobile retailing.

Adjusted profits of income corporations can be combined with the losses of non-income corporations. Then profit rates for the group can be computed. This can be done for each asset class. This final comparison has some merit for it adjusts the data for the overstatement of officers' salaries but assumes that the losses of non-income corporations in the lower asset classes are due to their non-optimal size. This comparison was made. These data suggest that economies are experienced as the firm reaches an asset size of $500,000. Further economies though modest, are probably experienced as the size of firm increases.

Now consider the problem of dealership survival. It is clear that the larger dealerships are in a superior position. These dealerships are large both in terms of assets and the number of new units retailed. The large dealerships have persistently earned higher profit rates and have avoided losses when new cars sales have declined.

---

[7] In the few studies which have been made of profitability of other industries adjusted profit rates of corporations in the smaller asset classes are frequently found to be higher than the adjusted profit rates of corporations in the larger asset classes.

7.9. Dealer Profitability by Corporation

Profit rates of General Motors and Ford dealers were placed in the record during several recent Congressional Hearings. Profit rates on net worth (after taxes) for General Motors dealers are available for each year in the postwar period. The profit rates are given below.[8]

RATE OF RETURN ON EQUITY (AFTER TAXES), GENERAL MOTORS CAR DEALERS

1940	27.2	1950	42.4
1946	87.2	1951	24.6
1947	98.5	1952	15.3
1948	64.8	1953	14.40
1949	38.0	1954	19.04
		1955	13.81 (9 months)

Source: *General Motors,* Hearings before the Subcommittee on Antitrust and Monopoly of the Committee on the Judiciary, U.S. Senate, 84th Cong., 1st Sess., pursuant to S. Res. 61, Part 8, p. 4055; 4470.

Information was also presented which showed profitability of General Motors dealers by division. Profits as a per cent of net worth for the first nine months of 1955 for all dealers in each division, for "big city" dealers and for large volume dealers are presented below.[9]

GENERAL MOTORS DEALERS PROFIT RATE ON NET WORTH BY MAKE (FIRST 9 MONTHS OF 1955)

	Total Dealers	Big City Dealers	High Volume Dealers
Chevrolet (total dealers)	16.1	15.0	43.7
Pontiac (exclusive)	19.6	18.7	78.6
Oldsmobile (exclusive)	28.0	27.3	62.1
Buick (exclusive)	27.5	27.3	73.7

Source: *General Motors,* Hearings before the Subcommittee on Antitrust and Monopoly of the Committee on the Judiciary, U.S. Senate, 84th Cong., 1st Sess., pursuant to S. Res. 61, Part 7, p. 3687.

----

[8] The profit rates were computed from net profit which included the total net profit from all sources including dealer finance income. Personal letter dated April 30, 1958 from Mr. R. F. Schreitmueller, Manager, Dealer Organization Department, Sales Section, General Motors Corporation.

[9] Profit rates are based on net profits before income taxes.

These data suggest that profit rates are not significantly different between dealerships in large and small markets.

The Ford Motor Company reported their dealers earned 11.27 per cent return on net worth (after taxes) in 1954 and 16.28 per cent [10] return on net worth (after taxes) in 1955.[11]

The profit figures reported by the Ford Motor Company and the General Motors Corporation differ substantially from those derived from *Statistics of Income* data. After-tax profits as a per cent of net worth for all corporations and for income corporations, as reported by the Internal Revenue Service, are compared with the after-tax profit rates of Ford Motor dealers and General Motors dealers in Table 66.

TABLE 66. PROFITS (AFTER TAXES) AS A PER CENT OF NET WORTH, AUTOMOBILE DEALERS

	All Corporations	Income Corporations	General Motors Car Dealers	Ford Motor Dealers
1940	8.0	12.9	27.2	
1941	15.2	17.5	n.a.	
1946	32.4	33.8	87.2	
1947	35.7	36.6	98.5	
1948	29.1	30.1	64.8	
1949	14.8	17.8	38.0	
1950	19.2	19.9	42.4	
1951	11.0	12.3	24.6	
1952	n.a.	n.a.	15.3	
1953	3.0	7.9	14.4	
1954	0.0	6.9	9.04	11.27
1955	4.6	8.7	13.81 (9 mo.)	16.28

Source: Profit data for all corporations and income corporations. See Table 60. Source of profit data of General Motors Corporation dealers and Ford Motor Company dealers described in text.

It is important to see if these differences can be reconciled. The discrepancy apparently results from the method of reporting

[10] *Automobile Dealer Franchises,* Hearings before the Antitrust Subcommittee (Subcommittee No. 5) of the Committee on the Judiciary, House of Representatives, 84th Cong., 2nd Sess. on H.R. 11360 and S. 3879, pp. 386–387.

[11] Subsequent correspondence with Mr. R. S. McNamara revealed the net profit figures include dealer finance income. Mr. McNamara did not release the profit figures. Personal letter dated May 5, 1958 from Mr. R. S. McNamara, Group Vice President, Car and Truck Divisions, Ford Motor Company.

officers' compensation. A statement by (former) President Harlow Curtice reported that General Motors dealers in the postwar period had profits before taxes of over five billion dollars, after deducting over one billion dollars of owners' salaries and bonuses.[12] Thus, the ratio of profits before taxes to officers' compensation is approximately equal to 5. If the ratio of total profits before tax of automobile dealers to total officers' compensation of automobile dealers is computed from *Statistics of Income* data from 1948 to 1955; this ratio is 1.36. Thus, this indicates either (1) dealers overstate payments to officers on their income statements to minimize their tax liability, or (2) General Motors (and presumably the other companies) require their dealers to understate their officers' compensation when reporting to the General Motors Corporation and thereby overstate their profits. The former seems to be a better explanation than the latter since it is not clear what advantage the automobile companies would gain by overstating their dealer profits especially if these data are used to determine internal corporate policy.

If the ratio of profits before taxes to officers' compensation is assumed to be equal to 5, this ratio can be used to revise *Statistics of Income* profits upward. Profit rates can be recomputed. Then these profit rates can be compared with profit data reported by the companies to determine their comparability. Computations have been completed and the data are presented in Table 67. The adjusted profit rates more closely approximate the profit rates reported by General Motors. Major differences exist in the 1948–1950 period which suggest General Motors dealers earned exceptionally high returns in the early postwar period. Apparently, dealers supply different returns to the Internal Revenue Service than they do to the companies.[13] The profit rate data

---

[12] See "The Development and Growth of General Motors," statement by Harlow H. Curtice, President, General Motors before Subcommittee on Antitrust and Monopoly of the U.S. Senate Committee on the Judiciary, December 2, 1955, p. 17 (mimeograph).

[13] Usually an accurate separation of profits from payments to management cannot be made. In such cases the best way of comparing the relative profitability in distribution industries is to lump payments to management with profits and then to consider the total return.

TABLE 67. PROFIT RATES IN AUTOMOBILE DISTRIBUTION, A COMPARISON OF THREE INDEPENDENT SOURCES OF PROFIT DATA [a]

(all rates expressed as a per cent of net worth)

	Before Tax				After Tax			
	Statistics of Income [a]				Statistics of Income [a]			
Year	Reported Net Profit Plus Officers' Compensation (1)	Reported Net Profit (2)	Adjusted Net Profit [b] (3)	Profit Rates Reported By N.A.D.A. and Whitney [c] (4)	Reported after tax Profits plus Officers' Compensation (5)	Adjusted after tax Profits [b] (6)	After tax Profits General Motors Dealers [d] (7)	After tax Profits Ford Dealers [d] (8)
1938	12.6	-5.9						
1939	26.4	5.0					27.2	
1940	32.5	10.9						
1941	49.5	25.0						
1946	67.3	51.4					87.2	57.1 e
1947	65.6	55.4					98.5	
1948	62.1	45.3	51.8		45.9	35.6	64.8	
1949	38.0	23.4	31.7		29.4	23.1	38.0	
1950	45.9	30.9	38.3	34.5	34.0	26.3	42.4	
1951	33.3	19.3	27.7	25.8	24.8	19.3	24.6	
1952	n.a.	n.a.	n.a.	19.0	n.a.	n.a.	15.3	
1953	19.9	7.5	16.6	13.9	15.4	12.1	14.4	
1954	14.6	3.0	12.2	8.2	11.6	9.1	9.04	11.27
1955	21.7	9.2	18.1	11.1	17.1	13.5	13.81	16.28

[a] Statistics of Income data, from 1938–1947, include data for major group "automotive dealers"; from 1948–1955, it includes data for minor group "automobiles and trucks, retail."
[b] Adjusted by assuming the ratio of profits before tax to officers compensation was equal to 5.
[c] For 1950–1953 profit rates computed by Whitney from N.A.D.A. data; for 1954–1955 profit rates were reported by N.A.D.A. See Simon N. Whitney, Antitrust Policies, (New York: The Twentieth Century Fund, 1958) Vol. 1, p. 513.
[d] For source of data see Table 66.
[e] Before tax, "The Rebirth of Ford," Fortune (May, 1947), p. 207.

from the N.A.D.A. (column 4 in Table 67) data also suggest that the *Statistics of Income* data understate total profits. In each year from 1950 to 1955 the profit rates reported or computed from N.A.D.A. data are higher than the profit rates computed from *Statistics of Income* data. Hence, these adjusted profit rates are probably better estimates of the actual earnings in automobile distribution.

CHAPTER 8

Distribution as a Barrier

to Entry in the

Automobile Industry

8.1. Introduction

The purpose of this chapter is to make several quantitative estimates of the relationship between the sales of a hypothetical automobile company and per unit distribution cost. The term "distribution cost" has been defined narrowly. It is defined as the cost incurred by the company's dealers from the sale of the company's autos. It does not include the cost of operating zone and regional offices. In fact, the reader may prefer to think of distribution costs as those selling costs which are incurred by dealerships owned and operated by a hypothetical automobile company. If there are economies of scale in automobile retailing, there would be a reduction in unit dealership cost as the sales of the dealership increase. The automobile company will find its unit cost decreases as the volume of each of its dealerships increases. Similarly, if the company owned and operated each of its dealerships, it would find its per unit distribution cost decreases as the volume of its dealerships increases.

217

8.2. The Establishment of a Dealer Organization as a Barrier to Entry

It is important to know the extent of these distribution economies, for they may restrict a manufacturer from entering the automobile industry. However, it is easy to overstate their importance. An example will clarify this. Economies in distribution cost cannot act as a barrier to entry unless there are concurrently significant economies in production cost. To begin, suppose the economies of scale in the production of automobiles are insignificant, that is, a manufacturer would be at no cost disadvantage even though it accounts for a small fraction of total industry sales. In contrast, suppose the extent of the economies of scale in retailing is such that a dealer operating in a small local market must have a large share of that market in order to exhaust these economies. Under such conditions the dealer of the new entrant will have difficulty displacing existing dealers because of his high cost position. Often, the new entrant will not be able to secure representation in these small markets. However, in a large local market, the dealer of the new entrant will be able to realize the economies of scale in retailing without displacing a large share of the existing market. In the large markets the new entrant will have less difficulty in securing representation. Suppose there are enough of these large markets so that combined sales of the dealers of the new entrant are equal to the production requirements of one optimum size plant. The new entrant will not be at a cost disadvantage and will be able to persist in the industry even though it is only represented in relatively large local markets and not in relatively small local markets. In this case the probability of successful entry will depend on the proportion of car sales recorded in large markets. It can be seen that entry can be successfully made if the new entrant is able to secure enough sales in these large markets to enable it to exhaust the production economies.[1]

However, what if production economies of scale require an even larger plant? Then, the combined sales of the new entrant's dealers will not equal the production requirements of one optimum size plant. In order to survive, the new entrant will need additional volume. However, the additional volume cannot be easily obtained because of the difficulty in securing representations in small markets. In this case entry will not be successful because the combined sales of the dealers located in relatively large markets are not sufficient to exhaust the production economies, and additional dealers cannot be placed in relatively small markets to obtain additional sales. Hence, economies of scale in retailing can only be an important barrier to entry if there are concurrent and significant production economies.

It is possible the new entrant may be just able to survive; that is, the combined sales in the large local markets and some sales in small local markets may enable the new entrant to realize a large proportion of these production economies. The new entrant's existence, however, will be touch and go. The new entrant will be in trouble if several years of depressed sales are encountered. Also, a further increase in its market share will be difficult to execute. Thus, a new entrant may enter the industry and secure a small share of industry output and continually persist, not being able to increase its share but not losing its share unless it commits a major error in product design.

A new entrant will have other difficulties in establishing a dealer organization. These difficulties will increase the cost level of the new entrant's dealerships above the level of dealerships of established companies. Usually these difficulties originate elsewhere. Thus, the new entrant is likely to obtain less capable and less experienced dealers. Their locations may be inefficient for

---

[1] Entry can be made relatively easier by differentiation of product and particularly so, if the extent of differentiation permits the dealers of the new entrant to secure premium prices.

sales promotion activities. Each of these factors will raise the costs of the new entrant's dealerships. However, these difficulties are most likely to arise because of the existence of product differentiation. The new entrant does not secure capable dealers because these dealers are aware of the difficulty of making "captive" sales, that is, sales to owners of a different make of auto. The probability that a new entrant will successfully disrupt existing consumer brand attachments is low. Judging from past experience, the probability that a new entrant could increase its market share in a short time to 5 per cent of the total market is very low. Kaiser-Fraser was able to increase its market share from zero to 4.8 per cent in three years during the immediate postwar period, but the company was able to do this only because of unusual demand conditions and supply restrictions on the other producers. The last time a new entrant was able to increase its market share by more than 5 per cent in a short period was the dramatic success of Plymouth during the 1928–1933 period. The recent success of Rambler is due in large part to the tardy awakening of an established oligopoly to a change in demand conditions.

In summary, economies of scale in retailing can only be important as a barrier to entry if there are also significant economies in production cost. Whether there are in fact economies is an empirical question which can only be determined by an industry-by-industry study. It is also evident the difficulties the new entrant will have to overcome will increase if there is differentiation of existing products. In the automobile industry the strength of these consumer-brand attachments is likely to cause the new entrant continuous difficulties.[2]

---

[2] For other views on distribution as a barrier to entry in the automobile industry see Simon N. Whitner, *Antitrust Policies* (New York: The Twentieth Century Fund, 1958), Vol. 1, p. 474, and Joe S. Bain, *Barriers to New Competition* (Cambridge: Harvard University Press), pp. 301–308.

8.3. Summary of Procedures Used to Measure Economies in Distribution Cost

To begin, assume the sales of a hypothetical company account for 20 per cent of an annual 6,000,000 automobile market, that is, 1,200,000 units, of which 15 per cent or 180,000 units are sold in cities with over 500,000 inhabitants. Also assume this company has 200 dealerships located in cities with 500,000 or more inhabitants so that the average number of new autos retailed by dealerships in these cities is 180,000 ÷ 200 or 900 units. By repeating this process it is possible to estimate the average number of new cars retailed by dealerships located in each size of city.

By determining the relationship between the sales of each dealership and unit dealership cost, it is possible to determine the behavior of unit distribution cost as the total sales of the manufacturer increase. This can be demonstrated algebraically. Let

$$(1) \qquad\qquad ac_d = f(q_d)$$

be the relationship between dealership sales and per unit cost where ac_d is per unit cost and q_d is the volume of the dealership.

The average number of new autos retailed by dealerships in i^{th} city size class is

$$(2) \qquad\qquad q_d^i = \frac{\overline{S}\alpha b_i}{D_i}$$

where $\overline{S}$ is total industry sales, assumed constant, α is the proportion of industry sales accounted for by the company, b_i is the proportion of the company's sales recorded in the ith city size class and D_i is the number of dealerships of the company in the ith city size class.

Then, the total cost incurred by the company's dealerships located in the ith city size class while selling $\overline{S}\alpha b_i$ cars is

$$(3) \qquad\qquad C^i = (\overline{S}\alpha b_i)(ac_d)$$

or

(3a) $$C^i = (\overline{S}\alpha b_i) \, f\left(\frac{\overline{S}\alpha b_i}{D_i}\right)$$

The total cost incurred by the company's dealers located in all cities and places can be determined by summing over all city size classes; that is,

(4) $$\sum_i C^i = \sum \overline{S}\alpha b_i \, f\left(\frac{\overline{S}\alpha b_i}{D_i}\right)$$

(4a) $$\sum_i C^i = \alpha\overline{S}\Sigma b_i \, f\left(\frac{\overline{S}\alpha b_i}{D_i}\right)$$

Per unit distribution cost, *A.C.*, of the company is given by

(5) $$A.C. = \frac{\sum\limits_i C^i}{\overline{S}\alpha} = \sum_i b_i \, f\left(\frac{\overline{S}\alpha b_i}{D_i}\right)$$

That is, per unit distribution cost is a weighted average of unit dealership cost in the different population size classes. Total sales $\overline{S}$ are assumed constant. Given the dealer cost function f, it can be seen that per unit distribution cost, *A.C.*, depends on the distribution of car sales among the different city size classes, that is, on the b_i's. The behavior of per unit distribution cost, as the company's sales increase, can be determined by allowing α to increase and become a larger and larger proportion.

Therefore, to determine per unit distribution cost, it is necessary to determine (1) the relationship between sales of the dealership and per unit cost, and (2) the distribution of sales by size of place.

Relationship between Dealership Sales and Per Unit Cost. The exact relationship between dealership sales and per unit cost is difficult to determine without an exhaustive cost study. However, it is possible to make several plausible estimates of this relationship.

Two relationships between dealership sales and per unit cost will be made. The first estimate will be referred to as the "standard" estimate. The per unit cost of a dealership selling 800 or more new units per annum was set equal to 100. Per unit cost of a dealership selling 600 new units was estimated to be equal to 110. For example, if the per unit cost of the dealership selling 800 units was $500, then the per unit cost of the dealership selling 600 units would be $550. Once sales decline below 600 new units, per unit cost increases sharply. If the dealership sells 400 units, per unit cost is estimated to be $625. The "standard" relationship is presented in Table 68 and Figure 9.

TABLE 68. ESTIMATED RELATIONSHIP BETWEEN THE NUMBER OF NEW UNITS RETAILED AND PER UNIT DEALERSHIP COST

	Per Unit Cost Index	
Number of New Units Retailed	Low Estimate	Standard Estimate
100	130	140
200	125	135
300	115	130
400	110	125
500	105	115
600	100	110
700	100	105
800	100	100
900	100	100
1,000	100	100
1,100	100	100
1,200	100	100

Source : Estimated by author.

This relationship was estimated after four sets of data were studied. The study of current market representation policies in city markets showed that the average dealership selling a low price make retails approximately 800 new units per year. The number of new units retailed tends to remain constant as the size of market increases.[3] It would be possible to decrease the average size of dealership by placing more dealers in these markets. However, the manufacturers have not adopted such policies. There-

---

[3] See Chapter 5.

fore, it is likely smaller dealerships are less efficient than dealerships selling about 800 new units per year.

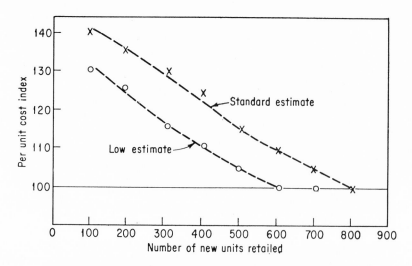

Fig. 9. Estimated relationship between per unit dealership cost and the number of new units retailed

Confidential cost data were studied. These data show per unit cost data for different size dealerships. However, no attempt was made to adjust these for differences in prices of factor inputs, in product mix, and so on. However, these data were adjusted for differences in location. Comparisons were then made of different size dealerships located in metropolitan areas. The relative cost position of dealerships of different sizes was estimated.

The study of the Cleveland local market indicated that the probability of survival was directly related to size. Furthermore, dealerships with fewer than 800 units per year experienced significantly higher turnover rates in the 1954–1957 period. However, the survival of several dealerships with 600 to 800 sales volume indicates that they are not at a large cost disadvantage.

The replies to the dealership questionnaire are not inconsistent with these cost estimates (see Appendix A). However, some dealers suggested that dealerships selling fewer than 800 units may be at no cost disadvantage with respect to larger dealers.

In general the "standard" estimate is consistent with these data. In several instances, however, there was some indication that a smaller dealership may be at no cost disadvantage with respect to a larger dealership.

For this reason, another estimate, hereafter referred to as the "low" estimate, will be made. This estimate will assume that a 600 unit dealership is at no cost disadvantage with respect to larger dealerships. However, dealerships with smaller volumes will be at a cost disadvantage which becomes progressively greater as volume declines. This relationship is presented in Table 68 and Figure 9.

Appropriate use of N.A.D.A. data and *Statistics of Income* data permits a crude independent check of these relationships. For the three years, 1954, 1955, and 1956, total receipts per corporation, and the profit rate on receipts (adjusted for overstatement of officers' and owners' salaries) were computed for each asset class from *Statistics of Income* data. The cost rate can be determined from the profit rate; that is,

$$(6) \qquad \frac{C}{S} = 1 - \frac{\pi}{S}$$

where S = total receipts, C = total cost, and π = total adjusted profits. The N.A.D.A. computes total receipts per new unit retailed of dealerships retailing 1–149, 150–399, 400–799 and 750 or more new cars and trucks annually.[4] It is also possible to estimate total receipts of dealerships in each of these classes. From *Statistics of Income* data total receipts per corporation of corporations in each asset class can be determined. Then, these corporations can be compared with those dealerships with equal total receipts as reported by the N.A.D.A. An example will make

---

[4] See *Operating Averages for the Automobile Retailing Industry* (Washington: National Automobile Dealers Association). Reports for entire year, 1954, 1955, and 1956.

this clear. In 1956 *Statistics of Income* corporations with assets between $250,000 and $500,000 averaged $1,801,000 in total receipts per corporation. Their adjusted profit rate on sales was 1.5 per cent. The N.A.D.A. reported those dealerships which retailed between 150 to 399 new units in 1956 averaged $1,408,000 in total receipts, the closest figure to the *Statistics of Income* figure of $1,801,000, and they received $5,120 per new unit retailed (in total receipts, that is parts, labor, used cars, and so on). The receipts per corporation, computed from the *Statistics of Income* data, are approximately equal to the receipts per dealership, computed from N.A.D.A. data. Then, it is necessary to make the strong assumption that the adjusted profit rate, computed from *Statistics of Income* data, is an accurate estimate of the actual adjusted profit rate of the dealerships in the 150–399 N.A.D.A. class. If this assumption is made, the adjusted profit rate can be used to estimate the cost rate by use of Equation (6). For example, in this case the cost rate is equal to 98.5, that is, 100.0 − 1.5. Multiplying this rate, 98.5, by the total receipts per new unit retailed, that is, $5,120, one obtains the cost per new unit retailed or $5,043. The reader should note this per unit cost figure includes all costs associated with the operation of a dealership including the purchasing of automobiles, parts, and so forth. By dividing the total receipts per corporation, $1,801,000, by the N.A.D.A. figure for total receipts per new unit retailed, $5,120, one can determine the number of new units sold. In this case it is 352 units. In this way a per unit cost figure can be associated with the total number of new units sold. This process can be repeated for each asset class. In this way several observations of per unit cost and new units sold can be obtained. These data are plotted in Figure 10.

Figure 10 indicates these estimates are not inconsistent with the previous estimates of the behavior of unit cost and dealership volume. However, these findings are subject to several limitations and should be accepted with much caution. In the author's view, the most important finding is that per unit cost does not appear to decrease significantly as volume increases above 800 units. In summary, the data plotted in Figure 10 do not contradict the estimates of the relationship between per unit cost and new units retailed.

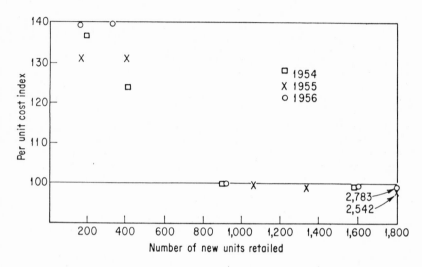

Fig. 10. Relationship between per unit cost and the number of new units retailed

The Distribution of Sales by Size of Place. As was noted earlier, per unit distribution cost depends on the distribution of automobile sales by size of place.

Data showing the distribution of car sales by size of city are practically non-existent. Existing data show the distribution of sales by size of metropolitan area. However, these data are not suitable for our purposes since the data showing the distribution of franchises by size of place, which will be used later, are by size of town or city. Thus, a compromise must be made and this will introduce some error in the estimates.

Consequently, chief reliance has been placed on data presented in the 1954 *Census of Business*. Data presented in the 1954 *Census of Business* show the distribution of total sales by new car dealers by size of place. The number of establishments and total sales of these establishments by size of place in 1948 and 1954 are presented in Table 69. The lower panel shows the per cent of total establishments and the per cent of total sales by size

TABLE 69. NUMBER OF DEALERSHIPS AND TOTAL DEALERSHIP SALES BY SIZE OF PLACE ($ MILLIONS)

Size of Place (Inhabitants)	1948		1954	
	Number	Sales	Number	Sales
Total	43,999	15,952.8	41,407	25,108.0
500,000 or more	2,354	2,596.3	2,214	4,036.4
250,000–499,999	791	1,139.2	948	1,857.9
100,000–249,999	1,380	1,443.6	1,387	2,185.4
50,000– 99,999	1,955	1,413.4	1,962	2,214.0
25,000– 49,999	⎰10,344	⎰4,096.1	2,973	2,445.2
10,000– 24,999	⎱	⎱	6,181	3,586.0
5,000– 9,999	6,693	1,652.1	5,897	2,491.6
2,500– 4,999	5,993	1,208.8	5,717	1,972.3
2,500 or less	14,489	2,403.3	14,128	4,319.2

Total	Per cent of Total			
	1948		1954	
	Number	Sales	Number	Sales
	100.0	100.0	100.0	100.0
500,000 or more	5.3	14.5	5.3	16.1
250,000–499,999	2.5	8.3	2.3	7.4
100,000–249,999	3.2	8.6	3.3	8.7
50,000– 99,999	4.1	9.1	4.7	8.8
25,000– 49,999	⎰20.4	⎰24.8	7.2	9.7
10,000– 24,999	⎱	⎱	14.9	14.3
5,000– 9,999	13.6	10.5	14.2	9.9
2,500– 4,999	13.6	8.4	13.8	7.9
2,500 or less	37.2	15.8	34.1	17.2

Source: *Census of Business*, 1948, 1954.

of place in each of these years. The distribution of sales by size of place has been relatively stable in the postwar period. These data also show the importance of the large city markets. Cities with 50,000 or more inhabitants accounted for 41.0 per cent of total sales of new car dealers in 1954. According to the Federal Reserve Board study of consumer credit, 65 per cent of total new car registrations were made in metropolitan areas and 26 per cent were made in central cities.[5] Thus, a large part of the automobile market is concentrated in the large local markets.

The percentages shown in Table 69 can be used as estimates of the distribution of car sales by size of city. Two objections may be raised to the use of these data to estimate the distribution of car sales by size of city. First, these percentages are based upon the total receipts of establishments classified as franchise dealers, that is, receipts from the sale of new and used cars, parts, and service. Small dealerships are known to receive a larger percentage of their total sales from the sale of parts and service. This has the effect of overstating the percentage of cars sold in the smaller markets. This is a valid objection. However, it does not necessarily mean these data are totally inadequate. The 1958 N.A.D.A. survey shows that dealerships selling 400 to 749 new units obtained 55.6 per cent of their total sales from the sales of new cars and trucks, whereas dealerships selling between 1 to 149 units obtained 48.8 per cent of their total sales from the sales of new cars and trucks, a difference of just 6.8 percentage points. Thus, the difference between large and small dealerships is not large.

A second objection is that the distribution of car sales by size of city differs by make and the Census data are biased because of this. In particular, the chief purpose of this chapter is to investigate the relationship between the sales of a company and unit distribution cost. For the most part, this analysis concentrates on a company producing an automobile in the low price class. Therefore, the desired relationship is the distribution of total sales of a low price auto by size of city. Census data show the distribution of sales of all franchise dealers. Since fewer middle price dealerships are found in the smaller markets, it is likely

---

[5] Consumer Installment Credit, Board of Governors of the Federal Reserve System, *Financing New Car Purchases,* Part IV (Washington, D.C.: Government Printing Office, 1957), p. 18.

that the use of the Census data overstates the sales of low price makes in the large cities. However, confidential data inspected by the author indicated the distribution of car sales by size of metropolitan area did not differ greatly between the low price class and the middle price class.

It is evident the two possible objections to the use of Census data to estimate the distribution of new car sales by size of place work against each other. One tends to overstate, and the other tends to understate the percentage of new car sales in the large markets.

The Distribution of Car Sales by Size of Place of a Hypothetical Company with Different Market Shares. The number of new cars sold by size of city (place) by a hypothetical company with 2, 5, 10, 20, or 30 per cent of a 6,000,000 unit total market is shown in Table 70. These estimates were derived by assuming the dis-

TABLE 70. ESTIMATED DISTRIBUTION OF NEW CAR SALES BY SIZE OF PLACE

Size of Place	Percentage Distribu- tion of Total Sales	Company's New Car Sales as Percentage of 6,000,000 Annual Market				
		2 Per cent	5 Per cent	10 Per cent	20 Per cent	30 Per cent
500,000 or more	16.1	19,320	48,300	96,600	193,200	289,000
250,000–499,999	7.4	8,880	22,200	44,400	88,800	133,200
100,000–249,999	8.7	10,440	26,100	52,200	104,400	156,600
50,000– 99,999	8.8	10,560	26,400	52,800	105,600	158,400
25,000– 49,999	9.7	11,640	29,100	58,200	116,400	174,600
10,000– 24,999	14.3	17,160	42,900	85,800	171,600	257,400
5,000– 9,999	9.9	11,880	29,700	59,400	118,800	178,200
2,500– 4,999	7.9	9,480	23,700	47,400	94,800	142,200
2,500 or less	17.2	20,640	51,600	103,200	206,400	309,600
Total	100.0	120,000	300,000	600,000	1,200,000	1,800,000

tribution of car sales by size of place does not change as the company's share of the market increases.

The Estimated Number of Franchises by Size of Place. The next step is to determine the number of franchises a company will need to sell a specified number of cars. The number of dealers a company will have and their distribution by size of city will depend on the total sales of the company. Obviously, it would be incorrect to assume a company with 5 per cent of the market would have as many franchises as a company with 30 per cent of the market. How can one estimate the number of franchises and their distribution by size of place that a company would have if it persistently accounted for (say) 2, 5, 10, 20, or 30 per cent of a 6,000,000 unit annual market? It is assumed that a company with 30 per cent of a 6,000,000 market would have the same number and distribution of franchises as Chevrolet; with 20 per cent of the market, the same number and distribution as Ford, with 10 per cent of the market, the same number and distribution as Dodge, with 5 per cent of the market, the same number and distribution as Pontiac and with 2 per cent of the market, the same number and distribution as Hudson. To summarize, it is assumed that a company would duplicate the market representation policies of the makes mentioned above as its market share increased from 2 to 30 per cent.

These makes were selected for two reasons. Other than Ford and Chevrolet, each can be considered a lower middle price auto. These makes most closely approximate the low price makes. Second, each make's share of the total market during the 1950–1952 period was approximately equal to the market share attributed it. For example, Dodge dealers with their share of Plymouth new car registrations accounted for 8 to 10 per cent of the market from 1950–1952. Pontiac accounted for about 6 per cent of the market during this period, and so on. The 1950–1952 period is selected for comparison because 1952 is the latest date for which the required franchise data are available. Consequently, the number of franchises of each make in 1952 would depend on the sales of that make during the 1950–1952 period.

The selection of the franchise policy of these specific makes should not bias the analysis. This can be seen by observing the number of franchises for each population size class as the market share increases. In Figure 11 the number of franchises of each

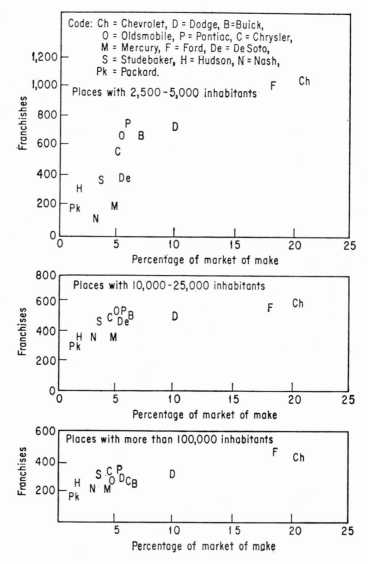

Fig. 11. Relationship between number of franchises and market share of make by size of place

make in 1952 has been plotted against the market share of the make in 1952 for selected sizes of cities (towns). There is little variability in the number of franchises once the market share of the make is known. Therefore, the selection of the specific makes, noted above, should not bias the results.[6] The distribution of franchises by size of place for Chevrolet, Ford, Dodge, Pontiac and Hudson are shown in Table 71. On the whole these data seem reasonable. There are some inconsistencies. For example, in the population size class with 50,000–99,999 inhabitants, the number of franchises declines from 132 to 117 as the market share increases from 5 to 10 per cent. By fitting curves to the data shown in Figure 11, a relationship between the number of franchises and market share could be established for each population size class. In this way the data in Table 71

TABLE 71. ESTIMATED RELATIONSHIP BETWEEN MARKET SHARE OF COMPANY AND THE DISTRIBUTION OF FRANCHISES BY SIZE OF PLACE [a]

	Market Share (Per cent)				
Size of Place	2 [b]	5 [c]	10 [d]	20 [e]	30 [f]
500,000 or more [g]	113	136	150	219	202
250,000–499,999 [g]	48	58	64	99	86
100,000–249,999 [g]	72	85	94	138	217
50,000– 99,999	91	132	117	148	136
25,000– 49,999	142	205	188	210	211
10,000– 24,999	376	536	523	583	592
5,000– 9,999	355	669	665	774	786
2,500– 4,999	308	768	719	1,107	1,136
2,500 or less	411	1,177	1,302	3,353	3,940
Total	1,916	3,766	3,822	6,626	7,216

[a] Franchise data based on 1952 figures.
[b] Hudson.
[c] Pontiac.
[d] Dodge.
[e] Ford.
[f] Chevrolet.
[g] Estimated from Census data.
Source: Trade List Department, Chilton Company.

[6] The number of franchises in the smaller towns may be under enumerated. Hence, the average number of new units retailed per dealership in these towns may be lower and unit cost higher. If so, the estimates of per unit distribution cost, to be presented shortly, understate the extent of the barriers to entry. However, dealerships in small markets are often able to lower costs by not providing as many services as do dealerships in large markets.

could be improved. However, these limitations do not appear important.[7]

The Average Number of New Units Retailed per Franchise by Size of Place. The average number of new units retailed per franchise by size place is shown in Table 72. The average num-

TABLE 72. ESTIMATED NUMBER OF NEW UNITS RETAILED PER FRANCHISE BY SIZE OF PLACE

	Market Share (Per cent)				
Size of Place	2	5	15	20	30
500,000 or more	171	355	644	882	1,435
250,500–499,999	185	383	694	945	1,549
100,000–249,999	145	307	555	757	1,233
50,000– 99,999	116	200	451	714	1,165
25,000– 49,999	82	142	310	554	827
10,000– 24,999	46	80	164	294	435
5,000– 9,999	33	44	89	153	227
2,500– 4,499	31	31	66	86	125
2,500 or less	50	44	79	62	78

ber of new units retailed per franchise in each size class can be computed by dividing the estimated number of new cars sold in that class by the number of franchises in that class.

8.4. The Behavior of per Unit Distribution Cost and Company Sales

The next step is to determine the behavior of per unit distribution cost as the company's sales increase. To do this, it is

---

[7] The author substituted Studebaker for Pontiac. Fewer inconsistencies could then be detected. However, the results of this analysis, to be presented shortly, are generally insensitive to this substitution.

Recently, the Chrysler Corporation announced that they would establish 4,000 Plymouth dealers most of whom are expected to sell Plymouths. Plymouth new car registrations plus the sales of DeSoto and Chrysler which may be attributed to these dealers would account for 10 to 12 per cent of the total market. This policy is consistent with the estimates in Table 71. See *Detroit News* (September 17, 1959), p. 1.

necessary to return and consider the two estimates of the relationship between per unit cost and the sales of the dealership.
Given (1) the relationship between per unit cost and dealership sales, (2) the average number of new units retailed by size
of place, and (3) the distribution of total sales by size of place,
per unit distribution cost can be estimated from Equation (5).
The procedure is straightforward though difficult to explain. For
any city size class, determine the average number of new units
retailed per franchise. This in turn determines the per unit cost
of dealerships in this population class (see Table 68). For example, if a company accounts for 20 per cent of the total market,
the average number of new units sold by each dealership in cities
with 500,000 or more inhabitants is 882. Since this is greater than
800 units, these dealerships are at no cost disadvantage; that is
the per unit cost of these dealerships would be equated to 100.0.
For each population class, the average number of new units retailed can be determined, and from this, the per unit cost of these
dealerships relative to the per unit cost of dealerships selling 800
units can be determined. The per unit distribution cost of a company with 20 per cent of the market can be determined by multiplying for each population class the relative cost position of the
dealerships in that class by the percentage of the total company
sales recorded in that class, and by adding these totals [see Equation (5)]. This procedure can then be repeated with one change.
The company is assumed to account for a different percentage of
the total market. In this way the relationship between per unit
distribution cost and total company sales can be generated.

Of course, every dealership which retails 800 new units per
year does not achieve minimum per unit cost. Some of these
dealerships will have higher costs, and some will have lower costs.
In practice, one should expect to find considerable dispersion in
the cost figures, even after an adjustment had been made for
dealership size. For a specified sales volume, there will be a frequency distribution of per unit cost observations with the mean
observation falling on the "standard" estimate. The distribution

arises from differences in entrepreneurial ability, differences in location, differences in product mix, and so on. Initially, the frequency distribution of unit cost observations of the new entrant's dealerships will be assumed to be identical with the frequency distribution of unit cost observations of the dealerships of an established firm. Granting this assumption for the moment, an estimate of the relationship between the per unit distribution cost and total company sales can be made. If this estimated relationship reveals the dealerships of the new entrant will be at a cost disadvantage, it can be inferred that this cost disadvantage will increase once the initial assumption is relaxed.

The relationship between per unit distribution cost and company sales is shown in Table 73. Two estimates of this relation-

TABLE 73. RELATIONSHIP BETWEEN COMPANY SALES AND PER UNIT DISTRIBUTION COST [a]

| | Per Unit Distribution Cost Index | |
Annual Sales of Company	Low Estimate [b]	Standard Estimate [c]
120,000	129	139
300,000	124	135
600,000	116	126
1,200,000	112	119
1,800,000	111	117

[a] Per unit distribution cost equals 100 when all dealers in all population classes operate at minimum per unit cost.
[b] Per unit dealer cost at minimum if dealer sales are equal or greater than 600 units.
[c] Per unit dealer cost at minimum if dealer sales are equal to or greater than 800 units.

ship are presented, one based on the "low" estimate and the other based on the "standard" estimate of the relationship between per unit cost and dealership sales. In each case an index of per unit cost is used as the dependent variable. Per unit distribution cost will equal 100 when all dealerships in all population size classes retail 800 units, in the case of the standard estimate, and 600 units, in the case of the low estimate, so that unit distribution (and dealership) cost is at a minimum. The data in Table 73 are plotted in Figure 12.

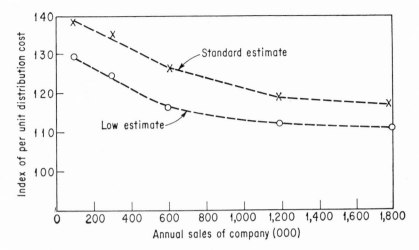

Fig. 12. Relationship between company sales and per unit distribution cost

It is evident that complete realization of distribution economies would require a very large firm. Even a company which accounts for 30 per cent of a 6,000,000 unit market has not completely exhausted these distribution economies. More important, a large part of the distribution economies are quickly realized as the company increases its market share from 2 to 10 per cent. Consider the "standard" estimate. A large part of the distribution economies are realized as the company's sales increase from 120,-000 units to 600,000 units. Further economies are realized as sales increase from 600,000 to 1,200,000 units. Beyond this, further economies are modest and gradually realized. A company with 10 per cent of the market would be at a moderate cost disadvantage compared to a company with 20 or 30 per cent market. Now, consider the "low" estimate. Again, a large part of the distribution economies are exhausted as sales increase from 120,000 to 600,000 units. The company with sales of 600,000 units is at a slight cost disadvantage compared to a company with sales of 1,200,000 or 1,800,000. All other things equal, a company with 10 per cent of the market should survive even if it was competing with one or more companies, each with 20 per cent of the market.

To translate these figures into actual dollar figures, an example has been worked out. The standard estimate of the relationship between unit dealership cost and dealership sales has been used. The per unit cost of the optimum size of dealership, that is, one which sells 800 or more units, is assumed to be $500. The relationship between a company's sales and per unit distribution cost is shown in Figure 13. Figure 13 shows that a large

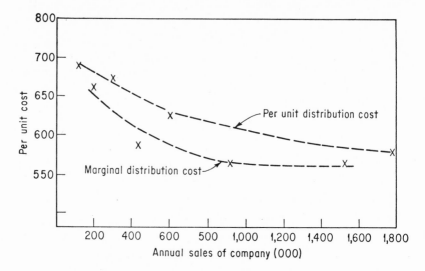

Fig. 13. Relationship between company sales and per unit distribution cost (minimum per unit distribution cost—$500)

part of the distribution economies are exhausted once the company's sales reach 1,200,000 units. Per unit cost for a company with sales of 600,000 would be $630. It would fall to $596, a decrease of $34, as the company's sales increased to 1,200,000 units. Per unit cost for a company with sales of 1,800,000 units would fall to $585, a decrease of just $11. Marginal distribution cost does not decrease significantly once sales increase beyond 900,000 units.

The Future of the Imports and Rambler. To summarize, economies in distribution cost are likely to extend beyond the point where production economies are exhausted. Most authorities believe that production economies are exhausted once 600,000 units are produced. There may be some additional economies as output increases to 1,000,000 units.[8]

Economies in distribution cost extend well beyond the optimum production unit. A company with 30 per cent of the market has not yet completely realized all distribution economies. Hence, it appears that the optimum production unit is smaller than the optimum marketing unit.

A large part of the distribution economies are exhausted once sales reach 600,000 units. A new entrant, retailing a low price auto, is not likely to be at a serious distribution cost disadvantage compared to larger producers once sales have been increased to 600,000 units. However, this represents 10 per cent of the market. It is unlikely a new entrant will succeed. The large volumes of Ford and Chevrolet make effective entry into the low price class difficult. A new entrant attempting to compete in the same price market as Ford and Chevrolet is likely to be at serious distribution and production cost disadvantages if volume is much less than 600,000. With the existing attachments of consumers to existing makes, it is unlikely a new entrant will be able to break into the low price market and boost sales to 600,000 units in any short period.[9]

It becomes more and more evident that successful entry into the low price market can only be achieved by a new entrant who is able to increase sales rapidly in a short period of time. Under what conditions is this likely to occur? A new entrant who is able to innovate continuously and to offer persistently a different product than existing producers might be able to achieve a rapid increase in sales. However, it does not seem likely that the new en-

---

[8] George Maxcy and Aubrey Silberston, *The Motor Industry* (Allen and Unwin, 1959), Chapter VI.

[9] This discussion has to a great extent neglected the middle price class. However, entry may be less difficult because the makes in this class have not as yet exhausted the distribution or production economies.

trant would be able to predict successive consumer response to product or style change correctly. One major mistake in product development or style change could be devastating. A somewhat different market situation may enable a new entrant to increase sales in a short period. A lag in the reaction of the established producers to a change in the composition of demand may allow the new entrant to increase sales before encountering the effects of the reaction of the established producers. The success of the Rambler in the late 50's is such an example. The events of the last few years have shown us how difficult it is to predict consumer demand and to realize how quickly consumer tastes change. If the established firms tend to be risk averters, that is, to wait until the future makes itself "clear," a new entrant may succeed in entering the industry. However, the new entrant will be adopting a very risky market policy for it is betting that it knows the way consumer tastes will change as well as the magnitude of the change better than the established firms in the industry.

Some may claim the success of the foreign autos in the United States in the last three years nullifies this analysis. Perhaps this is true, but, in the author's opinion, this view is not as yet warranted. Volkswagon and Renault have been successful in penetrating the United States market, but, their success is due to the failure of the American producers to forecast changes in American tastes accurately. The American producers will soon introduce their compact autos and, thereby, provide many features such as economy which are characteristic of foreign cars. The American compact autos are being priced a notch higher than the Renault or Volkswagon.[10] Nevertheless, the compact cars are similar to the foreign cars in several respects. It will be an interesting test case. The small foreign cars may be forced to relinquish their market shares. This would be consistent with the analysis presented in this chapter. The foreign autos may persist

---

[10] The author would not be surprised if Renault and Volkswagon are forced to counter by adding more quality and extras to their autos, for example more horsepower.

in direct competition with the American compact autos. If so, further analysis will be required to determine what errors have been made. The next five years or so should provide the necessary answers.[11]

The prediction for American Motors is more difficult to make. The sales of Ramblers have increased dramatically in the last few years. In 1960 new car registrations of Ramblers approached 440,000. This is under the estimated 600,000 units required for efficient distribution. However, if sales can be stabilized around the 500,000 figure in the next few years, the expansion of the total market in the near future should permit the sales of Ramblers to reach 600,000 units. If no obvious styling errors are made in the future, Rambler should be able to survive in the automobile market. The hedging on this prediction arises because the sales of Rambler have not yet reached 600,000 units and have increased to the 440,000 level in a very short time.[12] There is little information which shows the repeat performance of Rambler buyers. If this repeat performance is approximating the past repeat performance of other low price makes, there would be no reason to change the prediction. If the repeat performance of the Rambler is not measuring up to the past repeat performance of the other low price makes, it means that buyers shifted to Rambler only because the Big Three did not offer an economy automobile. Once they did, these buyers shifted back to the economy automobiles of the Big Three. This type of buyer behavior would mean that buyer attachments to the established automobile companies are much stronger than the data indicate and would suggest that successful entry into the automobile industry is virtually impossible.

---

[11] Many observers may wait in vain. The small car or compact car market now accounts for about 10 per cent of the total market, and it is divided up among many companies. Perhaps the small car market may not develop further and remain divided among several small producers. It is quite possible successful entry can be made if there are many small volume producers. However, entry may not be possible if there are one or two large volume producers.

[12] For the sake of this prediction and the future of the American Motors Corporation, let us hope that the 1961 recession proves to be a short and mild one.

CHAPTER 9

The Market Performance of Franchise Dealers in the Replacement Parts and Service Market

9.1. Introduction

The franchise dealer is one of several sellers of replacement parts and service labor. Replacement parts and service sales generally represent less than 20 per cent of the total sales of a dealership. The performance of the franchise dealer in the replacement parts and service market is of importance to the dealer and to the manufacturer.

Both the dealer and the manufacturer find the sale of replacement parts profitable. The manufacturer is interested in dealer performance in this market, for the dealer represents his primary distribution outlet. Each auto company manufactures a variety of parts, both for original equipment and for replacement needs. Some parts are purchased from independent producers for subsequent use either as original equipment or for replacement requirements. The independents sell to only one, or another, or both of these markets. To reach the replacement parts market, the auto companies and the independent parts producers sell to jobbers, warehouse distributors, direct retail outlets, oil companies (for their tire, battery, and accessory programs), and so on. Besides selling directly through their dealers, the automobile companies also sell through their own distributive organizations. For example, United Motor Service, a division of General Motors Corporation, has an independent distribution system. Such distribution organizations are used to reach the non-dealer service market.

Most industry observers believe the profit rate earned by the auto companies on the sale of parts and accessories has been relatively high and, at times has exceeded the profit rate on the sales of motor vehicles. The Federal Trade Commission reported similar findings.[1] In addition to being profitable, parts sales are more stable than motor vehicle sales and, hence, represent a more stable source of earnings for the auto companies.

The dealer is also interested in the parts and service market for the same reason as the manufacturer—it is profitable. If a dealer expects to operate a dealership for a long period, he will have to and want to offer service. True, some transient dealers open dealerships for a short period and neglect service. However, they are only interested in selling autos for a year or two at most. Also, there are not that many transient dealers. In such instances, the interests of the manufacturer and the dealer conflict. The manufacturer, with a longer time horizon, expects the dealer to have adequate service facilities and to develop the parts and service market. The dealer, being only interested in the sale of autos for a year or two, is willing to neglect service, but, in most instances, the interests of the manufacturer and the dealer do coincide.

The need to provide reliable service was quickly recognized by the companies early in the history of the automobile industry.

---

[1] U.S. Federal Trade Commission, *Report on Motor Vehicle Industry* (Washington, D.C.: U.S. Government Printing Office, 1939), p. 493.

The companies require their dealers to provide for adequate floor space, mechanics, and other service personnel. They evaluate the service performance of their dealer organization in terms of a concept referred to as "service absorption." The theoretical goal of each dealership is to attain 100 per cent absorption. This is achieved if the gross margin on parts and service sales offsets all fixed costs of the dealership. Sometimes officers' and owners' salaries are included in fixed costs and sometimes they are not. It is claimed that the parts and service operations "should pay" for all fixed costs of the dealership. This is a crude and essentially unjustified method of allocating all common costs to the parts and service department. It is claimed that a dealer with a high service absorption is more likely to lower prices and increase volume. Because of this allocation of common costs, the new car department appears profitable, while losses are frequently exhibited by the parts and service department since this latter department assumes the total fixed cost burden. Many have suggested this accounting procedure is adopted to encourage price cutting. Dealers often criticize this procedure, claiming that the accounting statements do not reflect actual costs of operating each department. It is doubtful whether devices of this nature actually are effective in inducing dealers to offer lower prices.

Service and parts sales have generally been profitable to the dealer. Nevertheless, discussions with company officials and dealers indicate a great deal of diversity in dealer emphasis on service. Many large volume dealerships (over 1,000 new units per year) have been criticized because they do not have facilities to service the cars they sell. In some instances, this may be a legitimate criticism. In my opinion, the point has been overemphasized.

The factory is interested in whether the car buyer returns to the dealership for service because the probability that factory parts will be used increases if the car is returned to the dealership. Whether customers of volume dealerships have their warranty and service work done elsewhere, and, if so, whether it is done at another dealership or an independent repair shop, is not known. There are many smaller dealerships in metropolitan area markets which may service the customers of the volume dealerships. If the service work is done at another dealership, it can be assumed that factory parts will be used, provided factory parts are suitable for the particular repair. In contrast, the probability that non-factory parts will be used increases if the car is serviced outside of the dealer organization.

9.2. Determinants of the Dealers' Share of the Replacement Parts and Service Market

In this section the determinants of the dealers' share of the replacement parts and service market are investigated.

The share of the total replacement parts and service market which is accounted for by franchise dealers will depend on

(1) the relationship between the annual repair expenditure per car and age of car;

(2) the relationship between the age of car and the place where service is performed;

(3) the age distribution of the total stock of cars.

Given these three relationships, it is possible to determine the dealers' share at any point in time.

It is generally recognized that repair expenditures per car increase with the age of car. Numerous surveys conducted by trade magazines indicate major repairs are experienced on cars in the four to ten year old age bracket. Cars less than four years old normally require minor repairs. Cars older than ten years are apt to be junked rather than repaired.

The relationship between repair cost per car and age of car is of interest because the outlet where cars are repaired also varies with the age of car. The probability that a car will be serviced by a dealer decreases as the age of car increases. In individual repair markets the new car dealers' share appears to be highest in the major repair market, somewhat lower in the adjustments and tune-up market, and lowest in the lubrication market. To summarize, repair costs per auto increase with the age of car. However, the probability that the car will be serviced by a dealer decreases with the age of car.

The relative position of the dealer, the independent repair shop, and the filling station in the repair market will depend on the age distribution of the *stock* of cars. Suppose the average age of the stock of cars is relatively low. Then, the dealers' share of the repair market should be relatively high. Conversely, the dealers' share of the repair market should be relatively low when the average age of the stock of autos is high.

To measure the performance of the dealer in the replacement parts and service market, it is necessary to correct for fluctuations in the age distribution of the stock of autos. Ideally, the dealers' performance in this market could be best determined by comparing several time series observations of the dealers' share during which the age distribution of the stock of autos had not changed. Another factor which makes time series comparisons difficult is the change in the product mix of repairs. Should tire, battery, and accessory sales increase in proportion to other repairs, they would cause the dealers' share of the total market to fall since their penetration in these repair areas is lower than in some other repair areas. Another example of such a change is the introduction of automatic transmissions, power brakes, and power steering during the postwar period. Consumers may believe that repairs connected with these systems can be best made by dealers.

As noted above, given these three relationships, it is possible to determine the fluctuations in dealers' share over time. Of course, this assumes these relationships are stable over time. Suppose the first two relationships are stable. Then, the dealers' share of the market would vary with the age distribution of the stock of autos, being higher, the younger the stock, and lower, the older the stock.

Unfortunately, little is known about the stability of these relationships. However, it is not likely the first two relationships will change greatly in any short period. The relationship between the age of car and the place where the service is performed does appear to be changing slowly over time. *Motor Age* reported that one factory believed the "zone of repair period," that is, the period in which new cars are returned to the original dealer for service, was increasing.[2] The reasons for this were that major repair jobs occurred at higher mileage, and a larger percentage of such sales was accident work where the dealer is the chief source of replacement parts. No adjustment for this change in the "zone of repair period" can be made. Quite probably, the change has been small and is, therefore, not likely to distort any time series comparisons seriously.

Less is known of possible changes in the relationship between repair cost per car and age of car. As the price of parts and labor has increased, repair cost per car have also increased, but this is not of interest. It is important to know whether the relative cost of repairing new models as compared to older models may have increased over time. This would tend to increase the dealers' share of the market. Unfortunately, the point can only be mentioned. Hence, it is necessary to assume these changes have been small and have taken place slowly over time.

As noted above, if the first two relationships are stable, the third relationship will determine the dealers' share of the market. The per cent of the total passenger car stock between three and ten years old and the weighted average age of autos in this age bracket are presented in Table 75. The per cent of autos in the three to ten year old age bracket decreased until 1952 and then continued to increase through 1956. The weighted average age of autos in this age bracket exhibited a similar pattern. Even so, the average auto in this age bracket was about two and one-half years younger in 1954 than it was in 1948. One might have expected to observe an increase in the dealers' share of the repair market from 1946 to 1952 and a decrease thereafter. Results

---

[2] *Motor Age* (May, 1959), p. 34.

TABLE 75. AGE OF PASSENGER CAR STOCK AND PER CENT OF PASSENGER CAR STOCK
BETWEEN THREE AND TEN YEARS OLD

Year	Per cent of Passenger Cars Between Three and Ten Years Old	Weighted Average Age of Passenger Cars Between Three and Ten Years Old
1947	39.1	8.0
1948	35.2	8.1
1949	31.1	7.7
1950	28.0	6.6
1951	23.1	4.9
1952	22.3	4.6
1953	45.0	4.9
1954	54.3	5.4
1955	57.1	5.9
1956	59.5	6.0

(1948 = 100)

1947	139	99
1948	100	100
1949	88	95
1950	80	81
1951	66	60
1952	63	57
1953	128	60
1954	154	67
1955	162	73
1956	169	74

Source: Automobile Manufacturers Association, *Automobile Facts and Figures* (Detroit: Automobile Manufacturers Association), annual issues.

from surveys conducted by Crowell-Collier indicate the dealers' share did rise and then did decline.[3] Between 1948 and 1955 there appears to have been a small net decrease in the dealers'

---

[3] The interested reader is referred to the annual issues of *Crowell-Collier Automotive Survey*, sponsored by the Crowell-Collier Publishing Company. Estimates of the dealers' share of the repair market are presented in the 1947–1951 and 1955 annual issues.

share of the service market. Thus, there is some evidence which suggests the dealers' share did increase in the immediate postwar period as the average age of the stock of autos decreased and then decreased as the average age of the stock of autos increased.

9.3. The Measurement of the Size of the National Replacement Parts and Service Market

The size of the replacement parts and service market is difficult to measure for several reasons. First, there are several data limitations. Second, many sellers perform wholesale-retail functions. Thus, double counting of sales is possible. For example, dealers sell replacement parts at wholesale and retail. Therefore, one must be careful not to double count these sales by simply adding the total sales of dealers to the total sales of (say) independent repair shops (as well as others) to determine the size of the market. Ideally, value added should be used. Unfortunately, these data are not available.

The size of the national replacement parts and service market can be estimated from data presented in the *Census of Business*. The 1948 *Census of Business* presents commodity line data by type of establishment. This information is used to develop a more detailed analysis of the replacement parts and service market. Unfortunately, the 1954 *Census of Business* did not present commodity line data. It is necessary to estimate parts and service sales of the principal competitors in order to develop estimates of the national replacement parts and service market in 1954. Prior to this study, Professor Davisson had used Census data to estimate the size of the national market. His study has made the author's task much easier.[4]

---

[4] Charles N. Davisson, *The Marketing of Automobile Parts* (Ann Arbor: University of Michigan, 1954). I have extended the analysis and included a wider range of services. This is by no means the only instance where I have found Professor Davisson's study useful. Limitations of the Census data are adequately discussed by Professor Davisson on pages 68–72 and are fully acknowledged.

The major competitors in the replacement parts and service market are franchised automobile dealers, used car dealers, gasoline service stations, independent repair shops, department stores, merchant wholesalers (sales to households), tire, battery and accessory dealers, and farm equipment dealers. Besides these groups, there are other miscellaneous groups who sell at retail, for example, second hand tire battery and accessory dealers. Other retail outlets principally engaged in other retailing classifications also sell some automotive parts and repair service sales.

By adding the total sales of replacement parts and service of each of these groups, an estimate of the national market can be made. This estimate would include some double counting, for example, sales of parts by dealers to independent repair shops [5] or sales by independent repair shops to dealers for subcontracted work. However, an adjustment can be made for some of these sales.

The eight groups sell a variety of goods and services, not all of which are automotive parts and services. Certain arbitrary decisions must be made to determine which products and services should be included in the definition of the replacement parts and service market. These decisions are important in the final determination of the size of the market and the dealers' share. For the interested reader, a detailed description of the procedures employed by the author is included in Appendix B.

9.4. The Size of the Replacement Parts and Service Market in 1948

The replacement parts and service sales of each group were computed and then added to determine the size of the total market. A similar procedure was adopted for each of nine Census

---

[5] For example, 15,610 General Motors dealers were wholesaling parts in 1954. See *General Motors,* Hearings Before the Subcommittee on Antitrust and Monopoly of the Committee on the Judiciary, U.S. Senate, 84th Cong., 1st Sess. pursuant to S. Res. 61, Pt. 8, p. 3866.

regions. These data are presented in Table 76. The market share of each group is shown in Table 77.

Before inspecting these data, several comments are necessary. In 1948, the Census classified each establishment by its principal source of revenue. If a dealer-owned-repair shop was at a different location than the dealership, it would be assigned to the repair shop category. Obviously, this would tend to understate the dealers' share of the market. Fortunately, this does not appear to be an important defect.[6] A similar problem arises in the midwest. Some farm equipment dealers also sell automobiles and often make automotive repairs. The new car dealers' share would be somewhat understated in these areas since many sellers of both farm equipment and automobiles may be classified as farm equipment dealers.

The total sales of replacement parts and service in 1948 are estimated to be $7,877 million.[7] The dealers' share of this market amounted to 42.1 per cent in 1948.

Adjustment for Inter-dealer Sales and Dealer Wholesale Sales. These estimates have been adjusted in a crude way for inter-dealer sales or dealer wholesale sales. A rough estimate can be made. Davisson reports one dollar of repair labor was sold with one dollar of parts in 1948.[8] The remainder of the parts and accessory sales by new car dealers is either over the counter or wholesale sales. Assume that one-half were wholesale sales. Then, wholesale sales of replacement parts would represent 3 per cent of total dealers' sales.[9] These wholesale sales by dealers

---

6 Mr. Harvey Kailin, Chief, Business Division, Bureau of the Census, suggested the number of dealer repair shops classified in the service trades to be insignificant, personal letter dated March 4, 1958.

7 This is a minimal estimate, see Davisson, *op. cit.*, pp. 68–72.

8 Davisson, *op. cit.*, p. 211.

9 A similar adjustment was made to the 1939 Census data. Dealer wholesale sales would be equal to 1.0 per cent of total dealers' sales. Data in the 1935 Census of Business indicated that 4 per cent of the sales of (new) motor vehicle dealers

TABLE 76. TOTAL SALES IN 1948 OF REPLACEMENT PARTS AND SERVICE BY COMPETING GROUP, UNITED STATES AND NINE REGIONS ($ millions)

Area	New and Used Dealers	Tire, Battery and Accessory Dealers	Gasoline Service Stations	Used Cars Dealers	Repair Shops	Department Stores	Wholesalers	Farm Equipment Dealers	Total [a]
U.S.	3,318.2	1,111.5	1,543.0	51.3	1,264.2	223.5	81.9	393.7	7,887.3
New England	180.4	53.0	98.6	3.6	79.2	8.2	4.2	4.2	431.2
Middle Atlantic	476.0	153.9	235.6	9.3	261.0	25.4	16.5	18.9	1,196.7
East No. Central	699.8	190.0	327.0	10.3	238.6	53.2	17.7	80.4	1,616.9
West No. Central	402.1	113.6	197.5	6.5	118.5	32.2	9.7	125.9	1,005.9
South Atlantic	418.4	125.5	180.7	5.3	145.8	19.8	8.9	25.0	929.4
East So. Central	198.0	63.6	86.4	2.8	61.4	10.6	3.8	17.4	444.1
West So. Central	365.2	143.7	148.4	3.9	117.2	22.2	7.4	49.4	857.3
Mountain	164.1	40.7	77.7	1.7	48.2	10.5	3.7	25.6	372.2
Pacific	406.3	127.9	191.9	7.4	194.4	36.1	10.1	46.7	1,020.7

[a] Columns do not add because of rounding or because of estimating method.
Source: *Census of Business, 1948.*

TABLE 77. MARKET SHARES IN 1948 BY COMPETING GROUP, NATIONAL AND REGIONAL MARKETS

(per cent)

Area	New and Used Dealers	Tire, Battery and Accessory Dealers	Gasoline Service Stations	Used Cars Dealers	Repair Shops	Department Stores	Wholesalers (retail sales)	Farm Equipment Dealers	Total [a]
U.S.	42.1	12.8	19.6	.7	16.0	2.8	1.0	5.0	100.0
New England	41.8	12.3	22.9	.8	18.4	1.9	1.0	1.0	100.0
Middle Atlantic	39.8	12.9	19.7	.8	21.8	2.1	1.4	1.6	100.0
East No. Central	43.3	11.8	20.2	.6	14.8	3.3	1.1	5.0	100.0
West No. Central	40.0	11.3	19.6	.6	11.8	3.2	1.0	12.5	100.0
South Atlantic	45.0	13.5	19.4	.6	15.7	2.1	1.0	2.7	100.0
East So. Central	44.6	14.3	19.5	.6	13.8	2.4	.9	3.9	100.0
West So. Central	42.6	16.8	17.3	.5	13.7	2.6	.9	5.8	100.0
Mountain	44.1	10.9	20.9	.5	12.9	2.8	1.0	6.9	100.0
Pacific	39.8	12.5	18.8	.7	19.0	3.5	1.0	4.6	100.0

[a] Rows do not add because of rounding.
Source: See Table 76.

should be excluded from the dealers' sales of replacement parts and services. Otherwise, they will be counted twice, once at the wholesale level and once at the retail level. Since this study is designed to measure the sales of replacement parts and service at the retail level, it would be incomplete unless an adjustment was made. An adjustment was made. The dealers' share of adjusted national market was 38.3 per cent.

9.5. Dealer Performance in Regional Markets in 1948

The dealers' performance in the replacement parts and service market varies among the nine Census regions. What factors determine the dealers' performance in these regional markets? Several hypotheses were tested. First, the relationship between the size of market and dealers' share was investigated. It is generally recognized that specialization in repair work by repair shops and others is only possible if the market size is large. If there are economies in repair services from specialization, there would be an inverse relationship between the size of market and the dealers' share. A rank correlation coefficient was computed. It was equal to —.45. The coefficient is not significantly different from zero at the 5 per cent probability level. However, the sign of the coefficient is negative and does at least suggest the existence of specialization effects.

Repair markets are local markets. The total sales of replacement parts and service within a region can be spread over many small towns and cities. Regional sales may be relatively high but

---

were made to other retailers. Wholesale sales of automobiles would make up the bulk of these sales. In 1954, 8,012 General Motors dealers did not participate in wholesaling. Only 2,966 sold 40 per cent or more of their parts at wholesale. General Motors officials claimed that in a great majority of cases wholesaling was a minor part of their dealers' total parts business. (See *General Motors,* Hearings Before the Subcommittee on Antitrust and Monopoly of the Committee on the Judiciary, U.S. Senate, 84th Cong., 1st Sess. pursuant to S. Res. 61, Part 8, pp. 3864–3866.) In summary, these data indicate wholesale sales of replacement parts account for negligible part of total dealers' sales. Furthermore, the 1948 estimate of 3 per cent is probably high.

not concentrated in urban markets. Hence, competition from independent repair shops and gasoline stations may not fully develop because each local market is small. Rather than use size of expenditure in the regional market as the independent variable, one can use the per cent of the region's population which is urbanized. Suppose a large per cent of the region's population is in urban centers. These centers would then be large repair markets, large enough to permit repair specialization and to overcome indivisibilities.[10] Thus, one would expect the dealers' share of the repair market to decrease as the degree of urbanization increased. A rank correlation coefficient was computed. The coefficient was equal to −.77 and is significantly different from zero at the five per cent probability level. Thus, there is an inverse relationship between the degree of population urbanization and the dealers' share of the repair market. This evidence does support the hypothesis that dealers have not been able to meet the competition of specialized shops and filling stations.

Another test of this hypothesis can be made. The 1948 *Census of Business* presents commodity line data for each group of competitors in 90 metropolitan areas, that is, over 50 per cent of all metropolitan areas. The size of the replacement parts and service market and the market share of each group of competitors was computed in each of 88 metropolitan areas.[11] Dealers' shares in metropolitan areas are compared with dealers' shares in non-metropolitan areas in each region in Table 78. In each region the dealers' share in the non-metropolitan areas was obtained by subtracting the total sales of replacement parts and service and

---

[10] Consider the following description of indivisibilities in equipment use. "For many types of equipment this rule of one is based on the fact that only one unit of each type of equipment is needed for even the larger shops. For example, one valve grinder is sufficient to take care of all the jobs that may be handled by a large shop, or only one brake tester or only one drive-on wheel aligning gauge may be necessary. Yet, these same pieces of equipment are needed in even small dealerships." See Motor Service Magazine, *Market Analysis of the Automotive Service Shop Industry* (place of publication not listed: Motor Service Magazine, 1951), p. 9.

[11] Two metropolitan areas were excluded because of data limitations.

dealers' sales of replacement parts and service in the metropolitan areas within the region from total sales of replacement parts and service and from total sales of parts and service of all new car dealers in the region. Inspection of these data indicates that the dealers' share in metropolitan areas is less than the dealers' share in non-metropolitan areas, except in the East North Central and West North Central regions. In the West North Central region, it is difficult to distinguish between a farm equipment dealer and a new car dealer. Many dealers in rural areas are probably classified by the Census as farm equipment dealers. Hence, the new car dealers' share in the non-metropolitan areas of this region will be relatively low. In general, these data are consistent with the hypothesis that the dealers' share of the repair market decreases with increasing urbanization and probably reflect specialization and/or availability effects.[12]

Although it is possible to explain dealers' performance in regional markets by considering the size of the market and the degree of urbanization within the region, it is much more difficult to explain the dealers' performance in individual metropolitan areas. The lack of data prevents any serious study. An analysis which relates the dealers' share in each metropolitan area to the age distribution of the stock of passenger cars in the area and density of population within the area would be interesting. Unfortunately, the age distribution of the stock of passenger cars is not available by metropolitan area. The dealers' share in the metropolitan area was not related to the size of repair market in the metropolitan area.

In summary, there is considerable support for the contention that the dealers' share of the repair market decreases with an increase in the degree of population urbanization within a region. Their share appears to be lower in metropolitan areas. Thus, as

---

[12] The preliminary surveys made by General Motors indicated buyers in rural areas returned to the selling dealer for service for a longer period than buyers in large metropolitan areas, personal letter dated March 5, 1958 from Mr. P. L. Paulson, Service Section, General Motors Corporation.

A COMPARISON OF NINE REGIONS, 1948
($ millions)

	Total Sales of Replacement Parts and Service	Dealers' Sales of Replacement Parts and Service	Dealers' Share of Total Market (Per cent)
New England	431.2	180.4	42.1
Metropolitan areas *a*	222.8	90.8	40.8
Non-metropolitan areas	208.4	89.6	43.0
Middle Atlantic	1,196.7	476.0	39.8
Metropolitan areas *b*	929.7	355.3	38.2
Non-metropolitan areas	267.0	120.7	45.2
Middle Atlantic (except NYC)	791.4	340.0	43.0
Metropolitan areas (except NYC)	524.4	219.3	41.8
Non-metropolitan areas	267.0	120.7	45.2
East North Central	1,616.9	699.8	43.3
Metropolitan areas *c*	760.4	333.2	43.8
Non-metropolitan areas	856.5	366.6	42.8
West North Central	1,005.9	402.1	40.0
Metropolitan areas *d*	296.1	127.0	42.9
Non-metropolitan areas	709.8	275.1	38.8
South Atlantic	929.4	418.4	45.0
Metropolitan areas *e*	270.6	111.8	41.3
Non-metropolitan areas	658.8	306.6	46.5
East South Central	444.1	198.0	44.6
Metropolitan areas *f*	119.8	46.4	38.7
Non-metropolitan areas	324.3	151.6	46.7
West South Central	857.3	365.2	42.6
Metropolitan areas *g*	221.0	84.9	38.6
Non-metropolitan areas	636.3	280.3	44.1
Mountain	372.2	164.1	44.1
Metropolitan areas *h*	106.6	41.0	38.5
Non-metropolitan areas	265.6	123.1	46.3
Pacific	1,020.7	406.3	39.8
Metropolitan areas *i*	686.4	269.3	39.2
Non-metropolitan areas	334.3	137.0	41.0

[a] Includes seven metropolitan ares.
[b] Includes eleven metropolitan areas.
[c] Includes sixteen metropolitan areas.
[d] Includes seven metropolitan areas
[e] Includes nine metropolitan areas.
[f] Includes eight metropolitan areas.
[g] Includes seven metropolitan areas.
[h] Includes four metropolitan areas.
[i] Includes twelve metropolitan areas.
Source: *U.S. Census of Business,* 1948. The data for metropolitan areas does not include all metropolitan areas since the Census did not provide commodity line data for all metropolitan areas.

the market grows in size, it encourages the entry of specialized shops and possibly more intensive geographical coverage by filling stations. The evidence suggests that these competitors have been successful in increasing their share of these repair markets. The implications of this analysis are of interest. To the extent that the car population becomes concentrated in metropolitan areas over time, the dealers' share can also be expected to decline with time. Inroads by repair shops and gasoline stations can be expected to continue in these markets.

9.6. The Size of the Replacement Parts and Service Market in 1954

Commodity line data (product mix data) were not collected in the 1954 *Census of Business.* Therefore, it is difficult to estimate the size of the replacement parts and service market in 1954. Nevertheless, several estimates can be made. To do this, changes in the product mix of each group of competitors from 1948 to 1954 must be estimated.

Changes in the product mix of each group of competitors from 1939 to 1948 was investigated. In most cases the changes were not large. However, there were some exceptions. In these instances the following procedures were adopted.

Product mix data for car dealers in 1939 and 1948 are presented in Table 79. In addition, parts and service sales as per cent of total sales for each year from 1954 to 1958, as reported by the National Automobile Dealers Association, are also presented.[13]

The N.A.D.A. data are subjected to error arising from nonresponse to their mail surveys. However, the constancy of the percentage figures and the decline in 1955 and the increase in 1958 provides some assurance concerning the accuracy of the data. At least, the changes are in the right direction. The de-

---

[13] National Automobile Dealers Association *Operating Averages for the Automobile Retailing Industry* (Washington, D.C.: National Automobile Dealers Association), annual issues 1954–1958.

TABLE 79. SERVICE AND PARTS SALES AS A PER CENT OF TOTAL SALES
(FRANCHISED DEALERS)

	Census	National Automobile Dealers Association
1939	12.7	
1948	20.8	
1954		17.4
1955		14.4
1956		16.1
1957		16.4
1958		18.0 (est.)

Sources: *U. S. Census of Business,* 1939 and 1948. *National Automobile Dealers Association Operating Averages for the Automobile Retailing Industry* (Washington, D.C.: National Automobile Dealers Association).

crease in 1955 and the increase in 1958 would be expected since 1955 was a large volume year, and 1958 was a low volume year.

Apparently, the percentage of dealership sales accounted for by sales of repairs, storage, service, and meals (non-merchandise sales) increased during the Second World War. Non-merchandise sales accounted for 5.6 per cent of total sales by new car dealers in 1935, 6.0 per cent in 1939, 8.7 per cent in 1948, and 7.4 per cent in 1954.[14]

These data suggest the product mix of dealerships changed during the Second World War. Before the Second World War, non-merchandise sales accounted for about 6.0 per cent of dealership sales. By 1948 this percentage had increased to 8.7 and had declined to 7.4 in 1954.

Non-merchandise sales can be used as an index of parts and service sales. Non-merchandise sales as a percentage of total sales decreased slightly from 1948 to 1954. Thus, it is likely dealership

---

[14] The source of the 1935, 1939, and 1948 figures is the *Census of Business.* The 1954 data were obtained from Mr. Harvey Kailen, Chief, Business Division, Bureau of Census through personal correspondence, letter dated March 4, 1958. The 1954 figure only includes those dealerships which excluded parts sales from service sales. Some returns included the sales of parts with service sales. The sales of parts and services accounted for 9.7 per cent of total sales for these dealerships. This low figure is difficult to explain.

parts and service sales as a percentage of total dealership sales also decreased from 1948 to 1954. This would be consistent with the N.A.D.A. data. The N.A.D.A. data indicate parts and service sales as a percentage of total sales were 17.4 in 1954 which is less than the 1948 Census figure of 20.8. By this check, N.A.D.A. data are consistent with Census data. Hence, the N.A.D.A. figure of 17.4 has been used.

For each group of competitors, the change in the product mix from 1939 to 1948 was determined and then projected linearly to 1954. A second method of estimating each group's product mix in 1954 was also adopted. The product mix of each group was assumed to be unchanged from 1948 to 1954. In several instances, product mix data were published in the 1954 *Census of Business* and were used.

Parts and service sales as a percentage of total sales of each group in 1939 and 1948 and the 1954 estimates are presented in Table 80.

Three estimates of 1954 national replacement parts and service parts market were made. The first estimate was obtained by using product mix estimates which would minimize the new car dealers' share. The second estimate was obtained by using product mix estimates which would maximize the new car dealers' share. The third estimate was obtained by using the product mix figures which prevailed in 1948 except where the 1954 Census presented product mix data (wholesalers) or where supplementary information was available (franchised dealers). The three estimates are presented in Table 82. The difference in the dealers' share between the highest and lowest estimate is 2.2 percentage points.

Adjustment for Inter-dealer Sales and Dealer Wholesale Sales. An adjustment for inter-dealer sales and dealer wholesale sales in 1954 should be made. Because product mix data were not collected by the 1954 Census, they cannot be used for the adjustment. Other data sources must be relied on.

In the 1954 automotive survey conducted by *Automotive*

TABLE 80. PARTS AND SERVICE SALES AS A PER CENT OF TOTAL SALES

Group	Actual 1939	Actual 1948	Estimate 1954
Used car dealers	1.8	2.1	$\left\{\begin{array}{l} 2.3 \\ 2.1 \end{array}\right.$
Gasoline service stations	19.6	23.8	$\left\{\begin{array}{l} 26.6 \\ 23.8 \end{array}\right.$
Battery dealers	85.0	74.4	$\left\{\begin{array}{l} 74.4 \\ 67.3 \end{array}\right.$
Farm equipment dealers	3.5 ᵃ	16.5	16.5
Department stores	1.2	2.1	$\left\{\begin{array}{l} 2.1 \\ .9^{b} \end{array}\right.$

ᵃ Sale of parts and accessories not reported separately.
ᵇ A recent study by Robert Entenberg suggests automotive parts sales by department stores were .9 per cent of total sales. Robert Entenberg, *The Changing Competitive Position of Department Stores in the United States* (Pittsburgh: Pittsburgh University Press, 1957) p. 172.

News, total sales of parts, accessories, and repair labor were reported as $156,345 per dealer. Of this amount, $65,002 represented customer labor sales.[15] Davisson assumed that one dollar of parts was sold with one dollar of customer labor in 1948.[16] *Motor Magazine* reported that 72 cents of parts were sold with one dollar of customer labor in 1956.[17] Suppose that 72 cents of parts are sold with one dollar of customer labor. Then, sales arising from repairs (including parts and customer labor) would equal $65,002 + 72/100($65,002) or $111,803 which is 71.51 per cent of total sales of parts, accessories, and customer labor. The remainder represents over the counter and wholesale sales. Assume that one-half of the remainder represent wholesale sales. Then, inter-dealer and wholesale sales would amount to $622.6 million ($4,368.8 × 14.25). This would represent 2.5 per cent of *total* sales of new car dealers in 1954. The low and high estimates of the national replacement parts and service market, adjusted for inter-dealer sales and dealer wholesale sales, are $9,812.1 mil-

---

[15] *How to Get Your Share of the Big Car Dealer Market* (Detroit: Slocum Publishing Co., 1955), p. 5.
[16] Davisson, *op. cit.,* p. 211.
[17] See *Motor Magazine* (December, 1956), p. 20.

TABLE 81. SIZE AND RELATIVE SHARES OF THE NATIONAL REPLACEMENT PARTS AND SERVICE MARKET, 1954

($ millions)

	Franchise Dealers	Tire, Battery and Accessory Dealers	Gasoline Service Stations	Used Car Dealers	Repair Shops	Dept. Stores	Wholesalers (Retail)	Farm Equipment Dealers	Total
Estimate 1	4,368.8	1,349.6	2,857.9	55.7	1,579.6	221.7	99.8	462.7	10,995.8
Per cent	39.7	12.3	25.7	.5	14.4	2.0	.9	4.2	100.0
Estimate 2	4,368.8	1,221.1	2,557.0	50.9	1,579.6	95.0	99.8	462.7	10,434.7
Per cent	41.9	11.7	24.5	.5	15.1	.9	1.0	4.4	100.0
Estimate 3	4,368.8	1,349.6	2,557.0	50.9	1,579.6	221.7	99.8	462.7	10,690.2
Per cent	40.9	12.6	23.9	.5	14.8	2.1	.9	4.3	100.0

Sources: *Census of Business*, 1939, 1948, and 1954; National Automobile Dealers Association, *Operating Averages for the Automobile Retailing Industry* (Washington, D.C.: National Automobile Dealers Association, 1954), p. 4.

lion and $10,373.2 million. Dealers' shares of these adjusted totals are 38.2 per cent and 36.1 per cent.

9.7. Changes in the Dealers' Share from 1948 to 1954

Unadjusted and adjusted dealers' shares in 1948 and 1954 are compared in Table 82.

TABLE 82. ESTIMATED CHANGE IN DEALERS' SHARES FROM 1948 TO 1954

	Unadjusted Estimates		Percentage Point Decrease
	1948	1954	
Dealers' Share	42.1	39.7–41.9	2.4–.2
	Adjusted Estimates		
	1948	1954	
Dealers' Share	38.3	36.1–38.2	2.2–.1

Source: See Tables 76 and 81.

As was noted above, it is difficult to estimate the absolute size of the national replacement parts and service market. Because of data limitations, it is likely that unadjusted and adjusted estimates understate the actual size of the market. This limitation need not be serious. It may mean that the absolute share of each group of competitors may not be accurate. However, the primary purpose of this chapter is to determine if changes have occurred in the dealers' share of the replacement parts and service market from 1948 to 1954. These data can be used to determine if any changes in market shares did occur.

In each year, two types of estimates were made: the unadjusted and adjusted estimates. Consider the unadjusted estimates. The dealers' share of the market has declined slightly; at most it has declined by 2.4 percentage points. Next, consider the adjusted estimates. Dealers' share of the market has declined at most by 2.2 percentage points. Thus, the best guess is that the dealers' share has declined slightly from 1948 to 1954. It is clear there has not been a major change in the dealers' performance.

Gasoline service stations are emerging as the dealers' major competitor. Apparently, gasoline service stations have increased their share of the market at the expense of each group of competitors. Each group has lost a part of the market to the gasoline service stations. The share of the gasoline service stations has increased anywhere from 4.3 percentage points to 6.1 percentage points. In general, these results are consistent with trade reports which have indicated the increasing importance of the gasoline service stations in the repair market.

The dealers' share of the national market did not decline by a large percentage from 1948 to 1954. However, it should not be inferred from this that new car dealers have been able to withstand the price and service competition of gasoline service stations, repair shops, and so on. What is surprising is that the dealers' share did not rise. Note that the dealers' share declined from 1948 to 1954 even though the weighted average age of cars in the three to ten year old age bracket declined from 8.1 years to 5.4 years. By 1954, the stock of automobiles was much younger than in 1948. As noted above, the younger the auto, the more likely it will be returned to a dealer for service. Therefore, the relatively small decline in the dealers' share from 1948 to 1954 is somewhat masked by the younger stock of autos in existence in 1954. Quite likely, the decline would have been larger had the average age of the stock of autos remained constant.

Viewed in this way, the decline in the dealers' share becomes more important. The inroads made by the gasoline service stations should not be considered insignificant nor attributable to chance fluctuations.

9.8. A Summary and a Prediction of the Future Replacement Parts and Service Market

In this chapter the determinants of the dealers' share of the replacement parts and service market have been specified. The probability that an auto will be returned to a dealer for service is inversely related to the age of car. Therefore, the dealers' share of this market will depend on the age distribution of the stock of autos.

The results from sample surveys indicate that the dealers' share of the replacement parts and service market increased and then decreased between 1948 and 1955. However, there was a net decrease between the two dates.

From Census data, the size of the replacement parts and service market in 1948 and 1954 was estimated. The unadjusted dealers' share declined from 42.1 per cent in 1948 to somewhere between 39.7 and 41.9 per cent in 1954. Thus, the dealers' share declined at most by 2.4 percentage points. The adjusted dealers' share declined at most by 2.2 percentage points. Thus, Census data indicate a small decline in the dealers' share from 1948 to 1954. The data do not support the view that there has been a large decline in the dealers' share. Some reports in the trade press have suggested the dealers' share has decreased substantially in the postwar period. Census data do not show this.

Gasoline service stations have become one of the principal competitors in the service market. They have increased their share of the market at the expense of each group of competitors. It will be interesting to see if this trend continues.

Some dealers have complained that service sales are not profitable. They have argued that large volume dealers with low overhead can underprice the market because they do not have to service the cars they sell. Suppose this argument is valid. Then, one would expect the dealers' share of the replacement parts and service market would decline because (1) volume-dealerships do not service the cars they sell or (2) dealers find service unprofitable and therefore do not actively develop the service market. However, there is little evidence which supports this contention. The dealers' share of this market has not declined by any large magnitude. Consequently, one must infer the dealers' share has not changed much because dealers have found it profitable to develop the service market.

The dealers' share of the replacement parts and service market is lower in metropolitan areas than in non-metropolitan areas. It appears that the dealers' share decreases as the size of the market increases. The gasoline service station and the independent repair shop have increased their shares in the metropolitan areas. There have also been some comments in the trade press of an increasing trend toward specialization by repair shops which may explain this decrease in the dealers' share.

These cross-sectional studies would suggest that the dealers' share of the replacement parts and service market will decline as the concentration of automobiles in metropolitan areas increases. The author would not be surprised to see the auto companies increase the parts availability to other sellers. More intensive coverage of the non-dealer market can be expected. It should be noted that General Motors has already moved in this direction.[18]

---

[18] United Motors Service has recently appointed Richfield Oil Corporation of California as a distributor for batteries, ignition, carburetor, and brake parts. Richfield has approximately 4,500 stations in six western states which is more than the number of General Motors franchises in these states. United Motor Service will also train Richfield mechanics. *Automotive News* (March 10, 1958), p. 31.

Dealer Replies to the Dealer Questionnaire

A.1. Introduction

Most of the conclusions which have been reached in this study have been made from an analysis of public or confidential data or from discussions and correspondence with company and N.A.D.A. officials. The author has held several discussions with some dealers and has read the testimony of dealers in several congressional hearings. However, it was felt that some information was being neglected by not obtaining a more systematic coverage of dealers' views. In particular, it was felt that evaluations by dealers could be used as an independent check of the results which had been derived by other methods.

With the cooperation of the N.A.D.A. and, in particular, Mr. Paul E. Herzog, Director of Research, N.A.D.A., a mail survey was conducted of N.A.D.A. members in eight metropolitan areas. The questionnaire was devised by the author and then reviewed by Mr. Herzog. This questionnaire was then sent to all N.A.D.A. members retailing Fords or Chevrolets in these markets. A copy of the questionnaire is presented in Table 84, page 274. The questionnaire was sent only to N.A.D.A. members who represent a large percentage of total franchise dealers, but not all franchised dealers.

Mail surveys are difficult to execute for two major reasons. First, it is difficult to state the questions simply so that the respondent is able to understand and answer them easily. Second, the non-response rate is usually high. In some instances, the response rate can be increased by successive mailings or by compensating the respondent.

As noted above, the dealer questionnaire was drawn up by the author. An attempt was made to state the questions clearly so that misunderstandings would be kept at a minimum.

A more serious difficulty was the low response rate. The questionnaire was four pages in length. It was one of the longest circulated by the N.A.D.A., and perhaps that was the reason for the low response rate. Two mailings were completed. The questionnaire was sent to 309 dealers. Fifty-five replies, or 18 per cent of the first mailing, were returned. Twenty-eight replies of the second mailing were received. In total, 83 replies were received for a total response rate of 27 per cent.

The response rate and the total number of dealers surveyed in each market area are shown in Table 85, page 278. The response rates in the smaller markets are generally higher. It would have been desirable to increase the response rate, but this would have involved considerable expense since further mailings were not likely to secure the desired result. It would have been desirable to sample the non-respondents to determine if they differed from the respondents. Again, this would have involved considerable expense. Hence, the findings must be considered tentative. However, the author feels that the findings are of sufficient interest and that they should be introduced.

A.2. Number and Size of Metropolitan Areas Surveyed

Before describing the results, a few comments on the selection of markets should be included. The markets included are large metropolitan areas. Markets A and B are among the five largest automobile markets in the United States. New car registrations in markets C or D are about one-half of the new car registrations in markets A or B. Markets C and D would be included in the ten largest metropolitan automobile markets. New car registrations in markets E, F, G, or H would be about one-fifth of the new car registrations in markets A or B. Markets E, F, G, and H would be included in the 25 largest metropolitan area automobile markets. Clearly, the sample of metropolitan areas only includes the larger metropolitan areas. Whether market and dealership characteristics differ in smaller metropolitan areas, is not known.

A.3. Description of Questionnaire

The questionnaire can be divided into three parts. The first part was designed to obtain basic information about the size and service characteristics of the dealership. The second part was designed to secure minimum information of market characteristics, that is, income of purchasers, repeat sales, distances buyers travel to purchase cars, demand characteristics, the extent of consumer attachments to existing dealerships, and the importance and effect of dealership service reputation. The third part of the questionnaire was designed to obtain several measures of the extent of economies of scale.

The remainder of this chapter will summarize the replies.

A.4. Economies of Scale

Generally it is difficult to estimate the relationship between unit cost and volume accurately by directing questions to businessmen. To obtain accurate estimates, it is necessary to undertake a cost investigation of major proportions. However, dealers can estimate and do know the number of cars which must be retailed to earn a profit. Dealers were asked, "From what you have observed in your metropolitan area, do you believe that a dealership selling your make and retailing the following amounts of new units per year can operate profitably in your area?" (Question VI-6.)

Dealerships in each market area were segregated into two groups: those in the city and those in the suburbs of the metropolitan area. The size of the dealerships in the two groups differs substantially. This can be seen by inspecting Table 86, page 278. Frequency distributions of new car sales in 1957 of each type of dealership were constructed. The median of each distribution is shown in Table 86. This procedure decreases the number of observations in each cell, but this classification is necessary since there is a large difference in the sales of the two groups of dealers. Clearly, the dealerships located in the city sell two to three times more new autos than the dealerships located in the suburbs.

Each return was studied and the minimum size dealership necessary for profitable operations, as specified by the dealer, was determined. Then, two frequency distributions were constructed for each market, one for each group of dealers. These data are reproduced in Table 87, page 279. Inspection of these data indicates that the dealer estimates of the minimum size necessary to operate profitably differ from market to market. Of the dealers located in the city, the median fell in the 800–1,200 class four times and on the 400–800 class three times. In general, dealers located in markets where the dealerships were relatively large selected the 800–1,200 class while dealers located in markets where the dealerships were relatively small selected the 400–800 class. Frequently, dealers selected the volume class just below the class their dealerships would be classified in on the basis of their 1957 sales. For example, a dealer who operated a dealership which sold (say) 1,300 new units in 1957 would select the 800–1,200 class as the minimum size necessary for profitable operations. This can be seen by comparing the median of actual dealership sales in 1957 in each market to the median of the minimum sales necessary to operate profitably. In each case, the median of actual dealership sales in 1957 is one class higher than the median of the minimum sales size necessary to operate profitably. Hence, dealer estimates depend on the actual size of dealerships in their markets. In some markets dealerships were relatively large. Dealers located in these markets selected higher estimates of the minimum size necessary to operate profitably. In other markets dealerships were small. Dealers located in these markets selected lower estimates of the minimum size necessary to operate profitably.

It is interesting to note that dealers in those markets where dealerships are large selected the 800–1,200 class and not the 400–800 class. It appears that small dealerships, that is, those dealerships with sales between 400–800, have not been able to operate profitably in those markets where dealerships are relatively large. Where small dealerships have had to compete with large dealerships in the same market, they have not been successful. However, dealers in the 800–1,200 class have been able to operate profitably.

Are these estimates consistent with the previous estimates of the extent of economies of scale in automobile retailing? In general, they support the previous estimates. Dealer estimates range from 400–800 units to 800–1,200 units. The mid-points of these classes are 600 and 1,000 units respectively. Then, in three markets, the minimum required size was estimated to be 600 units, and, in four other markets, the minimum required size was estimated to be 1,000 units. The dealer estimates are not precise enough to make exact comparisons, but, they do not contradict the estimates used in Chapter 8.

The profitability of a dealership may be influenced by differences in location and management ability. A hypothetical question was asked which attempted to hold location and management ability constant and then attempted to observe the relationship between the number of new units retailed and profitability. The respondent was asked, "If the quality of management were the same in two dealerships selling your make, one selling 400 new units per year and the other selling 1,000 new units per year, which dealership would be more likely to obtain a higher percentage return on its invested capital if both were lo-

cated on a main street in your metropolitan area?" (Question
VI-5.) Dealers found this question more difficult to answer. This
question received fewer responses. However, those that did reply
selected the larger dealership by a large majority (see Table 88,
page 280). Dealers located in the suburbs also selected the larger
dealership.

These responses are also consistent with the previous estimates of the extent of economies of scale. The author has assumed that differences in profitability result from differences in
costs. These differences could result from differences in the prices
charged. Larger dealerships could charge higher prices than small
dealerships and record higher profit rates, even though per unit
costs do not differ. However, it is generally thought that larger
dealerships do not charge higher prices, but rather, are more likely
to charge lower prices. Consequently, differences in profit rates
are likely to arise from differences in per unit costs. However, the
point can hardly be considered settled and warrants further study.

A.5. Repeat Sales

Do dealers located in the suburbs obtain a larger percentage
of repeat sales than dealers located in the city? The dealer was
asked to estimate the per cent of total retail sales in 1958 which
was made to customers who had previously bought a new car
from the dealership. (Question V-3.) Two frequency distributions of the percentage of repeat sales were constructed for each
market. The median of each distribution was determined and is
presented in Table 89, page 281. There are no significant differences between city or suburban dealers. This result is surprising.
The author expected dealers in the suburbs would obtain a higher
percentage of repeat sales.

A.6. Service Reputation and Price Premiums

Does a dealer with a service reputation charge higher prices
than a dealer without a service reputation? Are consumer at-

tachments to service dealerships strong enough to enable the service dealership to secure higher prices? Or, does a service reputation merely assure the dealer that the customer will return to the dealership to purchase but only if the customer cannot purchase at a lower price elsewhere?

The dealer was asked, "Does a better service reputation enable a dealer to get higher prices for his new cars than his competitors without as good a service reputation?" (Question V-7.) The replies to the question are presented in Table 90, page 281. Both city and suburban dealers reported service dealers were able to obtain higher prices than non-service dealers. This result is consistent with reports made by industry officials who note small differences. No attempt was made to determine the extent of the difference in prices. However, many dealers commented the differences were "slight" or "small" or that higher prices were obtained "sometimes" or "not often." One dealer summarized his views quite distinctly by noting "money is all that counts." Apparently, a dealership with a service reputation can charge higher prices, perhaps $50 or so more.

No relationship was observed between the percentage of repeat sales and the ability to charge higher prices by developing a service reputation. Those dealers who thought a service reputation enabled them to charge higher prices did not operate dealerships which obtained a higher percentage of repeat sales. Thus, some dealers who operated dealerships with a high percentage of repeat sales were able to charge higher prices, but some others were not able to.

A.7. Consumer Attachments to Existing Dealerships

If consumers are closely attached to existing dealerships, they can only be bid away by a new dealership if the new entrant offers lower prices or undertakes higher sales promotion expense. Do new dealerships face entry barriers?

The dealer was asked, "In your opinion, are car buyers strongly inclined to purchase new cars from existing dealership selling your make so that a new dealership would have to offer substantially lower prices or undertake higher sales promotion costs per new unit retailed in order to secure a share of the market proportional to its capacity?" (Question VI-9.) Dealer responses to this question are shown in Table 91, page 282. Dealer responses indicate a new dealership would have to overcome an entry barrier. Dealers thought the new dealership would have to offer lower prices or engage in higher sales promotion expenditure. However, existing dealers can be expected to overestimate the problems a new dealership will face. Dealers who have recently opened a dealership should be free from this bias. Therefore, the responses of all dealers who had been operating at their present locations for less than five years were selected. Of course, there were few dealers in this class. In fact, there were seven city dealers and ten suburban dealers. Four of the city dealers and six of the suburban dealers thought a new dealership would be at a price or cost disadvantage. Hence, these dealers do not consider the entry barriers to be as important as those dealers who have been in the automobile retailing for longer than five years. However, even those dealers who opened dealerships within the last five years thought a new dealer would encounter an entry barrier.[1]

TABLE 84. DEALER QUESTIONNAIRE

Section I: General Data
    1. Location of Dealership:
        Name of City
        Name of County
        Name of State
    2. Name of Principal Make Handled:
    3. How many years have you been retailing the above
       make?   _____ Years
    4. How many years have you been at your present
       location?   _____ Years
    5. Total Unit Sales of Dealership:

---

[1] Several dealers felt that a new dealer would be at a cost or price disadvantage for a year or two.

Number of Units Sold During Year

	1955	1956	1957	1958
Total New Cars (Including Fleet)	___	___	___	___
Total Used Cars	___	___	___	___
Per cent of Used Cars Wholesaled	___	___	___	___

Section II: Statistical Data

1. Dollar Value Of:

(End of Year)

	1955	1956	1957	1958
Total Assets	$____	$____	$____	$____
Net Worth	$____	$____	$____	$____

Section III: Physical Data

1. Do you own or rent your building? (Please check one)   ☐ Own   ☐ Rent
2. How many full-time service mechanics do you normally employ in your service department?   _____ Service Mechanics
3. How many service stalls do you currently have in your service department?   _____ Service Stalls

Section IV: Market Data

1. What were the total new car registrations of your make in your metropolitan area in each of the last four years?

   This includes: _____, | 1955 | 1956 | 1957 | 1958 |

   _____, _____ Counties.
2. How many dealers are currently selling your make in your metropolitan area?   _____ Dealers
3. Of the dealers selling your make in your metropolitan area, estimate the number of new cars retailed by the largest dealer in 1958   _____ Units

Section V: Economic Characteristics of Dealership

1. Is your dealership located in: (Please check one)
   ☐ Central business district
   ☐ Outside of central business district but not in suburbs
   ☐ In suburbs
   ☐ Other (please specify) _____
2. Is your dealership located in an area where most families have incomes of:
   ☐ less than $5,000   ☐ $5,000–$9,999   ☐ $10,000 or more

3. Please estimate what per cent of your total retail car sales in 1958 was sold to customers who had previously bought a new car from your dealership.

_____ Per cent

4. In your opinion, do you have a larger per cent of repeat customers than most other dealers selling your make in your metropolitan area? □ Yes □ No

5. If you believe you have a larger per cent of repeat customers than most other dealers, is this because: (Please check one)

   □ You have a better reputation for service than other dealers

   □ You generally sell your cars at a lower gross profit than other dealers selling your make

   □ Other (please specify) _____

6. Do you believe that dealerships with good service reputations win greater customer loyalty than dealerships without good service reputations? □ Yes □ No

7. Does a better service reputation enable a dealer to get higher prices for his new cars than his competitors without as good a service reputation? □ Yes □ No

8. How far do you believe the average customer will travel to purchase a new auto from a dealer? (Please check one)
   □ Less than 5 miles   □ 5–10 miles   □ More than 10 miles

9. If you believe that over 50 per cent of your 1958 retail sales were made to customers who live more than 5 miles from your dealership, is this: (Please check one)

   □ Because your dealership is located in a business district where many of your customers work but do not live.

   □ Because you generally sell your cars at a lower gross profit than other dealers selling your make.

   □ Because you generally find it more profitable to advertise more than other dealers selling your make.

   □ Because you have a better service reputation than other dealers selling your make.

Section VI: Efficiency in Automobile Distribution

1. Would you regard your chief competitors as: (Please check one)
   □ (a) Other dealers selling your make
   □ (b) Dealers selling another make in your price class
   □ (c) No difference between (a) or (b)

2. If you sold your new cars at a slightly higher price than other dealers selling your make, would you lose the greater part of your customers? □ Yes □ No

3. If you were selling your new cars at slightly lower prices than other dealers selling your make, would you take the greater part of their customers away from them? ☐ Yes ☐ No

4. Have you a group of regular customers who purchase new cars from you because they have confidence in you and are not very sensitive to price differentials? ☐ Yes ☐ No

5. If the quality of management were the same in two dealerships selling your make, one selling 400 new units per year and the other selling 1,000 new units per year, which dealership would be more likely to obtain a higher percentage return on its invested capital if both were located on a main street in your metropolitan area?

   ☐ Dealership selling 400 new units per year

   ☐ Dealership selling 1,000 new units per year

   ☐ No difference

6. From what you have observed in your metropolitan area, do you believe that a dealership selling your make and retailing the following amounts of new units per year can operate profitably in your area?

   Fewer than 400 ☐ Yes ☐ No   Between 800–1,199 ☐ Yes ☐ No

   Between 400–799 ☐ Yes ☐ No   More than 1,200   ☐ Yes ☐ No

7. Which one of the following dealerships do you think would have been the most successful financially during a poor new car selling year? (Please check one of the four blocks)

	Dealership Selling Less Than 500 New Units Per Year	Dealership Selling 500 or More New Units Per Year
Dealership generally getting lower parts and customer labor sales per new unit retailed.		
Dealership generally getting higher parts and customer labor sales per new unit retailed.		

8. In the last four years, in your market area, which of the following size dealerships has had the greatest ownership turnover? (Of your own make only) (Please check one):

   ☐ Less than 400 new units per year

   ☐ 400–799 new units per year

   ☐ 800–1,199 new units per year

   ☐ 1,200 or more new units per year

9. In your opinion, are car buyers strongly inclined to purchase new cars from existing dealerships selling your make so that a new dealership would have to offer substantially lower prices or undertake higher sales promotion costs per new unit retailed in order to secure a share of the market proportional to its capacity? ☐ Yes ☐ No

TABLE 85. NUMBER OF DEALERS SURVEYED AND RESPONSE RATE AFTER SECOND MAILING

Market	Total Dealers Surveyed	Response Rate (Per cent)
A	93	23
B	80	12
C	49	35
D	36	36
E	13	46
F	9	44
G	14	57
H	15	27
Total	309	27

TABLE 86. MEDIAN OF SALES IN 1957 OF DEALERSHIPS LOCATED IN MARKETS SURVEYED
(New Units Retailed)

Market	Dealerships in Central Business District or within City Limits (Units)	Dealerships in Suburbs (Units)
A	800–1,200	400
B	1,200+	400
C	1,200+	400–800
D	800–1,200	0–400
E	1,200+	a
F	1,200+	b
G	800–1,200	a
H	a	400–800

a Denotes no observations.
b Denotes too few observations.

TABLE 87. MINIMUM NUMBER OF NEW UNITS RETAILED NECESSARY TO OPERATE
PROFITABLY—FREQUENCY DISTRIBUTION OF DEALER REPLIES

New Units Per Year

Market	0–400	400–800	800–1,200	1,200 or more	Median
Dealerships located in city:					
A	1	6	2	—	400– 800
B	—	—	5	1	800–1,200
C	—	2	5	2	800–1,200
D	1	5	4	—	400– 800
E	—	—	3	1	800–1,200
F	—	—	2	2	800–1,200
G	—	4	1	1	400– 800
H					[b]
Total	2	17	23[a]	7	800–1,200
Dealerships located in suburbs:					
A	7	3	2	—	000– 400
B	1	2	1	—	400– 800
C	5	2	—	—	000– 400
D	1	3	—	—	400– 800
E					[b]
F					[b]
G					[b]
H	3	—	—	—	000– 400
Total	20[a]	10	3	—	000– 400

[a] Columns may not add. All returns included in totals.
[b] Denotes too few observations.

TABLE 88. DEALER ESTIMATES OF THE SIZE OF DEALERSHIP WITH HIGHEST PROFIT RATE—
NUMBER OF RESPONSES

Size of Dealership with Highest Profit Rate
(see Question VI-5)

Markets	Dealership Selling 400 New Units per Year or "No Difference"	Dealership Selling 1,000 New Units per Year
Dealerships located in city:		
A	3	7
B	—	6
C	—	7
D	4	5
E	1	3
F	—	4
G	—	6
H	a	a
Total	8	39 b
Dealerships located in suburbs:		
A	4	5
B	1	2
C	3	6
D	2	1
E	a	a
F	a	a
G	a	a
H	—	3
Total	11 b	19 b

a Denotes too few observations.
b Columns may not add. All returns included in totals.

TABLE 89. REPEAT SALES AS A PERCENTAGE OF TOTAL SALES
(Median Percentage)

Market	Dealerships Located in City	Dealerships Located in Suburbs
A	40–50	40–50
B	50–60	50–60
C	40–50	40–50
D	40–50	40–50
E	a	a
F	a	a
G	40–50	a
H	a	a

TABLE 90. RELATIONSHIP BETWEEN SERVICE REPUTATION AND PRICE
Premiums "Do Dealerships with Service Reputations Charge
Higher Prices than Dealership without Service Reputations?"

Market	Dealerships Located in City		Dealerships Located in Suburbs	
	Yes	No	Yes	No
A	6	2	8	5
B	3	3	1	3
C	5	4	5	4
D	7	3	4	0
E	3	1	2	0
F	1	2	a	a
G	3	3	a	a
H	a	a	3	0
Total	29 [b]	18	24 [b]	12

a Denotes too few observations.
b Columns may not add. All returns included in totals.

TABLE 91. THE IMPORTANCE OF CONSUMER ATTACHMENTS TO EXISTING DEALERSHIPS "Are Consumers Strongly Inclined to Purchase New Cars from Existing Dealerships Selling Your Make so that a new Dealership Would Have to Offer Substantially Lower Prices or Undertake Higher Sales Promotion Costs per New Unit Retailed in order to Secure a Share of the Market Proportional to its Capacity?"

	Dealerships Located in City		Dealerships Located in Suburbs	
	Number of Dealers Answering	Number of Dealers Answering	Number of Dealers Answering	Number of Dealers Answering
Market	Yes	No	Yes	No
A	6	2	7	5
B	4	2	2	1
C	8	2	6	3
D	8	2	3	1
E	3	—	*a*	*a*
F	3	1	*a*	*a*
G	5	1	*a*	*a*
H	*a*	*a*	3	—
Total	37	11 *b*	23 *b*	11 *b*

a Denotes too few observations.
b Columns may not add. All returns included in totals.

Products and Services Included in the Definition of the Replacement Parts and Service Market

B.1. Franchised Dealers

The sales of parts and accessories and shop or service sales were included in the definition of the replacement parts and service market. According to recent dealer accounting practices, this would not include factory installed accessories or dealer installed accessories on new car sales. It is believed this practice was also followed in 1948. The total sales of dealers reporting commodity line data as a per cent of total sales of all dealers (hereafter referred to as the coverage ratio) were *99.4* per cent in 1948. Parts and accessories and shop or service sales as a per cent of total sales of those dealers reporting commodity line sales (hereafter P.C.L., per cent of sales of those dealers reporting commodity line sales) are listed below.

P.C.L.	Per cent
Parts and accessory sales	13.4
Shop or service sales	7.4
Total	20.8

B.2. Tire, Battery, and Accessory Dealers

The sales of tires (new and used), tire recapping, batteries and accessories, lubrication, and services were included. 1948 U.S. Coverage Ratio was *97.2*.

P.C.L.	Per cent
Tires (new and used)	32.8
Tire (recapping)	4.1
Batteries and accessories	32.0
Lubrication	.9
Services	4.6
Total	74.4

B.3. Gasoline Service Stations

The sales of lubrication, fuel oil, tires (new and used), recapping, batteries, and services were included. 1948 U.S. Coverage Ratio was *97.5*.

P.C.L.	Per cent
Lubrication	6.8
Fuel Oil	2.0
Tires (new and used)	4.1
Tires (recapping)	.5
Batteries	5.0
Service	5.4
Total	23.8

B.4. Used Car Dealers

The sales of parts and accessories and service were included. 1948 U.S. Coverage Ratio was *98.7*.

P.C.L.	Per cent
Parts and accessories	1.2
Service	.9
Total	2.1

B.5. Department Stores

The sales of tires, batteries and accessories were included. 1948 U.S. Coverage Ratio was *99.9*.

P.C.L.	Per cent
Tires, batteries, and accessories	2.1
Total	2.1

B.6. Merchant Wholesalers

The sales of automotive parts and accessories, garage equipment, tools, tires and tubes were included. Sales to households in 1948 represented 3.4 per cent of total sales by merchant wholesalers. In 1954 sales to consumers and farmers represented 3.5 per cent of total sales. In 1948, 89.9 per cent of the sales of merchant wholesalers classified in the *Automotive Equipment: Tire-Tube Wholesalers* group were sales of automotive parts and accessories. If 89.8 per cent of total sales to consumers are assumed to consist of automotive parts and accessories, then 3.1 per cent of total sales of merchant wholesalers in this classification were automotive parts sales.

B.7. Farm Equipment Dealers

The sales of tires and tubes, automotive parts, and accessories (new) were included. 1948 U.S. Coverage Ratio was *98.9.*

P.C.L.	Per cent
Parts and accessories	12.2
Shop or service labor sales	4.3
Total	16.5

B.8. Independent Repair Shops and Garages

The sales of repairs and service and parts and accessories merchandise sales were included. 1948 U.S. Coverage Ratio was *100.0.*

P.C.L.	Per cent
Repairs and service	76.5
Parts and accessories (merchandise sales)	4.5
Total	81.0

The coverage ratios, though high, are often less than 100 per cent. Rather than exclude the sales of sellers in each category who did not report commodity line data, the per cent of total sales which were accounted for by parts and service sales of those sellers reporting commodity line data was applied to the total sales of all sellers in that group. The coverage ratios are generally high. So, this procedure is not likely to lead to major errors. However, there may be a more serious data limitation. Small businessmen seldom keep business records in sufficient detail. Quite probably, some parts and service sales are lumped together with some other sales category. Hence, these sales are not properly recorded by the Census. Also, the Census may not have been able to enumerate all independent repair shops because of their high turnover. Unfortunately, these points can only be mentioned.

A Comparison of Actual Ford Franchises with Chilton Estimates

	Actual Ford Franchises	Chilton Estimates
1927	8.8	9.4
1928	8.3	8.7
1929	8.2	8.6
1930	9.4	8.8
1931	8.4	8.7
1932	8.7	8.2
1933	8.8	7.5
1934	10.8	7.3
1935	11.8	7.9
1936	11.3	8.3
1937	9.1	8.2
1938	7.8	7.8
1939	7.5	7.4
1940	7.8	7.2

Sources : Actual franchises are from a personal letter dated December 6, 1960 from R. J. Eggert, Marketing Research Manager, Ford Motor Company; Chilton estimates are from Trade List Department, Chilton Company.

SELECTIVE BIBLIOGRAPHY

Books

1. Bain, Joe S., *Barriers to New Competition*. Cambridge: Harvard University Press, 1956.

2. ———, *Price Theory*. New York: Henry Holt and Company, 1952.

3. ———, *The Economics of Pacific Coast Petroleum Industry*. Berkeley: University of California Press, 1944.

4. Davisson, Charles N., *The Marketing of Automotive Parts*. Ann Arbor: University of Michigan Press, 1954.

5. Entenberg, Robert, *The Changing Competitive Position of Department Stores in the United States*. Pittsburgh: Pittsburgh University Press, 1957.

6. Henderson, James M., and Richard E. Quandt, *Microeconomic Theory*. New York: McGraw-Hill Book Company, Inc., 1958.

7. Maxcy, George, and Aubrey Silberston, *The Motor Industry*. London: Allen and Unwin, 1959.

8. Nicholls, William H., *Imperfect Competition Within Agricultural Industries*. Ames, Iowa: The Iowa State College Press, 1941.

9. Robinson, E. A. G., *The Structure of Competitive Industry*. London: Cambridge University Press, 1953.

10. Whitney, Simon N., *Antitrust Policies*. New York: The Twentieth Century Fund, 1958.

Articles

11. Adelman, M. A., "The 'Product' and 'Price' in Distribution," *American Economic Review* (May, 1957), pp. 266–273.

12. Alexander, Sidney, "The Effect of Size of Manufacturing Corporation on the Distribution of the Rate of Return," *Review of Economics and Statistics* (August, 1949), pp. 229–235.

13. Churchill, Betty C., "Recent Business Population Movements," *Survey of Current Business* (January, 1954), pp. 11–16.

14. Fellner, William, "Prices and Wages Under Bilateral Monopoly," *Quarterly Journal of Economics* (August, 1947), pp. 503–532.

15. Griffin, Clare E., "Wholesale Organization in the Automobile Industry," *Harvard Business Review*, II (July, 1925), pp. 424–435

16. Niehaus, Jürg, "Ein Messziffer Sür Betriebsgüssen," *Zietschrift Sür die Gesamte Stuatswissenschaft*, III, pp. 529–542.

17. Suits, Daniel S., "The Demand for New Automobiles in the United States 1929–1956," *The Review of Economics and Statistics* (August, 1958), pp. 273–280.

18. Winston, Clement, and Mabel Smith, "Income Sensitivity of Consumption Expenditure," *Survey of Current Business* (January, 1950), pp. 17–20.

Public Documents

19. Board of Governors of the Federal Reserve System, *Financing New Car Purchases, Consumer Installment Credit*, Part IV. Washington, D.C.: U.S. Government Printing Office, 1957.

20. Congress, House of Representatives, *Automobile Dealer Franchises*, Hearings before the Antitrust Subcommittee of the Committee on the Judiciary, 84th Cong., on H.R. 11360 and S. 3879, 1956.

21. Congress, House of Representatives, *Automobile Labeling*, Hearings before the Subcommittee of the Committee on Interstate and Foreign Commerce, 85th Cong., on S. 3500, 1958.

22. Congress, Senate, *Automobile Marketing Practices*, Hearings before the Subcommittee on Interstate and Foreign Commerce, 84th Cong., pursuant to S. Res. 13 continued by S. Res. 163, 1956.

23. Congress, Senate, *Automobile Price Labeling*, Hearings before the Automobile Marketing Subcommittee of the Committee on Interstate and Foreign Commerce, 85th Cong., on S. 3500, 1958.

24. Congress, Senate, *Administered Prices*, Hearings before the Subcommittee on Antitrust and Monopoly of the Committee on the Judiciary, 85th Cong., pursuant to S. Res. 57 and S. Res. 231, 1958.

25. Congress, Senate, *General Motors*, Hearings before the Subcommittee on Antitrust and Monopoly of the Committee on the Judiciary, 84th Cong., pursuant to S. Res. 61, 1956.

26. Federal Trade Commission, *Report on Motor Vehicle Industry*. Washington, D.C.: U.S. Government Printing Office, 1939.

27. Internal Revenue Service, *Statistics of Income*, Part II. Washington, D.C.: U.S. Government Printing Office, annual issues.

DATE DUE

MAY 13 '73			
F H			
APR 26 '83			
MAY 11 1985			
MAY 24 '88			
DE 18 '91			
GAYLORD			PRINTED IN U.S.A.